Africans at Home and in the
United States

Africans at Home and in the United States

One People, One Problem, One Destiny

Emeka C. Anaedozie

LEXINGTON BOOKS
Lanham • Boulder • New York • London

Published by Lexington Books
An imprint of The Rowman & Littlefield Publishing Group, Inc.
4501 Forbes Boulevard, Suite 200, Lanham, Maryland 20706
www.rowman.com

6 Tinworth Street, London SE11 5AL, United Kingdom

Copyright © 2021 by The Rowman & Littlefield Publishing Group, Inc.

All rights reserved. No part of this book may be reproduced in any form or by any electronic or mechanical means, including information storage and retrieval systems, without written permission from the publisher, except by a reviewer who may quote passages in a review.

British Library Cataloguing in Publication Information Available

Library of Congress Cataloging-in-Publication Data

Names: Anaedozie, Emeka C., 1982- author.
Title: Africans at home and in the United States : one people, one problem, one destiny / Emeka C. Anaedozie.
Description: Lanham : Lexington Books, [2021] | Includes bibliographical references and index. | Summary: "In Africans at Home and in the United States: One People, One Problem, One Destiny, Emeka C. Anaedozie examines Pan-African history, focusing on sociocultural commonalities and challenges facing African people. Anaedozie argues that Pan-African resistance to oppression represents the best future for Africans both on the African continent and abroad in the United States"—Provided by publisher.
Identifiers: LCCN 2020050259 (print) | LCCN 2020050260 (ebook) | ISBN 9781793634863 (cloth) | ISBN 9781793634870 (epub)
Subjects: LCSH: Pan-Africanism—History. | African diaspora—History. | Africans—United States—History. | United States—Race relations—History. | Racism—United States—History.
Classification: LCC DT30.5 .A56 2021 (print) | LCC DT30.5 (ebook) | DDC 909/.0496—dc23
LC record available at https://lccn.loc.gov/2020050259
LC ebook record available at https://lccn.loc.gov/2020050260

∞™ The paper used in this publication meets the minimum requirements of American National Standard for Information Sciences Permanence of Paper for Printed Library Materials, ANSI/NISO Z39.48-1992.

Contents

Introduction		vii
1	Oppression in Context	1
2	African People's History: Challenge to the Standard Narratives	21
3	Popular Oppression in Entertainment and Public Places	35
4	The New Jim Crow and Neocolonialism	57
5	Swimming Against the Tide	79
6	Using Multiperspectivity Theory to Confront Monoperspectivity in the U.S. History Pedagogics	103
7	From Oppression to Freedom	121
Conclusion		141
Bibliography		145
Index		157
About the Author		161

Introduction

Pan-Africanism is an ideological and philosophical movement that serves as an antidote to the oppression of physical and mental separation. It seeks to unite Africa descended people who have been forcefully dispersed and trafficked across the globe. As an intellectual movement, it serves to remedy the mental divide occasioned by sociocultural and psychological oppression by seeking to collapse the oppressive wall that sustains that division. According to the African Union, "the ideology asserts that the fates of all African peoples and countries are intertwined. At its core, Pan-Africanism is 'a belief that African peoples both on the continent and in the Diaspora, share not merely a common history but a common destiny.'"[1]

In the same vein, this study is geared toward investigating the history of African people from the ideological and paradigmatic scaffolding of Pan-Africanism. It is held here that the obstacles facing African people know no geographical or national boundaries; why would the study of the latter respect boundaries? In fact, these challenges often have common ideological origins, goals, and the results and impacts are consistently similar. The crux of this book is to critically interrogate existing narratives and ideologies, since the Emancipation Proclamation in the diaspora and the emergence of European imperialism on the continent, so as to present a coherent Pan-African history thematically. To this end, it is a form of cultural cum intellectual history that explores ideologies and notions relating to African descendants to chart a historically accurate path for the latter. Within this globalized paradigm, geography and nationality become less significant as the intersectionality of social phenomena becomes glaring. This book, further, contends that African people are one people based on shared ancestry, history, and the reality of oppression. When their lives and realities are studied from the context of the first two, the history unravels in the context of continuum and interconnectivity. However, when approached from the prism of oppression, the latter defines them by naturalizing their separation and justifying the same unconsciously. The paradox of studying African people's history outside the Pan-African framework is that one is trapped by the same phenomenon he set out to confront.

African people have experienced a variegated modes of oppression that have caused internalization of self-destructive behaviors on the continent and in the diaspora. Instances of these abound as African people inadvertently and instinctively work against their cultural and existential interests. To encapsulate its operation and significance, racist oppression preying on African people is conceptualized within the framework of Cognitive Dissonance and its effects on the oppressed can be interpreted as manifesting as Stockholm Syndrome and classism. These resultant effects are responsible for African people's metaphoric swim against the tide:

> Speaking at the 7th Annual International Igbo Conference Chimamanda Ngozi Adichie revealed that she only speaks to her daughter in Igbo, a practice that shocks many [African] parents. . . . Many homes on the continent still deliberately don't speak their local languages. . . . It is even surprising that parents who both come from the same ethnic group do not speak their indigenous language to their children. As Adichie pointed out in her presentation, some of these parents argue that they don't want to confuse the child with learning two languages but paradoxically enrol [sic] the child in French and German lessons simultaneously.[2]

They, throughout ages, have been known and have identified with multiple uncomplimentary names. Many of these terms were imposed and signify repression as well as serve as a reminder to the perpetuity of oppression. While virtually every race has discarded color as a mark of group identity, African people and indeed Caucasians have held onto theirs for two diametrically opposing reasons. The latter consciously christened themselves "white" while at the same time imposed "black," "dark," and "negro" on African people. To them, whiteness signifies purity, beauty, and immaculacy, while blackness connotes ugliness, evil, or negativity. Justifiably, tagging an Asian "yellow" or an Indigenous American "red" equates to racial opprobrium since the second half of the twentieth century. African people, nevertheless, since the turn of the same century have embraced the imposed color identifier and sought to glamourize it since the Pan-African movement of the 1920s to the Human Rights Movement of the 1960s, hence phrases like "black is beautiful," " I am black and proud," among others. The Afrocentric Movement of the 1980s, inaugurated and advanced by Molefi Kete Asante, has rejected any imposition on African people in the spirit of Pan-Africanism and has sought to dignify and humanize Africa descended people as Africans irrespective of nationality and cultural leaning. The import is that Africa, like

Asia, is the proper racial identifier for it connects the identified people to a location (their ancestral land), history, and culture. Certainly, this notion builds on the emotional calls made by Pan-Africanists, starting in the nineteenth century with David Walker and Martin Delaney and in the twentieth century, Marcus Garvey, for African descendants to unite ideologically and otherwise against their intractable torturous oppression.

CONCEPTUAL FRAMEWORK

Cognitive dissonance state is induced when an individual's action is incongruent with his stated precepts, he then strives to cover his tracts to escape charges of duplicity. It involves one being in a contradictory state with his beliefs and behaviors causing an attitudinal imbalance. This psychology theory was promulgated by Festinger in the 1950s and used to argue that humans strive to balance and harmonize their attitudes and behaviors to combat disharmony (dissonance). Some possible scenarios have been suggested where this hypocritical state could be potentially forgiven—when new information emerges that challenges conventional wisdom and "very few things are all black and white . . . ."[3]

However, this research utilizes this cognitive dissonance theory to investigate and interrogate the dialectics of externally induced oppression, while employing the "Talented Tenth" philosophy to dissect its internal component. The latter serves well in exposing how the oppressed, due to the dictates of oppression, are imitating the culture of oppression. The validity of the former is found its ability to neutrally expose the duplicitous nature of historic oppression ravaging Africa-descended people around the world in the past and present, in all spheres of life. Since the theory has stood the test of time, it serves a veritable tool in examining the exegesis of oppression, the intergenerational nature of it, and its double standards, as well as how it remains covert in some instances and overt in others. To this end, this theory is useful in examining the commonality and intersectionality of challenges facing African people on the continent and in the diaspora.

Festinger's contention that the emergence of new data validates possible reversal of opinions and attitudes is not completely applicable to African people in the context of their relationship with oppression. The latter's oppression is not based on lack of information on their humanity and ability, it is more about the hypocritical construction of oppression victims as inferior to justify and sustain their dehumanization.

Methodologically, the textual analytical–qualitative model is employed to examine various ideologies and mantras of oppression as well as evaluate the philosophies utilized to fight against the former. To this end, pertinent primary and secondary sources are utilized to thread and convey the Pan-

African narrative. It employs the bottom-up rather than the elitist and traditionalist top-to-bottom approach. With this populist paradigm, it seeks to explore the commonalities in traits, themes, and phenomena among African descendants at home and in the diaspora. The bottom-up paradigm is also employed to critique the classism fostered by the "Talented Tenth"—an internal component of oppression—that has ravaged African people globally sapping them off needed cohesion and leadership.

EXTERNAL AND INTERNAL OPPRESSION IN CONTEXT

Oppression

Oppression is the cruel and unjustified treatment of another causing bodily, emotional, and property harm. It represents a reprehensive and injurious treatment of another human sometimes codified in law or norm. Some of the damages occasioned are as unquantifiable as they are immeasurable by any barometer. Oppressors often find ways to bury their tracks and justify their actions when exposed. The oppression that targets its victims because of their racial identity is evidently racism. In this book, this syndrome is categorized into Popular and Unpopular Oppression. The former represents the forms of racist attacks on African people that are subliminal, entrenched, and institutionalized. This type of oppression is invisible and has been defined as *The New Jim Crow* by Alexander and as "Process Racism" by Asante.[4] The latter contends that it is hidden deep within the bureaucratic process that makes the socioeconomic system of the west seem fair and innocuous. Popular Oppression is very normative in western societies, but unfortunately, it is detrimental to the destinies, human rights, and economic prospects of African people. The type of oppression that is more commonly attacked these days in sports and the media is the Unpopular Oppression. This involves verbal and or gesticular assault on African people. For the most part, this type of oppression, unlike the former, attracts censure from the mainstream western leaders, media, and entities. Culprits are swiftly and rightly labeled racists. However, labeling only these types of offenders racist limits the meaning of racism as a form of oppression. It further shields the perpetrators and defenders of "Process Racism," *New Jim Crow* and indeed Popular Oppression, placing them on the high moral ground while codifying subtle racial oppression.

It is worth reiterating that racial oppression has no geographical or cultural boundary, but in some cases, it seems to target African people based on socioeconomic class. In other words, low-income African people or the downtrodden are the most vulnerable to its scourge. Mostly, the only difference between oppression at home and abroad is the mode of oppression; the intent, the impact, and the results are usually similar for African people regardless of geography. For example, in the United States, one of the most debilitating effects of racist oppression can be found in America's justice system starting with the disproportionate police arrest and murder of African Americans. It is pertinent to reiterate that within the latter's community, the most vulnerable to oppression—especially police brutality—is the downtrodden, the ordinary men and women. The elite are less likely to be harassed, brutalized, and killed by the U.S. police. This is not to argue that all racial oppression targeting African people respect social status. The case of Dr. Henry Louis Gates, Jr. is illustrative of the fact that regardless of your status in America, if one is of African descent, he is not immune from racial profiling. The distinguished professor at Harvard University was arrested and jailed for trying to break into his own home in 2009.[5] Although it became a national headline at that time in the U.S., sparking an outcry for criminal justice reform, for ordinary African Americans on the streets of the United States this is their daily reality, not necessarily for the elites.

On the continent, the police serve as protectors and security for the elites while working as tools of oppression for the masses. Nigeria, for instance, operates a centralized police system, a legacy of the British colonialists. The institution has a track record of corruption and human rights abuses, especially during the military dictatorship. The brunt of the aforementioned vices is felt mostly by ordinary Nigerians who are abused and sometimes killed extrajudicially.[6] The Nigerian elites, like their African American counterparts, are less likely to be impacted by these. Rather than be victimized, they use their influences to employ the services of police bodyguards—the latter serves as a buffer between them and the victimized masses.[7] According to a Nigerian police chief, Rasheed Akintunde, as much as 80 percent of Nigerian police personnel are deployed to protect political leaders and their elite cronies.[8] Like in the U.S., from time to time, there are few reports of police arrests and attacks on elites but it is not an everyday occurrence.

On the surface, there seems to be a difference in the two scenarios above. A critical examination reveals more commonalities than differences. While the white communities in the U.S. generally perceive the police in good light, as protectors and defenders, the African American victims largely perceive the former as oppressive, an arm of oppression. Whereas the faces of oppression of the masses of African people on the continent are "black," in the diaspora the face is usually "white." The commonality lies in the class of the victims—always the ordinary masses, the downtrodden. The latter perceive the police as the enemy and tend to try to avoid them because of their track record. In the same vein, the police tend to treat the masses of African people at home and in the diaspora as dangerous. This factor is underscored by the former's tendency to escalate any security situation involving the latter. On the continent, the police treatment of the ordinary African as dangerous is derivative from the European colonial policies. Unlike in the West where the

THE "TALENTED TENTH"

The concept of the "Talented Tenth" as a panacea toward the liberation of African people was one of the myriad of remedies proffered by African people toward socioeconomic and cultural emancipation from unretractable oppression. In this book, it is employed and applied broadly to African elites both the intellectuals and politicoeconomic leaders at home and in the diaspora to explain how oppression has caused the oppressed to oppress rather than liberate himself and his race. Generally, those who are household names fall under the category of the "Talented Tenth" in this research. W. E. B. Du Bois proposed and popularized the "Talented Tenth" mantra at the turn of the twentieth century insisting that it was the duty of the elites—the gifted elites, the educated ones, and the intellectually talented to lead the rest of the race out of socioeconomic oppression.[9] The phrase had been used by Henry Lyman Morehouse (Morehouse College was named for him) seven years before DuBois employed it. Accordingly:

> The Negro race, like all races, is going to be saved by its exceptional men. The problem of education, then, among Negroes must first of all deal with the Talented Tenth; it is the problem of developing the Best of this race that they may guide the Mass away from contamination and death of the Worst, in their own and other races . . . . If we make money the object of man-training, we shall develop money-makers but not necessarily men; if we make technical skill the object of education, we may possess artisans but not, in nature, men.[10]

Undoubtedly, Du Bois proffered what he believed to be a sincere treatise toward the emancipation of the beleaguered African people. His solution was at odds and vehemently critical of Booker T. Washington's practical education-to-entrepreneurship blueprint. Unfortunately, while suggesting his plan, Du Bois dissipated energy detracting Washington, who ironically shared the same end-goal as he—social emancipation. The former also failed to appreciate the fact that not everyone would obtain liberal arts or university education as well as the fact that Washington's scheme perfectly served the skill sets of African people coming out of enslavement. On the other hand, it was Washington whose practical nationalism in education and economics that has had enduring socioeconomic effects on the lives of African Americans with the multiplication of Tuskegee Institute's model and attendant employment and educational opportunities.

Du Bois's proposal, expectedly, continues to be well received and romanticized in the academy. Scholars and African American elites naturally admire Du Bois's "Talented Tenth" philosophy and often find ways to prove its relevance. To Battle, the "Talented Tenth" are fulfilling their call to duty especially in politics:

> According to Du Bois's original theoretical formulation, the Talented Tenth were [sic] to sacrifice their personal interests and endeavors to provide leadership for the African American community. Following in Du Bois's footsteps, this inquiry uses the National Black Politics Study to examine the attitudes of today's Talented Tenth concerning their responsibilities as leaders of their respective communities. Multivariate findings indicate that among other things, the Talented Tenth report being more politically active and more involved in their communities and are suspect of the motives of the Black middle class. The authors' results suggest that the Talented Tenth are [sic] fulfilling the charge placed before them by W. E. B. Du Bois.[11]

This assessment ignores the reality on the ground. It disregards the fact that the post-1960s "Talented Tenth" is behaviorally antithetical to their forebearers. While the likes of Harriet Tubman, David Walker, Martin Delaney, and indeed Frederick Douglass, devoted their talents and resources toward uplifting and emancipating the rest of the race, the contemporary ones do the opposite. They are usually the first to abandon the African American communities, and in doing so they take their "smart kids" with them in their desire to integrate. They set a reprehensible precedent that causes all talented people to want to leave the African American community or institution. In politics, they are usually inseparably married to the Democratic Party, resulting in the latter's lackadaisical treatment of the former. They are mostly interested in get-out-the-vote initiatives, but not in getting the party to account for the promises made to African American communities in the previous election cycle.

On the continent, the same selfish attitude prevails. While the "Talented Tenth" of the late nineteenth century organized resistance against the European aggressive colonialism and resultant exploitation, the post-colonial ones starting from the 1960s to the present have been self-serving. Rather than invest in healthcare and functional education that serve the needs of Africa, they prefer to let the institutions rot. Simultaneously, they support their "mentor's" own institutions in the West to the detriment of their countries' existential interests. These elites ensure that all their immediate family members' health and educational needs are taken care of abroad rather than at home. Their negative precedence forces ordinary Africans to desire to leave the continent even at the expense of drowning in the Mediterranean. Others who made it to the West prefer to let European nations and America reap the benefits of their talents in science, sports, and entertainment.

Recent and past research have thrown more lights into the secluded and elitist lives of the twentieth and twenty-first centuries' "Talented Tenth." Frazier's remains a classic in unmasking these upper and middle-class African Americans in their desperate bid to imitate their oppressors' classism and detach themselves from their race. Without self-confidence, they sought validation from the former which was not forthcoming, and they ended up consumed by an inferiority complex.[12] Graham's seminal work exposes their reclusivity and exclusivity. These African American millionaires and some billionaires, scattered across the American cities, live lives that mimic European aristocracy. Such lifestyles, while implicitly exalting and venerating material possessions, seemingly mocks the downtrodden in the society by sheer flamboyance and extravagance. That reality combines to puncture the argument in support of the "Talented Tenth" as the predestined emancipators.[13]

Oppression, by design, causes unmeasurable agony for the oppressed including shaping the latter's perception of reality and response to the former. In response to this scourge, African descendants have evolved varied operational theories and ideologies toward asserting their bastardized humanity and heritage. There is no doubt that the dialectical charges of the early twentieth century were led by sôme of the selfless "Talented Tenth" including Marcus Garvey, Aimé Césaire, and Leopold Senghor. They utilized movements like Pan-Africanism and Negritude to chart paths of collective action against racial oppression. Negritude, a literary movement, conceived African descendants as one and sought a united front against the oppressive regime of colonialism. The movement also made pride in one's ancestry, history, and African identity grossly imperative. By design, it was an antidote to a diagnosed ailment—an illness of the mind that specifically preyed on Africa-descended people causing them to devalue themselves and their essences. It is not surprising that the diasporic Africans always lead the charge for a conscious and united Africa as represented in the aforementioned movements.

Awkwardly, some "Talented Tenth" at home were unmindful of the reality of various shades of racist oppression in the diaspora that birthed Negritude. The French equivalent of the New Jim Crow meant that African people in France continued to be socioeconomically deprived and culturally emasculated, leading to an inferiority complex. They unconsciously sought to become more French as a means of social mobility and validation. Negritude, emerging in the 1930's France and French colonized Africa began to not only critique the Eurocentric debasement of African values but also to emphasize the imperatives of Africans embracing their Africanness. Soyinka, a Nobel Laurette, is a notable critique of Negritude dismissing its efforts as "retrogressive" in an interview.[14] The Poet had in the 1960s sarcastically rebuked the ideology stating that a tiger does not need to assert its "Tigeritude."[15] These types of censure, as was the case with DuBois over Booker T. Washington, are not only misguided, they sap the energy needed to build a collective action against a common conundrum.

LITERATURE REVIEW

Pan-Africanism as an intellectual notion, and like similar ideologies, has elicited several debates not only on the question of its meaning, but also on its function, significance, and relevance. While some Pan-Africanist thinkers and researchers approach the ideal from a regional and organizational standpoint, others search for its significance in African people's culture, resistance, and pursuit of happiness. It is worth reiterating that this book represents an attempt at examining the cultural and intellectual history of African people rather than that of the elites who often get more than their fair share of attention. Jaji's cultural discourse of Pan-Africanism is very crucial and is paradigmatically similar to the conceptual attempt made in this book. The latter's work and this book both de-emphasized elitism and also explore Pan-Africanism in the cultural realm. Jaji focuses on Pan-African cultural relations in music between 1890 and 2011, highlighting how Africans at home bonded with their kith abroad through various music genres.[16]

Sadly, the Pan-African and African historiography is flush with paradigmatic delineation methodology that perpetuates the injustices of forced separation. Amoah and Williams fell victim to the traditional historical approach by equating and conceiving Pan-African history as synonymous with elitist and the elites' history. The former overwhelmingly concentrated on the study of nation-states, the political class, and their whims in his conception of "New Pan-Africanism," which is anything but new.[17] Unfortunately, the latter toes the same line in studying the state of Pan-Africanism in Ghana. His study, a very substantive contribution and exploration of the fate of Pan-Africanism in post-Nkrumah's Ghana, is top-to-bottom research paradigmatically.[18] It explores the operation and application of Pan-African ideals by the political leaders, their failures and successes rather than the destiny of the Ghanaian masses who are supposedly the subject of these thoughts.

Adi makes a crucial historical contribution to the Pan-African discourse by surveying the evolution and maturation of the movement, thereby providing a chronological context. Thus, people, as well as organizations that fought to liberate Africans starting in the diaspora, are presented. Also important is the crucial role of the African Union (AU) in the Pan-African struggle. The AU is seemingly disposed to serving the interest of all African people both at home and in the diaspora, unlike its defunct predecessor.[19] Ture and Abu-Jamal, in the same vein, demonstrated philosophical evolution and progression into Pan-Africanism at the individual level. The former, a foremost Black Nationalist grew conceptually to appreciate the indispensability of unity in the fight against oppression. As a result, like W. E. B. DuBois, he matured from parochialism into Pan-Africanism understanding that African American liberation struggle could not be divorced from that of the rest of the African world.[20]

Walters carefully threaded through otherwise sociocultural disparities among Africans in the diaspora to present a coherent and consistent Pan-African masterpiece. His discourse on Pan-Africanism is largely on the diasporan variant, and less on the continent. The author demonstrates that the external factor that shaped and continues to shape African people's culture and reality is racial oppression starting with slavery. While oppression in the diaspora is largely uniform in effect, the victim's response or resistance is also identical irrespective of nationality.[21]

James', in the same vein, has always been a classic in articulating African resistance to western oppression in a globalized paradigm and seminal in appreciating the inevitability of a unified approach to resisting oppression. His work on Pan-African revolt, originally published in 1938 and later expanded and reprinted in 1969, is a template on how to Pan-Africanly interpret and contextualize African people's history. James demonstrated sagacity by seeing beneath the national and geographical boundaries that tend to obscure the views of some Africanists. He masterfully threaded and conveyed the history of African people's resistance to global European oppression demonstrating continuity rather than discontinuity—in Haiti, the United States, and in on the continent of Africa and beyond.[22] This illustrates the fact that slavery in the diaspora is servitude at home despite the disparity in space and time, despite apparent nomenclatural distinction. Leslie James, in the same vein, showcases how Pan-African effort ignited the fire that culminated in the razing down of colonialism in Africa. The author explores the selfless efforts of George Padmore duly situating him within the league of Pan-African intellectual warriors.[23]

Few authors who scrutinized Pan-Africanism from Afrocentric lenses have dismissed the notion as inherently Eurocentric and segregative. Nantambu contends that the idea of Pan-Africanism is Eurocentric and needs a rethink. He avers that Pan-African Nationalism is not only the desirable panacea but the most actionable when perceived from an African prism. The former, he contends, is emotional and limited while the latter is revolutionary in that it treats oppression holistically not in Eurocentric segmented trapping.[24]

ORGANIZATION

To this end, this book is roughly divided into three parts: oppression, results of oppression, and attaining victory over oppression. Chapter 1 grapples with the meaning, biting significance, and the multifaceted operational guises of racial oppression comparatively both on the continent and in the diaspora. It attempts to contextualize and therefore contrasts racism with other forms of oppression highlighting the hypocrisies and inconsistencies in the approach to different kinds of oppression. Chapter 2 critically delves into the narrative issues in African history contending that both sides of the Atlantic are one and therefore should be treated as such in research. It contends that it was oppression that physically separated its victims and sustains such separation via miseducation and paradigmatic divisiveness. Chapter 3 engages and attempts to expose often unnoticed and concealed forms of oppression in popular culture targeting African people in the electronic and print media, as well as in public places. Thus, the history of such denigrating and offensive social construction is unmasked. Chapter 4 contends that the phenomenon of the New Jim Crow in the diaspora is the equivalent of Neocolonialism at home. While the old regime was bold and conspicuous, the new order deludes and masquerades in operation, yet unleashing the same amount of venom as the former.

Chapter 5 focuses on the results of oppression on African people at home and abroad. It exposes the torturous impacts of new and old regimes of oppression as they collude to cause slave mentality abroad and colonial mentality at home. The chapter, essentially, argues that both phenomena are the same—have identical origins and are symptomatically the same. Chapter 6 attempts to deconstruct intellectual oppression by exposing the mono-perspectivity of U.S. survey history textbooks. It demonstrates that U.S. history continues to portray one side of the story and present the same as all-encompassing. The chapter, using the multiperspectivity theory, pushes for a switch from monoperspectivity to multiperspectivity to represent a truly multiracial society in the classroom and on textbooks. Chapter 7 offers suggestive tips on how African people could overcome oppression. It contends that the oppressed must strive to expose acts of racial oppression and work to obtain social justice to assert their humanity.

NOTES

1. Hakim Adi, "Pan-Africanism: An Ideology and a Movement," in *Global Africa: Into the Twenty-First Century*, edited by Dorothy L. Hodgson and Judith A. Byfield (Oakland, California: University of California Press, 2017), 90.

2. "The Fading Use of Indigenous Languages in African Households," *This is Africa*, May 17, 2018, https://thisisafrica.me/arts-and-culture/the-fading-use-of-indigenous-languages-in-african-households/ (accessed January 17, 2020).

3. Leon Festinger, *A Theory of Cognitive Dissonance* (Palo Alto, CA: Stanford University Press, 1957), 1–6.

4. Molefi Kete Asante, *Afrocentricity* (Trenton, NJ: Africa World Press, Inc., 1988), 35.

5. Abby Goodnough, "Harvard Professor Jailed; Officer Is Accused of Bias," *The New York Times*, July 20, 2009, https://www.nytimes.com/2009/07/21/us/21gates.html (accessed January 17, 2020).

6. Otwin Marenin, "Policing Nigeria: Control and Autonomy in the Exercise of Coercion,"*African Studies Review* 28, no. 1 (1985): 73–93.

7. "Nigeria: Corruption Fueling Police Abuses," *Human Right Watch*, August 17, 2010, https://www.hrw.org/news/2010/08/17/nigeria-corruption-fueling-police-abuses (accessed January 17, 2020).

8. "80 percent Of Our Policemen Are Deployed To Protect Politicians And VIPS, Says Nigeria Police Chief," *Sahara Reporters*, February 8, 2018, http://saharareporters.com/2018/02/08/80-percent-our-policemen-are-deployed-protect-politicians-and-vips-says-nigeria-police (accessed January 17, 2020).

9. Henry Louis Gates, "Who Really Invented the 'Talented Tenth'?" *PBS*, https://www.pbs.org/wnet/african-americans-many-rivers-to-cross/history/who-really-invented-the-talented-tenth/ (accessed January 17,2020).

10. W.E.B. Du Bois, *The Talented Tenth* (Scotts Valley, CA: CreateSpace Independent Publishing Platform, 2017), 2.

11. Juan Battle and Earl Wright, "W. E. B. Du Bois's Talented Tenth: A Quantitative Assessment," *Journal of Black Studies* 32, no. 6 (2002): 654.

12. E. Franklin Frazier, *Black Bourgeoisie: The Book That Brought the Shock of Self-Revelation to Middle-Class Blacks in America* (New York: Free Press, 1997).

13. See Lawrence Otis Graham, *Our Kind of People: Inside America's Black Upper Class* (New York: Harper Perennial, 1999); Elizabeth Dowling Taylor, *The Original Black Elite: Daniel Murray and the Story of a Forgotten Era* (New York: Amistad, 2017).

14. "Negritude: A Dialogue BetweenWole Soyinka and Senghor - Trailer - Available from TWN," https://www.youtube.com/watch?v=VPjmRGvkFZE (accessed January 17, 2020).

15. Biodun Jeyifo, "Wole Soyinka and Tropes of Disalienation," in Biodun Jeyifo (ed.), *Perspectives on Wole Soyinka: Freedom and Complexity* (Jackson: University Press of Mississippi, 2001), 109.

16. Tsitsi Ella Jaji, *Africa in Stereo: Modernism, Music, And Pan-African Solidarity* (New York and Oxford: Oxford University Press, 2014).

17. Michael Amoah, *The New Pan-Africanism: Globalism and the Nation State in Africa* (New York: I. B. Tauris, 2019).

18. Justin Williams, *Pan-Africanism in Ghana: African Socialism, Neoliberalism, and Globalization* (Durham, NC: Carolina Academic Press, 2016).

19. Hakim Adi, *Pan-Africanism: A History* (London: Bloomsbury Academic, 2018).

20. Kwame Ture and Mumia Abu-Jamal, *Stokely Speaks: From Black Power to Pan-Africanism* (Chicago: Lawrence Hill Books, 2007).

21. Ronald Walters, *Pan Africanism in the African Diaspora: An Analysis of Modern Afrocentric Political Movements* (Detroit, MI: Wayne State University Press, 1997).

22. C. L. R. James, *A History of Pan-African Revolt* (Oakland, CA: P.M. Press, 2012).

23. Leslie James, *George Padmore and Decolonization from Below: Pan-Africanism, the Cold War, and the End of Empire* (London: Palgrave Macmillan, 2015).

24. Kwame Nantambu, "Pan-Africanism Versus Pan-African Nationalism: An Afrocentric Analysis," *Journal of Black Studies*, 28, no. 5 (May, 1998): 561–74.

Chapter One

Oppression in Context

Oppression, literally, stands for an unjust and inhuman treatment or control of a human being. This is not to argue that humans cannot mete out injustice against animals, but it is hard to fathom a scenario where a wild animal unjustly treats another. When we adjudge wild animals from our own moral standards, some may contend that there are situations when an animal oppresses another. Conversely, human's oppressive attitudes toward another are as old as human life itself. It manifests in multiple forms and not limited to racism, xenophobia, theft, rape, torture, pedophilia, and harassment. Often, oppression surfaces in the physical and tangible forms, other times it unravels in a more discreet way, all still sinister. The residues and pains of mistreatments cannot always be measured.

Life, undoubtedly, involves constant strives—strives for survival, to thrive, and for perfection. Every living being is born with an inherent instinct to defend itself from oppressive forces of life—survivalism, and then the desire to thrive is the natural next step for humans. Unfortunately, for African people around the world survival is the perpetual mode. Repression, seemingly, has conditioned the oppressed to perceive survival as the end-goal of life. Oppression dehumanizes the oppressed, often working psychically to convince the latter that he is of a lesser being, hence the tendency of the oppressed to try to imitate the oppressor on one hand, and perceive survival as the only attainable goal on the other.[1] It is not surprising that people who are clustered in the American prisons, for instance, tend to fight and engage in more social vices than those outside of it because the walls of prison represent oppression for the wrongfully convicted.

In modern times, especially since the second half of the twentieth century, various degrees of oppression codified in law and normalized in certain cultures have been gradually, grudgingly, reluctantly, and relatively rejected and denounced. Some of the notable ones include war crimes. This was made possible with the formation of the United Nations in 1945 to help make the world more·"democratic," help the marginalized nations and peoples of the world seek freedom within the legal parameters, and importantly to tackle the incessant cases of wartime brutalities. According to the global body's definition of what constitutes a war crime,

The term "war crimes" refers to serious breaches of international humanitarian law committed against civilians or enemy combatants during an international or domestic armed conflict, for which the perpetrators may be held criminally liable on an individual basis. Such crimes are derived primarily from the Geneva Conventions of August 12,1 1949 and their Additional Protocols I and II of 1977, and the Hague Conventions of 1899 and 1907. Their most recent codification can be found in article 8 of the 1998 Rome Statute for the International Criminal Court (ICC). The vast majority of incidents listed in the report could, if investigated and proven in a judicial process,

> point to the commission of prohibited acts such as murder, willfully causing great suffering, or serious injury to body or health, rape, intentional attacks on the civilian population, pillage, and unlawful and arbitrary destruction of civilian goods, including some which were essential to the survival of the civilian population. The vast majority of these acts were committed against protected persons, as defined in the Geneva Conventions, primarily people who did not take part in the hostilities, particularly civilian populations and those put out of combat. This applies in particular to people living in refugee camps, who constitute a civilian population that is not participating in the hostilities, in spite of the presence of military personnel among them in some cases.[2]

Prior to the inauguration of the Geneva Convention and the establishment of the International Criminal Court at Hague, Netherlands, there were no universally accepted standards for the treatment of civilians caught in war zones. The latter, like the military personnel, were also "fair game" and were therefore targeted, brutalized, and raped. These sets of laws outline the responsibilities of each warring faction as well as the penalties due to potential criminals who violate the human rights of defenseless civilians including women, children and non-combatant men.

During the Nigeria Civil War (1967–70) there were multiple reports of war crimes and atrocities committed against the Biafran secessionists of southeastern Nigeria. Unlike the war criminals of the Second World War and subsequent ones, there were neither an investigation nor convictions. Defenseless Biafran masses, women, children, the elderly, and non-combatant men were slaughtered barbarously at different times and stages of the war. For example, there was a report about the infamous Asaba Massacre, whereby the people of Asaba town along the Niger River were lined up and slaughtered.[3] There are multiple accounts of captured Biafran civilians who were summarily executed by the overzealous Nigerian soldiers. In one of such incidents, a shirtless Biafran man, who identified himself as Matthias Kanu, of Igbo ethnicity was seen in a YouTube video, tied and shot several times in the head as he pleaded with the Nigerian soldiers to spare his life after a western journalist had interviewed him as he was being tied for execution.[4]

Although governments exist to ensure order and protect humans and their properties through its laws and law enforcement, there are no codes or means that punish the government and its agencies for not fulfilling its part of the social contract. The United Nations, like governments of the world, have applied selective justice when it comes to war crimes and international criminality within its jurisdiction.

While the international statutes and conventions serve a veritable need in ensuring wartime accountability, responsibility, and justice, they make no effort or pretend to illegalize the act of war. Certainly, warring and combat is natural not only within the human community and families, it is also prevalent among other living organisms. Modernity, unfortunately, seems to revel in the act of war depicting it as a form of drama and reenacting it to the entertainment of gullible audiences. In movies and video games, the act of war is prevalent and naturalized as fun, acceptable, and as a sport. Many historical societies and centers in the U.S. reenact various wars and war strategies and do so to engage their numerous audiences. According to the American Civil War Society (ACWS), they provide "absorbing hobby" for members. In their published mission statement,

> Formed in 1975, the ACWS has been going from strength to strength ever since. We have strong connections with American Civil War re-enactors from all over the world. The Society provides an absorbing hobby for its members, spectacular battles and historical displays for audiences. The ACWS is essentially a historical society, with many members acknowledged as experts on the history of the period who give talks to schools, colleges and other organisations. ACWS caters for all interests in the subject from military modelling to music of the period and live shooting period black powder weapons.[5]

Undoubtedly, what is lost in all these war reenactments is the real meaning and consequences of war. The prevailing paradigm embellishes the act of combat, giving the general public, most of whom have not had a wartime experience at the war zone, a false sense of recreation. It is critical to add that war literally means tragedy and death! It means untimely death for millions of innocent men, women, and children. It precipitates epidemic, starvation, rape, corruption, deprivation, and countless other oppressive regimes. Certainly, most wars can safely be assessed as acts of oppression. Moralism and humanism have to take precedence in assessing war stories to fully appreciate the full cost of wars. By so doing, it will be easier to perceive war as a form of oppression rather than a competition.

The Greek historian, Thucydides played a foundational role in European historiography's conception and interpretation of wars. Thucydides' accounts of various wars and battles the Greek city-states fought including the Peloponnesian war was dramatic and generally glorifying to the act of war. He blatantly chastised certain wars for being too short and therefore offering less entertainment and drama to people on the metaphorical pavement. Like the modern-day war historians and war reenactors, Thucydides neither showed interest nor compassion to the thousands of lives lost during the cause of the battles he chronicled.[6]

MORAL CRITIQUE OF OPPRESSION

Certainly, there are levels of oppression, but all forms of oppression are evil, every evil abhorrent, reprehensible, despicable, and abominable, when viewed from moral lenses. From a legal perspective, while some acts are morally unjust, they could be legally permissible. The best barometer of assessment of a potentially unjust law or tradition is through role reversal. If the perpetrator is placed in the role of the victim, will he find it offensive, detestable, or amusing?

One of the most enduring cases of oppression in the world is the issue of chattel slavery, especially the European enslavement of African people. This topic has always elicited heated debates and emotions for obvious reasons. Some defenders of slavery have used quasi and pseudo-science to argue that African people were inherently and genetically inferior and therefore perfect beasts of burden. Leading this charge were many of the renowned nineteenth century Caucasian doctors including Samuel George Morton who inferred that the African brain was nine cubic inches less than that of the Caucasian.[7]

In the same vein Eurocentrist scholars have argued that slavery was in the past and should remain there, while others have tended to imply that it was the victims themselves, Africans, who sold each other or that the latter was a partner in his own annihilation. Some African people on the continent have bought into this misleading tale by apologizing for slavery.[8] Apologies would have been useful if indeed Africans started and ended it. In other words, if Africans were the subjects of the trade rather than objects. But without knowledge of the past and a grasp of the politics of the present, this sort of apologies does more harm than good as it absolves the Europeans of their culpability while putting the burden of guilt on the victims. It also undermines and tarnishes the justified quest for reparations. The question is if Europeans did not conquer the Western Hemisphere would they need African bodies or labors, or for that matter would there have been that inhuman trafficking of African people across the Atlantic? Without the land would there have been any need for labor? The answers to these questions are evidently in the negative. African people, obviously, did not invest in shipbuilding and various tools of slavery to enslave themselves nor were they consulted after the alleged "discovery of the Americas."

It has to be acknowledged that some Africans, very few, were part of this dastardly act. These Africans who joined Europeans in hunting and trafficking on African bodies were enemies of the people, and their actions do not reflect that of the generality of Africans. Millions of defenseless African people who lost relatives—parents, children, uncles, aunts, *et al.*, are they victims or predators too? Certainly, victims of oppression! It amounts to mischief to suggest that the infamous "House Negro," "Coons," or "Judases" who worked to sabotage the efforts of the rest of the enslaved Africans on the plantations, were responsible for slavocracy in the diaspora. The reality is that the argument about "African participation" blames the victim while exonerating the initiator, perpetrator, and the beneficiary of the trade. Every other person was used as tools in the advancement of the former's agenda.

The infamous Willie Lynch letter, which has been debated because of its unascertained origins and wording, is instructive, nevertheless. The validity of it lies in the fact that it paints a vivid picture of the mindset of the enslavers and above all their efforts and strategies of maintaining control of the mind of the enslaved Africans. The real debate should be on the substance of the letter. If the strategies of divide and conquer Lynch proffered were ever applied, then it is a worthwhile debate. While the letter showcases the devious and insidious ways Africans were controlled—dehumanizing techniques—it also illustrates the possibility that this tactic was also applied on the continent to ensure uninterrupted supply of human cargoes during the course of the human trafficking across the Atlantic.[9]

The crucial question should be, was chattel slavery morally upright, not legally because the victor always makes the rules? Therefore, to assess slavery impartially and to ascertain its place as an oppressive regime or otherwise, it is pertinent to dissect it with a moral compass. Since Europeans were predominantly Christians during the era of their enslavement of Africans, using the Bible as the barometer seems appropriate.

Certainly, the Bible did not condemn slavery; there were enslaved people during the era of the Old and New Testaments. But chattel slavery, dehumanizing slavery, not indentured servitude, were condemned implicitly and explicitly by the Old and the New Testaments. Some of the instances of such condemnation of slavery, especially the types aforementioned, are Deuteronomy 24:7—"If someone is caught kidnapping another Israelite, enslaving or selling the Israelite, then that kidnaper shall die. So you shall purge the evil from your midst;" in Exodus 21:20-21—" Anyone who beats their male or female slave with a rod must be punished if the slave dies as a direct result, but they are not to be punished if the slave recovers after a day or two, since the slave is their property." There are multiple instances where the Bible clearly instructed wealthy people on how to be humane with their servants or the enslaved.

Generally, the Bible emphasizes love over hate as well as the virtues of giving and sacrifice. The central theme of the scripture can be summed up in love. That God out of all creatures created humans with his hands and unlike other beings, gave the latter a breath of life. Also, the book of Genesis is emphatic on the fact that God created humans in his image and likeness. The implication is that God created humans last, yet placed them above all other beings including angels, who were never created in the image of God. The latter, accordingly, are messengers of God and man. In a demonstration of His love, when humans sinned, God sent His beloved son, Jesus, as a sacrificial lamb and to save those He loves. Thus, from the Old to the New Testament themes of love and sacrifice abound. Given the above, one wonders why Christian Europe ignored these thematic injunctions and moral lessons on love and kindness to traffic on African people for over 400 years and double up on it with other forms of oppression.

A closer examination of the contents of the Willie Lynch letter as well as documented and undocumented facts about slavery show that enslaved African people were tortured, raped, killed, forced to work, and were intergenerationally enslaved and subjugated. Exodus 20:13 and Matthew 5:21, as well as many other portions, condemn murder or lynching. Deuteronomy 22:23-29 condemns rape, different chapters and verses of the Bible condemns torturous treatment meted out to African people during slavery.

How the enslavers were able to ignore the moral injunctions of God and His Son, Christ, to unleash these oppressive and dehumanizing regimes on other humans and hypocritically justified them in the name of the same God that had promised heaven to the righteous and hell to sinners, is astonishing as it is contradictory. Thomas Jefferson was a man who epitomized double standards. In the Declaration of Independence document, he persuasively made the case that "all men are created equal and have the inalienable rights of life, liberty, and the pursuit of happiness."[10] Unfortunately, he meant all Caucasian men, not even their women. To grasp the full extent of this irony, one has to consider the fact that Jefferson portrayed himself through his writings as a spiritual man—a man who believed in God Almighty as well as the existence of heaven and hell for the righteous and sinners respectively.[11] Yet, somehow he and his contemporaries ignored the reality and humanity of African people by perpetuating their slavery as well as denying them human and civil rights as fellow Americans.

Oppression has been used in different forms and shapes to harass and torment African people on the continent and in the diaspora. The post-slavery oppression is commonly known as Jim Crow in the U.S. It involves the use of racist laws and ignoble tradition to subjugate Africans, dehumanizing them as sub-humans, as well as perpetually and publicly executing the defenseless victims. The paradox of this kind of oppression was that the oppressors tagged their victims as savages, wild, and uncivilized. Of course, civility to the former denotes material enrichment. This definition and perception ignore morality--discounting the fact that butchering innocent people and hanging them on trees as well as cutting off their body parts as souvenirs are the height of barbarity, savagery, and callousness. The first step in civility is the appreciation of the sanctity of human lives instead of the exaltation of material acquisitions.

In recent times, especially after the Human Rights Movement (incorrectly called the Civil Rights Movement), Jim Crow has persisted, although in different forms and has become more sophisticated. Whenever reports of certain kinds of oppression such as rape, child-trafficking, bullying, or child molestation, there is usually a universal condemnation of such crime as not only illegal but also abhorrently immoral. Unfortunately, when reports of police brutality, killing, harassment, or any kind of racist victimization of an African descendant occurs, the outcry is usually sectional. It begs the questions, are certain oppressions more heinous than others? Are some individuals and demography more American than others? Why the double standards? This attitude is consistent with the white American attitudes during slavery and the height of visible Jim Crow.

According to a research paper published by *CityLab* and conducted by Frank Edwards of Rutgers University's School of Criminal Justice, Hedwig Lee, of Washington University in St. Louis's Department of Sociology, and Michael Esposito, of the University of Michigan's Institute for Social Research, African American men are 2.5 times more likely to be killed by police than white people. For African American women, the figure is still astonishingly high—higher than white men—1.4 times. Their research used ascertained data of police killings between 2013 and 2018 to arrive at their inference. Accordingly, 1 in every 1,000 or 100 in every 100,000 black boys/men are likely to be murdered in their lifetime by the police, while for whites it is 39 in every 100,000.[12]

In the incarceration category similar trend prevails. According to data from the Prison Policy Initiative (PPI), 2207 African Americans in every 100,000 are incarcerated. For Latinos, the figure is high but not close—966, while the figure for Caucasians stands at 380 for every 100,000. This statistical data was a comparative study of June 30, 2010, and December 31, 2010, from the Correctional Population in the United States and from U.S. Census Summary according to PPI. In the same vein, during stops that do not lead to an arrest in New York City, African Americans are more than 12 times likely to be violently victimized than Caucasians.[13]

The pertinent question is, are African people more prone to crime genetically or are there social factors in the legal system, law enforcement, among others that engineer these unwelcome statistics? No doubt the answer is glaring. Social policies that disproportionately marginalize and criminalize Africa-descended people are at the root of this including police racial profiling of young black men and boys. One such policy has been exposed in New York City termed, "Stop and Frisk." Through this policy, the New York Police Department (NYPD) targeted African American males for harassment and arrest. Despite the Fourth Amendment's stipulation and requirement for the police to have a "reasonable suspicion" before stopping an individual, the NYPD and many other police departments across the U.S. have, as a matter of policy and tradition, been infringing on the human rights of African Americans.[14] The NYPD has been exposed numerous times for cultivating and harboring a culture of racism, sleaze, and corruption. Some of its members have summoned the courage and defied the odds to expose the institution's entrenched corrupt practices. Recently, a group of twelve morally upright NYPD officers filed a lawsuit against the establishment for compelling them to meet stipulated arrest quotas each day. This was in spite of a 2010 statewide ban of the corrupt practice. Sergeant Raymond, who was one of the plaintiffs, lamented thus; " . . . they can't enforce [quotas] in Park Slope, predominantly white areas . . . .But yet here they are in Flatbush, in Crown Heights, in Harlem, Mott Haven, south side of Jamaica, enforcing these things."[15]

This sinister and mendacious program is not the only oppression that is reminiscent of the nineteenth century racism; another worrisome trend of oppressive attitude is the celebration of predators and killers of African American boys and men in the twenty-first century. Trayvon Martin, whose story made national and international headlines, was a seventeen-year-old African American who was walking home at night in 2012 but was harassed and accosted by one overzealous neighborhood watchman, George Zimmermann. The latter, who is Caucasian, profiled the innocent teen determining that he fit the profile of a criminal based on his race. As a result, Zimmermann called the police. The dispatchers advised him to not confront the boy, but he ignored them and a fight ensued. Afraid of losing the fight he started, Zimmermann shot and killed Martin.

When the case was adjudged in court, Zimmermann used the self-defense argument claiming that he feared for his life during the fight and had to defend himself by pulling the trigger. The jury concurred and Zimmermann was acquitted in 2013. Ever since, he has been exposed for who he is—a violent narcissistic man that can hardly keep a job. To make matters worse, he has consistently taunted the dead boy, his family, and African people. Zimmermann has been acting erratically ever since he was acquitted in 2013.

On September 28, 2015, he tweeted a photo of Trayvon Martin's lifeless body, the same photo that was used as evidence in court.[16]

List of George Zimmermann's Run-ins with the Law

- July 2005, Zimmerman was arrested and accused of resisting an officer with violence near the University of Central Florida campus after a scuffle with police. The charges were eventually dropped after Zimmerman entered an alcohol education program.
- August 2005, Zimmerman's former fiancée filed for a restraining order against him, alleging domestic violence. Zimmerman responded by requesting a restraining order against her. Both requests were granted. No criminal charges were filed.
- February 2012, Zimmerman fatally shot 17-year-old Trayvon Martin during a confrontation in the community where Zimmerman was a neighborhood watch volunteer. Zimmerman was charged with second-degree murder but acquitted after a trial in July 2013.
- July 2013, police in Foley, Texas, stop Zimmerman for speeding in a 60-mph zone. Zimmerman is let go with just a warning.
- September 2013, Zimmerman is stopped by police in Lake Mary, Fla., and given a ticket for doing 60-mph in a 45-mph zone.
- September 2013, Zimmerman's estranged wife, Shellie, dials 911 and tells a police dispatcher that he punched her father and threatened her with a gun. She later decides against pressing charges and authorities announced in November they are dropping the case.
- September 2013, a Florida Highway Patrol trooper stops Zimmerman along Interstate 95 and issues a warning because the vehicle's tag cover and windows were too darkly tinted.
- November 2013, Zimmerman is arrested by Seminole County authorities after a disturbance at a home in Apopka.[17]

Surprisingly, considering Zimmermann's antecedents, he became a cult-hero to some white Americans who exalted the former. According to multiple news reports, Zimmermann placed the gun that he used to kill Martin in an auction and the quest to buy the weapon as a trophy was unprecedented. CNN's report stated that the last bidder, who eventually won the bid, got it for $138,900 on Tuesday, May 17, 2016.[18] Similarly, another African American teen, Mike Brown, who was gunned down by a Caucasian police officer Darren Wilson elicited tremendous news coverage. In the end, Wilson was not even tried for the cold murder. Not only was the prosecutor's decision shocking, the portrayal of Officer Wilson as a victim is equally appalling. Like Zimmermann, Wilson profited handsomely from the murder of Brown, raising between $250,000 and $500,000 online.[19] Evidently, those who donated these monies and gloried these un-convicted killers derive pleasure in African Americans' misery, pain, and oppression. It seems quite barbaric. Like Officer Wilson, Zimmermann also raised money online for killing a black boy. The former, according to the British paper, *The Telegraph*, raised about $200,000 to fund his defense team.[20]

TYPES OF OPPRESSION

There are various types of oppression, which range from racism, sexism, rape, harassment, and pedophilia, among others. But for this book, oppression will be assessed based on the approaches and attitudes of the oppressors to oppression and the oppressed. When incidents of bully occur in the U.S., for instance, it gets wide coverage in the media as well as justified attention and sympathy for the victim. There are multiple campaigns and sponsored programs geared toward eradicating bullying in the school system as well as those that advise victims on how best to respond to such incidents.

Stopbully.gov is a U.S. government website designed to sensitize people about the impact of bullying, how to prevent the scourge, as well as to expose various types of it. In combatting it, the website proffers prevention as the best form of defense. According to it, " . . . Prevention: Teach kids how to identify bullying and how to stand up to it safely . . . Be aware of what your kids are doing online." Stopbully.gov further advises potential victims and witnesses to endeavor to stop it on the spot. For adults, it counsels thus,

> When adults respond quickly and consistently to bullying behavior, they send the message that it is not acceptable. Research shows this can stop bullying behavior over time. Parents, school staff, and other adults in the community can help kids prevent bullying by talking about it, building a safe school environment, and creating a community-wide bullying prevention strategy.[21]

The website is flushed with data on types of bullying including cyber one as well as the definition of what constitutes bullying. It defines the act as an " . . . unwanted, aggressive behavior among school-aged children that involves a real or perceived power imbalance. The behavior is repeated, or has the potential to be repeated, over time. Both kids who are bullied and who bully others may have serious, lasting problems." To determine a bullying scenario, it opines that two critical components must be involved: "An Imbalance of Power," and "Repetition."

While this campaign is justified morally and otherwise, it is shortsighted conceptually in scope, reach, and definitionally. If racism, which is a fundamental part of oppression that affects disproportionately African descendants, is not a form of bullying what else is? Clearly, African people have been bullied in the past and are still being bullied in the present. There is a socioeconomic, political, and cultural power imbalance between European descendants and African people. There are intergenerational repetition and reoccurrence of racist victimization of African people around the world. If "bullying includes actions such as making threats, spreading rumors, attacking someone physically or verbally, and excluding someone from a group on purpose . . . ," what is the definition of racial oppression?

Why is the whole world united on certain kinds of oppression that are not peculiar to a race, but hypocritically turn a blind eye to the ones that affect a particular race? A global poll by UReport identified a double standard when it comes to oppression. Accordingly, in 2016, out 3,055 peopled polled around the world, only 477 responded. Among the respondents, 97 percent of them said, 'Yes bullying is a problem,' while only a paltry 3 percent said no. On the question of "have you ever been bullied?" it was 67 to 33 percent. When asked, "what does bullying most affect?" 91 percent said it affected them emotionally, physically, and their social life.[22] The balance of 9 percent said education. The unfortunate thing about this survey is that racism is separated from the notion of bullying and this is misguided. A racist victim is a bully victim and, in some instances, worse than a victim of a bully using the conventional definition. A September 2019 UNICEF report indicated that one in three young people in 30 countries admitted that they have been a victim of cyberbullying and as many as one in five has skipped class as a result. When black men and women and boys and girls are put into the equation as well as their experiences and bullying properly defined, the data will be dramatically different.

UNICEF has also launched a program tagged "End Violence" in schools. The program, which started in 2018 was aimed at combatting violence in and around schools especially those that affect children and teens. It also calls on teachers, parents, and the government to synergize to help end oppressive violence thereby making school environment conducive.[23] Like the short-sightedness of the anti-bullying campaign, this end school violence, while admirable, is not far-reaching and all-encompassing. The problem is that the whole world unites and supports the fight against other forms of oppression, including the world bodies, but when the issue is with African people it is largely ignored and pushed under the table. While we talk about school violence, why ignore the incessant shooting of defenseless and unarmed black men and women by police? Is one type of violence or oppression superior to the other?

In the same vein, the rape of women, children, and men is as atrocious as it is abominable. When such an incident occurs, there is always outcry not only from the victim and family for justice, the public rises in solidarity with the victim and against the oppressor. According to the Rape Crisis Center's report,

Prevalence of Assault

- Every 98 seconds, another American is sexually assaulted.
- 1 out of every 6 American women has been the victim of an attempted or completed rape in her lifetime.
- 1 out of every 33 American men has been the victim of an attempted or completed rape in his lifetime.
- A majority of child victims are ages 12–17.

Where Assaults Typically Occur

- 55 percent at or near the victim's home
- 15 percent in an open public space
- 12 percent at or near a relative's home
- 10 percent in an enclosed but public parking area, such as a garage or parking lot
- 8 percent on school property

Common Activities Before an Assault

- 48 percent sleeping or performing another activity at home
- 29 percent traveling to and from work or school or to shop or run errands
- 12 percent at work
- 7 percent at school
- 5 percent doing an unknown or other activity

Age of Victims

- 15 percent ages 12–17
- 54 percent ages 18–34
- 28 percent ages 35–64
- 3 percent ages 65+

The worrisome part of this report is that the perpetrators are less likely to go to jail or prison, and out of every 1,000 rape cases, 994 offenders are likely to walk free. Some of the reasons for this are: (1) the victim does not always report because of lack of support or fear of stigmatization; (2) some family members desire to protect the survivor and immediate family from further crime and therefore may not like to report to the police; (3) the victim believes that she is unable to get justice; (4) 7 percent do not want to get the perpetrator in trouble; (5) 13 percent believed it was a personal matter.[24]

The above report is damning and unflattering at all, and like in the case of school violence and bullying, there is unquestionably universal support for the fight against rape. This is not surprising as the syndrome transcends race and ethnicity. It begs the question once more, why is there lopsided sympathy, attention, action, and policies toward oppression that dehumanizes African people; that steals their dignity and peoplehood? Evidence suggests that since the 1960s revolutionary period in the African world against western oppression of Imperialism, Jim Crow, Apartheid, and Caste System, there is a redefinition of what constitutes racism and racial oppression.

POPULAR AND UNPOPULAR OPPRESSION

Popular oppression, in this book, involves cruel and persecutory policies and traditions that are acceptable to the hegemonic powers, naturalized as the norm, and somewhat absorbed by the victims as their destiny. To illustrate this properly, a look at what could be considered unpopular oppression will suffice. Public use of racial epithet or slurs is generally unpopular and therefore condemned as an act of racial oppression by most people irrespective of race. Unpopular oppression usually occurs at an individual level or is typically unleashed by an individual bigot against a victim or a group. It could also be unleashed by a group against another group or a person.

This type of oppression still prevails around the world and African people or non-Europeans are usually the targets. Samuel Eto'o, a Cameroonian-born former soccer player, was a constant victim of racial abuse by opposing fans while he played for FC Barcelona. It was typical for these racists to make monkey chants or throw bananas into the soccer pitch to try to distract and humiliate Eto'o. In one of such incidents in 2006, in a match between FC Barcelona and Real Zaragoza, he could not take it anymore. After 77 minutes of play, he walked off the field and headed to the exit. On his way out, he mouthed, "No more. No more. No more!" Unfortunately, rather than support Eto'o, the Barcelona coach, Frank Rijkaard, a black Dutchman of Surinam origin, persuaded him to play on and endure the torture. In this case, as in many others, the game, and the entertainment it offers, become more important than the humanity of the players.[25]

The racist chanting and abuse of African players and people had always been the culture of a lot of European teams. It began to subside since the 1980s and 1990s, but even in the twenty-first century, this scourge still prevails not only in Eastern Europe where it is institutionally entrenched but also in the west. This disease is so endemic that from time to time some fans racially abuse an African player within the team they supposedly support. Christie Cyrus, who plays for Fulham FC, a soccer team based in London reported that his sister was not only verbally abused, that she was also physically hit by some sections of the so-called Fulham fans after their team lost 1–0 to Barnsley in August 2019.[26]

Romelu Lukaku, who plays for Inter Milan of Italy as of 2019, has constantly endured similar abuse even when he played for Manchester United of England. His Manchester United fans had severally used his male organ to compose a misandric and sexualized song that is explicitly racist as it is chauvinistic.[27] As much it is absurd, some debauched journalists thought the song was amusing and entertaining. A writer for an online tabloid, Ben Green, described the song as "a hilarious new Romelu Lukaku song."[28] How depraved can one be? In a game against Cagliari, after joining Inter Milan in the summer of 2019, as Lukaku stepped up to take a penalty, "some in the crowd began to bellow ape-like grunts and monkey chants that did not abate after he scored." The worst part of this inhumane treatment was that his own fans dismissed the chants arguing that racism is not really a problem in Italy compared to northern Europe. In a social media statement by an Inter Milan support group, "you have to understand that Italy is not like many other Northern European countries where racism is a real problem"[29] This statement hurts as much as when an incompetent, yet arrogant doctor tells his patient that, "you do not have any problem because I could not see it through my tests."

Another layer of the problem is with the reportage on oppression. Nick Charles who reported the Lukaku incident for NBC NEWS is as dismissive, as unsympathetic, and apathetic as the Milan fans. This can be seen in the title of his report whereby he labeled the bigots "ignorant" thus, suggesting that it was because of a lack of awareness that caused them to be racially abusive. Certainly, this line of thought consciously or unconsciously bolsters oppression as it treats predators like victims. Paradigmatically, it treats oppression and, indeed, racism as a problem that requires management rather than total deracination and obliteration.

Meanwhile, these two scenarios and many more epitomize unpopular oppression—not popular because it is unacceptable in the mainstream western media and institutions; also because it is the type that is generally used to illustrate racism because it is overt, obvious, and somewhat hides the reality of institutionalized oppression. It gives people who demonstrate popular oppression cum racism unjustified high moral stand.

Examples of Popular Oppression abound in sports and other spheres of life. To grasp its operational reach and impacts in America one has to contrast the U.S. leagues with that of the rest of the world. The English soccer league, which is the oldest in the world, was formed in 1888 with twelve member teams. It has now evolved into multiple divisions; at the top is the Premier League followed by the Championship, League One, Two, and so forth. The Premier League consists of 20 teams, while the lower leagues' numbers vary, each vying for the Championship trophy within their division.

Within a season, every team will play one another twice home and away between August and May of the following year. Each win attracts a maximum of three points and a loss of zero points, while a draw or tie means each team goes home with a point apiece. At the end of the season, whoever accumulates the most points goes home with the league trophy. For the teams in the Premier League, the top four teams also qualify for the European elite competition, the UEFA Champions League to be played the following season. The ones that finished fifth and sixth play in the less prestigious European League, the Europa League. There are variables that time and space do not permit to discuss here. The last three of the twenty are relegated into the Championship division. This scenario is repeated in the Championship and other lower leagues, but the only difference is that only the top threes of each lower leagues are promoted into the upper league, while the last three drops down. There is no European league at the lower divisions. Thus, the top three from League Two goes to League One, those from League One promoted to the Championship division, and so on. Relegation, follows the same format.

Spanish League, La Liga, the German Bundesliga, the Nigerian, South African, Brazilian, and Ghanaian Leagues all follow the same template, which ensures sports democracy. Democratic because there is a healthy competition. There is also a clear path toward entrance and exit. Soccer teams are usually rooted in the communities they were formed; they are often named for the towns where they were created where they exist. For example, Manchester United, FC Barcelona, Real Madrid, Inter Milan, Ajax Amsterdam, etc. While ownership could change, the teams remain rooted in the city of its founding. A group of soccer fans or local interest groups could pull resources together to establish their own team today. They have a clear path to rise from the lowest entry-level to the zenith. An incredible example can be found in Germany with RB Leipzig which was born in 2009 in Saxony. By 2016, the young team had climbed four steps and were into the fifth, the Bundesliga, and have remained competitive ever since.[30]

In the United States, however, the league structure of all sports ranging from soccer to Basketball, to American Football is eccentric. The NFL, for example, consists of 32 teams that are grouped equally into divisions. The league consists of 17 playing weeks with each team playing against 16 teams during the regular season. Each team plays teams within their division twice, home and away with every team having one bye week. Top six teams from each conference square off in playoffs and the champion is the winner of the Super Bowl. Unlike the other leagues of the world, the American leagues perpetually remain the same, no relegation, no promotion, therefore undemocratic. No room or clear path for new entrants. The teams are not traditionally rooted in the communities of their founding as their history and destiny center around their owners. Many teams throughout the history of the NFL have relocated from city to city and state to state with the latest being the

L.A. Rams who moved from Los Angeles to St. Louis in 1995 and then back to L.A. after the 2015 season.

Although there are lower-division leagues in the U.S., they function as development leagues rather than proper leagues capable of producing top division teams. The NFL has no affiliation or relationship with other lower leagues, which means there is no competition as with other leagues of the world. The implication is that there is hardly any chance of the miracle of RB Leipzig of Saxony occurring anytime soon if the league structures remain the same.

America's sporting league structure is as vexatious as it is undemocratic. Unlike other league formats reviewed in this chapter, it rewards failure. Other leagues around the world stimulate competition by rewarding success with a championship and punishing failure with relegation, the U.S. leagues do the opposite—rewarding the least performing team with the first-round pick in the next draft of upcoming players. This makes failure attractive, especially compared to being a mediocre team. Without relegation and promotion the NBA, NFL, and MLB appear less competitive and forecloses the opportunity for further strengthening of the leagues via competitive relegation and promotion system that offers citizens a chance to form their own teams.

Thus, African people are confined to the field of play without the ability to shape the destiny of the leagues they supposedly dominate. This type of institutionalized oppression that systematically and strategically restricts African descendants on the field, where they neither control nor significantly influence the industry they dominate, is a form of Popular Oppression. It is not even perceived and counted as oppressive because it is entrenched, codified, and normalized. For African people who dominate the league at playing level, the possibility of a group of enthusiastic fans and players coming together and forming a team, growing the team, with the help of sponsors is remote or nonexistent because as the NFL, NBA, and MLB among others are constituted there is no way in. The party was already on and therefore the door has been shot.[31]

TYPES OF OPPRESSORS

Oppressors often appear in multiple ways, but operationally this notion can be grouped or divided into two according to their modus operandi—Active and Passive Oppressor. An Active Oppressor is an individual who perpetrates and unleashes venoms of repression and persecution against a victim. Such toxic actions, as noted, include verbal, racist policies and programs, as well as subscribe to an ideology that dehumanizes other humans or groups. Individuals like these cannot often exert their actions without the backing and assistance of a group. Thus, for an Active Oppression to take place, individuals belonging to a group or acting independently with the help of institutions enact policies and or unleash harmful strokes that undermine an individual or group victims' humanity. Active Oppressor unravels their ignoble exploits in both Popular Oppression and in Unpopular Oppression.

Passive Oppressor operates more discreetly, often masquerading as free-minded, liberal, or color-blind. This type observes and supervises an act of oppression but ignores it because that type of oppression is popular and therefore acceptable. This particular oppressor is as vicious and insidious as the other one. Besides, he/she is hypocritical about it but assumes a position of high moral ground when an incident of Unpopular Oppression is uncovered. A Passive Oppressor can overlook Unpopular Oppression sometimes; the individual or group of individuals ignore Popular Oppression most, if not all the time. It is convenient or easy for them to deny the fact that they are racist or an oppressor because certain oppressive acts against African people are considered normal. This normative situation fortifies them in their hypocrisy because when an act of oppression that is race neutral occurs such as rape, violence, theft, or murder, the individual reports it, criticizes it, and supports the victim.

Why is it normal for the mainstream media to call incidents of racial slurring in sports or in other public places racism, but fail to do so when it comes to the disproportionate number of black coaches versus black players in every sport? This trend is alarming and is not limited to the United States. The same trend can be seen in European soccer. In 2017, the percentage of black players in England was 33 percent, it was 16.5 percent in 1992.[32] Of those black players who have ventured into coaching, only five former England players have successfully done so since 1990.[33]

In the United States, the same alarming trend prevails. African Americans are overrepresented in two main areas in the United States, in the sports arena and in the prisons. While their playing population is astronomic in the NBA, NFL, as well as college sports, their representation in the coaching department, team ownership, as is the case in England is staggeringly and astonishingly low. Accordingly,

> While it is clear that African Americans are overrepresented in the commercialized prison system of the United States, in sports the same trend can be seen. Black overrepresentation in sports is only discernible in the playing category rather than in all other sectors such as team ownership, coaching, refereeing, sports administration, and sports journalism. Racial disparity in the above category is staggering according to the data provided by the Institute for Diversity and Ethics in Sports of the University of Central Florida. According to them, in the 2010–2011 season, 78 percent of the playing staff of NBA was black, while only about eighteen percent was white. The trend reverses sharply when it comes to management and other non-playing parts of the NBA. For

example, during the 2010–2011 season, the thirty-team NBA had only six black CEOs/presidents representing just eleven percent. Out of these thirty teams, only nine had black head coaches, while one had an Asian. In the team ownership department, it is even gloomier for blacks as only one team had a black majority shareholder—the Bobcats.[34]

The moral question to accompany this data is, why does it happen? Whose fault? Certainly, since slavery, Europeans have been content with restricting African people to physical tasks as well as entertaining acts. Coaching, apparently, is more of mental activity than it is physical therefore it seems like a convenient, yet unjustified, illogical reason to consider less African people in those positions. The oppressed African people have seemingly resigned and accepted the order. On the continent, many have naturalized the misnomer that they have to have a coach of European descent even in teams that are 100 percent black in ownership, playing staff, and so on. A lot of African National teams have a culture of always employing obscure Europeans to manage their national teams at the expense of indigenous coaches. Some pay African coaches less, give them excessive restrictions, but pay Europeans more and offer them luxury, that was consciously denied to the indigenous coaches.[35]

Different people at various levels of decision making in America, Europe, and around the world saw this syndrome developing but chose to ignore it because it is considered an acceptable form of oppression, nay, Popular Oppression. They hypocritically call out Unpopular Oppression when it occurs. The ongoing FIFA, UEFA, Premier League campaign against racism are clear examples. It is laudable that they are all fighting overt or Unpopular racism in soccer. On the other hand, it hypocritical that these soccer governing bodies are fighting oppression selectively. How could they fight Unpopular Oppression of verbalized racism by fans and ignore institutionalized racism in member nations as well as the racist composition and structure of FIFA itself? How could Europe have nearly half of the slots allocated to all the continents in the FIFA World Cup? Currently, thirty-two teams play in the senior World Cup, Europe alone has 13 ½ slots, Africa 5, and so on.[36]

Certainly, these inconsistencies and double-standard approach to oppression indicate that certain forms of oppression are popularly accepted by the hegemonic powers, while others are less tolerated. Unfortunately for African people, both forms dehumanize. In addition to dehumanization, Popular Oppression bites hard on African people's finances and social mobility. The Active Oppressor must eschew his abhorrent behavior, while the Passive Oppressor, who overlooks Popular Oppression must act with responsibility and integrity. The infamous European trafficking on Africans termed "Trans-Atlantic Slave Trade" represented a form of Popular Oppression while it lasted.

NOTES

1. Paulo Freire, *Pedagogy of the Oppressed*, https://selforganizedseminar.files.wordpress.com/2011/08/freire_pedagogy_oppresed1.pdf (accessed March 17, 2020).
2. "Democratic Republic of the Congo, 1993–2003 UN Mapping Report," *United Nations Human Rights, Office of the High Commissioner*, https://www.ohchr.org/Documents/Countries/CD/FS-2_Crimes_Final.pdf (accessed March 17, 2020).
3. See, Emeka Anaedozie, "American Media, Public Opinion, and the Nigerian Civil War, 1967–1970," *OFO: Journal of Transatlantic Studies* 4 no. 2 (2014):1–20; Elizabeth Bird and Fraser Ottanelli, *The Asaba Massacre: Trauma, Memory, and the Nigerian Civil War* (Cambridge, UK: Cambridge University Press, 2017); Elizabeth Bird and Fraser Ottanelli, "The Asaba Massacre and the Nigerian Civil War: Reclaiming Hidden History" *Journal of Genocide Research* 16 Issue 2–3(2014): 379–99.
4. "Execution of Mathias Kanu, A Biafran by Nigeria Army," *YouTube*, https://www.youtube.com/watch?v=Yb7Z_7AiGr8 (accessed March 17, 2020).
5. "The American Civil War Society," *ACWS*, https://acws.co.uk/historyalive/ACWS_InfoPack.pdf (accessed March 17, 2020).
6. See Ann Curthoys and John Docker, *Is History Fiction?* (Sydney: University of New South Wales, 2006).
7. Samuel Morton, "Observations on the Size of the Brain in Various Races and Families of Man," From the Proceedings of the Academy of Natural Sciences, October, 1849.
8. "Benin seeks forgiveness for role in slave trade," *Final Call*, last modified. October 8, 2002, http://www.finalcall.com/national/slave_trade10-08-2002.htm (accessed March 17, 2020); "African Chiefs Urged to Apologise for Slave Trade," *The Guardian*, November 18, 2009, https://www.theguardian.com/world/2009/nov/18/africans-apologise-slave-trade (accessed March 17, 2020); Alan Boyle, "Genetic Quest Leads to African Apology for Role in Slave Trade," NBC NEWS, October 13, 2013, https://www.nbcnews.com/sciencemain/genetic-quest-leads-african-apology-role-slave-trade-8C11467842 (accessed March 17, 2020).
9. "Willie Lynch letter: The Making of a Slave," *Final Call*, last Modified May 22, 2009, http://www.finalcall.com/artman/publish/Perspectives_1/Willie_Lynch_letter_The_Making_of_a_Slave.shtml (accessed March 17, 2020).
10. Thomas Jefferson—"Declaration of Independence: Right to Institute New Government," *Library of Congress*, https://www.loc.gov/exhibits/jefferson/jeffdec.html (accessed March 17, 2020).
11. "Jefferson's Religious Beliefs," *Monticello.org*, https://www.monticello.org/site/research-and-collections/jeffersons-religious-beliefs (accessed March 17, 2020).
12. Brentin Mock, "What New Research Says About Race and Police Shootings," *CityLab*, last modified August 6, 2019, https://www.citylab.com/equity/2019/08/police-officer-shootings-gun-violence-racial-bias-crime-data/595528/ (accessed March 17, 2020).
13. "United States Incarceration Rates by Race and Ethnicity, 2010," *Prison Policy Initiative*, https://www.prisonpolicy.org/graphs/raceinc.html (accessed March 17, 2020).
14. "Stop and Frisk," *Cornel Law School: Legal Information Institute*, https://www.law.cornell.edu/wex/stop_and_frisk (accessed March 17, 2020).
15. Dorothy Wickenden, "NYPD Sergeant Blows the Whistle on Quotas," *The New Yorker*, last modified August 27, 2018, https://www.newyorker.com/podcast/political-scene/an-nypd-sergeant-blows-the-whistle-on-quotas (accessed March 17, 2020).
16. Jason Silverstein, "George Zimmerman Goes on Depraved Twitter Rant after Retweeting Picture of Trayvon Martin's Corpse," *New York Daily News*, last modified September 28, 2015, https://www.nydailynews.com/news/national/george-zimmerman-retweets-picture-trayvon-martin-corpse-article-1.2376777 (accessed March 17, 2020).
17. "A list of George Zimmerman's past run-ins with the law," *Fox News Channel*, last modified January 13, 2015, https://www.foxnews.com/us/a-list-of-george-zimmermans-past-run-ins-with-the-law (accessed March 17, 2020).
18. Eliott C. McLaughlin, "George Zimmerman's Auction for Gun that Killed Trayvon Martin Ends," *CNN*, last modified May 18, 2016, https://www.cnn.com/2016/05/18/us/george-zimmerman-gun-auction/index.html (accessed March 17, 2020).

19. Carolyn Brown, "Over $500,000 in Crowdfunding Raised For Ferguson Officer Darren Wilson," *Black Enterprise*, last modified September 5, 2014, https://www.blackenterprise.com/over-500000-raised-for-ferguson-officer-darren-wilson-before-sites-shut-down/ (accessed March 17, 2020).

20. "George Zimmerman Raises $200,000 in Donations," *The Telegraph*, last modified April 27, 2012, https://www.telegraph.co.uk/news/worldnews/northamerica/usa/9230457/George-Zimmerman-raises-200000-in-donations.html (accessed March 17, 2020).

21. https://www.stopbullying.gov/ (accessed March 17, 2020).

22. https://ureport.in/v2/opinion/575/ (accessed March 17, 2020).

23. "UNICEF poll: More than a third of young people in 30 countries report being a victim of online bullying," *UNICEF*, last modified September 3, 2019, https://www.unicef.org/press-releases/unicef-poll-more-third-young-people-30-countries-report-being-victim-online-bullying (accessed March 17, 2020).

24. "Statistics," *Rape Crisis Center*, https://rapecrisis.com/statistics/ (accessed March 17, 2020).

25. Rob Hughes, "Soccer: Racist Spanish Fans Push Eto'o to Edge," *New York Times*, last modified February 26, 2006, https://www.nytimes.com/2006/02/26/sports/soccer-racist-spanish-fans-push-etoo-to-edge.html (accessed March 17, 2020).

26. "Christie Claims Sister was Racially Abused by Own Fans," *RTE*, last modified August 3, 2019, https://www.rte.ie/sport/soccer/2019/0803/1066855-christie-claims-sister-was-racially-abused-by-own-fans/ (accessed March 17, 2020).

27. Neil Wilkes, "Manchester United Fans to Keep Singing About Romelu Lukaku's Penis," *SportsMole*, https://www.sportsmole.co.uk/off-the-pitch/man-utd/racism-in-football/news/fans-to-keep-singing-about-lukaku-penis_307734.html (accessed March 17, 2020).

28. Ben Green, "Manchester United Fans Have a Hilarious New Romelu Lukaku Song," *101 Great Goals*, last modified September 19, 2017, https://www.101greatgoals.com/news/social/new-romelu-lukaku-song/ (accessed March 17, 2020).

29. Nick Charles, "Racist Abuse of Inter Milan Star Romelu Lukaku Shows 'Widespread Ignorance' Persists in Soccer," *NBC NEWS*, last modified September 25, 2019, https://www.nbcnews.com/news/nbcblk/racism-soccer-widespread-ignorance-n1056921 (accessed March 17, 2020).

30. Jefferson Chase, "RB Leipzig Seal Promotion to First Division," *DW*, last modified May 8, 2016, https://www.dw.com/en/rb-leipzig-seal-promotion-to-first-division/a-19243190 (accessed March 17, 2020).

31. Emeka Anaedozie, *Nuwaubian Pan-Africanism: Back to Our Root* (Lanham, MD: Lexington Books, 2019), 112–13.

32. Dave Fraser, "Testament to The Game: Proportion of British Premier League Players from Black, Asian and Minority Ethnic Backgrounds Has Doubled Since the 1992–93 Season," *The Sun*, last modified August 15, 2017, https://www.thesun.co.uk/sport/football/4246535/premier-league-black-asian-minority-ethnic-backgrounds-doubled-since-1992/ (accessed March 17, 2020).

33. Jonathan Liew, Football Must Face up to an Indisputable Truth: Black Managers do not get the Same Chances as White Managers," *Independent*, last modified June 1, 2018, https://www.independent.co.uk/sport/football/news-and-comment/rooney-rule-black-managers-indisputable-data-football-jonathan-liew-a8379111.html (accessed March 17, 2020).

34. Anaedozie, *Nuwaubian Pan-Africanism*, 113.

35. "The Foreign Coach Nigeria Needs!," *Complete Sports*, last modified July 19, 2015, https://www.completesports.com/the-foreign-coach-nigeria-needs/ (accessed March 17, 2020).

36. https://www.fifa.com/ (accessed March 17, 2020).

Chapter Two

African People's History

Challenge to the Standard Narratives

Various aspects of African people's history have been oppressively narrated by non-Africans and by some African people themselves that the stories oppress in the present as much as oppression did and is doing currently. Thus, these kinds of interpretations tend to either embellish, misinform, mis-educate, or do all. On the continent, various colonial and racist literature emerged to give impetus to imperialism. In the diaspora, they served to justify slavery and serve as intellectual tools that sustained oppression. Some of these literary works were fiction such as *King Solomon's Mines* and "The Birth of a Nation" movie, among others. In the academy, the same racist paradigm prevailed working complementarily to naturalize the oppression of African people. Sadly, even in the twenty-first century, the reverberating effects of these thoughts still shape some Africans' perception of themselves, their ancestral land, and their capabilities. The most worrisome part is that even the elite in the diaspora and on the continent, who are supposedly educated and wealthy, are not immune to this externally produced, internally consumed self-hate syndrome.

KING SOLOMON'S MINES

The novel, *King Solomon's Mines* was an unapologetically racist piece that reveled on two main themes; denigrating Africans while riding on their shoulders to forge an Anglo-Saxon identity, and shoring up support for the west's voracious quest for empires and resources in Africa.[1] The author's strategy, like other pro-colonial novels and movies, was to utilize witty, salacious, and imaginatively captivating prose to encapsulate his audience and to persuasively induce them to be sympathetic to the Europeans' imperialist cause.[2] In this case, Haggard presented himself and his co-adventurers as virtuous men, who were principled, pious and whose mission helped convey some glimpses of enlightenment to a group of "heathen," blood-thirsty "savages." The narrative followed the Eurocentric playbook and narratives of the nineteenth and early twenty-first century European imperialism that misrepresented Africans by disingenuously constructing them as childlike, "barbaric," uncultured, and in urgent need of European paternalistic grooming.Thus, to make it convincing, these fictions were somewhat presented as factual and made to complement the works of racist science.[3]

The Haggard carefully misrepresented Africans, casting them as passively lacking intellectual capability and morality to implicitly justify the European need to colonize and dominate the Africans. The author invented a fantasized Solomon's road and mines; that these were erected and established by some "Caucasian" Egyptians or Jews, thereby building on other familiar hypotheses, notably the Hamitic that tied African accomplishments to European origins. By so doing, Haggard reinforced the then-prevailing condescending racial stereotype that claimed that African people were "cursed" by God to be perpetual slaves of Europeans. Hence, he created an image of Africa as barren, the people as savages living in forests like wild animals, cannibalized one another, did not appreciate nor recognize the sanctity of life, and who were innately inferior and morally bankrupt. This picture contrasted with the self-glorifying image he crafted for his countrymen and race—an image of Anglo-Saxon cultural and moral superiority, a noble race that had the mandate to bear the burden of propagating civilization. In narrating his travels and encounters with different Bantu ethnic groups, Haggard portrayed Africa as culturally homogenous and out of touch with modernity. Thus, his construction, predictably placed Anglo-Saxons at the top echelon of the racial and ethnic pyramid and Africa at the periphery, a position he inferred the latter cannot climb out of due to inherent genetic inferiority.[4]

This flagrant colonial apologetic piece might have served to galvanize support for the British colonial ventures into different parts of Africa including South Africa.[5] By embodying fictive tales of adventures, the book presented to the European audience a "dark continent" and "jungle"—a gaming spot for potential adventurers. It also highlighted economic potentials including mineral resources inviting European corporations to exploit the people and their material possessions. Haggard implied that Africa was idling away in primitivity, having not mastered its environment—they live in a state of nature caring only about what to eat and how to outdo each other, he contended. The author invented and described the fictional Kukuanland as ruled by a despotic Twala, who was blood-thirsty and freakily promiscuous, having married hundreds of wives like the biblical Solomon. The inference here is, therefore, that Africa was anachronistically thousands of years behind Europe, tied to biblical Israel of the past in vices only. This type of depiction, at the height of British imperialism in Africa, served to encourage and inspire more conquest. It was suggestive to the British to extend its rule beyond Cape Town and coastal areas into the interiors of South Africa. To fortify his argument, the author viciously painted a falsified mental picture about incessant ritual killings, starvation, and epidemic rampant on the continent to perhaps make a moral case for imperialism. This can also be understood as a tactical plea to the British religious arm of imperialism—the Anglican church to join and support the mission in a supposed attempt to salvage the continent from internal implosion and self-destruction.

Haggard in aiming to galvanize support for the British imperial mission in Africa sought to exalt the Anglo-Saxons above other Europeans culturally and in terms of acumen. The Portuguese, who were the pioneers in the enslavement and human trafficking of Africans across the Atlantic, were especially depicted as culturally and anatomically inferior to the English. Silvestre, a character in the novel, was depicted as having died en route to the Solomon's mines. Unlike the British trio of Good, Quatermain, and Sir Henry, Silvestre could not obtain the precious stones because of the aforementioned deficiencies. He died on the treacherous and mountainous terrain. His death heralded the author's narrative that like the Egyptians, Jews, and Romans, the Portuguese civilization were less encompassing and sophisticated, but the English's were. To drive home this point, Haggard made sure that the trio, despite terrible encounters with the "savages" in Kukuanland, with Gagool and inside the cave, came out successfully on top even with the odds were against them. Their lights shone in the "darkest" Africa successfully enthroning a "good savage"—Ignosi as the benevolent ruler of Kukuanland.[6] Certainly, the function of this tragicomedy was to paint imperialism as noble rather than a scheme for economic and cultural exploitation.

Africa and African women, in particular, were sexualized, exploited as sources of cheap entertainment for middle-class English men. Haggard presented both literarily as sexual objects which were always and readily available to the English man.[7] Although these African women, he posited, would cherish the once in a lifetime opportunity to have sex with white men, Caucasian men do not desire them because they were "dirty," "barbaric" and could not take the place of white women. In some instances, the author portrayed African women positively and humanized them as pretty, like Foulata, yet Haggard did not miss the chance to remind his audience that the former was still African and therefore a "savage." This point in the novel was crucial as it was a way of reminding the British authorities of the need to facilitate the immigration of white women in the colonized land to perpetuate the Caucasian race. This also served to maintain the sexual boundary between the two worlds. The African land was not spared either; it was portrayed as femininely virgin, in need of the white man's penetration and exploitation.[8] The Solomon's mines map illustration underscores this. In it, the mountains around the mines were anatomized as consisting of breasts and being Sheba's, while the mines itself was sexually tagged as the mouth of the treasure, implying the feminine sexual organ. This sexualization and feminization of land, especially of other lands, is not uncommon for European imperialists and adventurists. They often use words like, "virgin," and "penetration" to denigrate and feminize places intended for colonization.[9] By describing the land in these terms, Europeans empowered themselves as potent men and the potential colony as females available for penetration by the "powerful" Anglo-Saxon men.

The book, like "The Birth of a Nation" movie, was vehemently racist; it embodied overt white supremacist and Manifest Destiny ideology of the era.[10] By purporting that Africans believed in the myth that whites were gods and that they descended from the moon, the author did not bother to blur his supremacist narrative. Throughout the book, accounts and the theme of Englishmen's successes abound—the English triumph over Africans; of English guns over Kukuan magic, of Good over Twala; civilization over "barbarism" and of light over darkness. These extreme racist paradigms explain the reasons for the book's virality in Britain and all over the western world. It not only vehemently promoted racial bigotry, but it also normalized oppressive patriarchy while objectifying women which paradoxically appealed to European men of the era.

IN THE WESTERN ACADEMY

Instances of such a racist paradigm abound in the theme of slavery, imperialism, emancipation, decolonization, and independence. Western scholars of the nineteenth and early twentieth centuries played pivotal roles in the falsified and misleading interpretation of African history. One of the notable authors and scholars in this regard includes U. B. Phillips who was educated at both the University of Georgia and Columbia University. Like his contemporaries, Phillips presented Africa in an unscrupulous light, somehow arguing that tropical Africa was a "curse" to its inhabitants. Of course, he conveniently left out the fact that tropical weather meant an abundance of rain and sunshine, hence an abundance of food and expertise in agriculture. The latter skill set was decisive in helping Europeans, who were by no means experts in farming (between the 1500s and 1800s), reap the full benefits of imperialism and slavery in the Western Hemisphere.

Accordingly, Phillips argued that tropical land encouraged redundancy while discouraging mental alertness. To him, this resulted in a lack of innovation and led to superstition. He dismissed African spirituality as coming in the way of productivity as nature intersected with spirituality. Rivers, trees, and other inanimate objects, according to him had guiding or specialty spirits:

> No people is without its philosophy and religion. To the Africans the forces of nature were often injurious and always impressive. To invest them with spirits disposed to do evil but capable of being placated was perhaps an obvious recourse; and this investiture grew into an elaborate system of superstition. Not only did the wind and the rain have their gods but each river and precipice, and each tribe and family and person, a tutelary spirit. These might be kept benevolent by appropriate fetish ceremonies; they might be used for evil by persons having specially great powers over them. The proper course for common-place persons at ordinary times was to follow routine fetish observances; but when beset by witch-work the only escape lay in the services of witch-doctors or priests. Sacrifices were called for, and on the greatest occasions nothing short of human sacrifice was acceptable.[11]

The author demonstrates his arrogance that was fussed with ignorance leading to the convoluted and vexatious narrative. Clearly, his Eurocentric perspective was at play in his supposed scholarly research. What he and his contemporaries could not grasp about other races is usually dismissed as superstitious or a mark of regression. The author, like in recent times, attempted fruitlessly to export European phenomena, in this case, patriarchy. This can be seen in his description of the African family structure and gender dynamics. While he falsely and collectively painted Africa as an epitome of patriarchy, where wives were virtually enslaved to their husbands, his audience would have known exactly which continent and people he was ironically talking about:

> In African economy nearly all routine work, including agriculture, was classed as domestic service and assigned to the women for performance. The wife, bought with a price at the time of marriage, was virtually a slave;her husband her master. Now one woman might keep her husband and children in but moderate comfort. Two or more could perform the family tasks much better. Thus a man who could pay the customary price would be inclined to add a second wife, whom the first would probably welcome as a lightener of her burdens. Polygamy prevailed almost everywhere.[12]

In the same vein, Phillips argued unequivocally that slavery was cultural, indigenous, and naturally an African phenomenon. Apparently, he was referencing the indentured servitude and debtor versus creditor work relationship but misleadingly termed it slavery to help exonerate Europeans from the guilt of four hundred years of human trafficking across the Atlantic. It is not surprising that this author in virtually all his publications, books and journal articles, demonized Africans in the diaspora while also disparaging those on the continent. To him, slavery was not as evil as the white liberals had made it out to be. And without the Civil War, it would have died a natural death for as of 1860, it had reached its peak and diminishing return was inevitable.[13]

SELF-INCRIMINATION

Views and thoughts as the ones above have worked and continue to work negatively on the minds of African people at home and in the diaspora. This level of miseducation, a form of educational abuse, manifests in different forms among African people. The most excruciating impact of this plague is felt when a black leader, elite, or role model espouses views about their history that is not only false but injurious to her people's collective destiny. Kimberly Daniels, an African American politician, Christian minister, gave a remarkable church sermon in 2008. She was the guest speaker at the Solid Rock Church in Monroe, Ohio, when she made the contentious remarks. Daniels, a Florida State House of Representatives member, admonished the audience to identify as Christians rather than as African Americans, perhaps in the spirit of racial blindness. Of course, this counsel, a liberal talking-point, implies that race is the problem rather than racism—oppression based on race or racial differences. She seemingly made a case against social justice for African Americans inferring that their reward should be in heaven and delivered by God. In her words, "And you can talk about the Holocaust, but the Jews own everything. We go through some things, but let me tell you something—when you go through, you qualify to get paid back. You don't need the government to give it back, God will give it back."[14] Thus, effectively shutting down the clamor for reparations. She also did not mention the fact that the same Bible exalted hard work, that the essence of Jesus's message was on justice. Therefore, justice is always shadowed by peace. Also, she seemed to not recognize the fact that part of the reasons for the successes the Jews are recording stem from reparations on earth rather than in heaven.

Astonishingly, Dr. Daniels also said the following in appreciation for her pastoral career and redemption from drugs:

> I thank God for slavery . . . . Huh! I thank God for the crack house. . . . If it wasn't for the crack house, come on somebody, God wouldn't have never been able to use me how He's able to use me now. And if it wasn't for slavery, I might be somewhere in Africa worshipping a tree.[15]

Dr. Daniels, who holds both masters and doctorate degrees, ministers to thousands of African Americans who inevitably look up to her as a model of success, spiritually and otherwise.[16] Comments like this, however, cause concern especially when they come from a person occupying a leadership position in the African American community. Certainly, this is the result of the cumulative intergenerational miseducation that Dr. Carter G. Woodson painstakingly articulated in his seminal classic *Miseducation of the Negro*.

In the same vein, Pastor James David Manning, Ph.D., made another disparaging and equally problematic comment that further exposed the menace of miseducation among the supposed "Talented Tenth." According to him,

> That Africa, the big old continent over there, they never built one boat that was sea-worthy, not one! There's not one monument in Africa, in all of Africa. I know you are talking about Egypt; Egypt is not Africa. There were no great cities that were built, even before the fresh colonization of white people, coming to the shores of Africa or the slave ships. Black men built nothing! No sewage system! No houses above one level. And none of them made out of stone. All of them made out of grass and wood. Black men, before the white men, ever got to Africa. The worst thing that could ever happen to South Africa was when they gave it to Nelson Mandela and black folk. That was a great nation. I understand that Apartheid was wrong, we all know it's wrong. I'm against it, there should have been other resolutions though than turning it over to Nelson Mandela.[17]

This is a synopsis of one of Dr. Manning's thoughts available on YouTube. He claimed that African descendants do not know how to run a nation, thus, as soon as Africans took over, diseases became rife all over the major cities, including Johannesburg. These problematic instances are microcosms of the bigger picture. Leaders are viewed as authority figures and revered by their teeming followers. If he or she err on a sociopolitical topic, it could cause serious damage to the communities the latter is working to promote.

DECONSTRUCTING THE PARLANCE OF SLAVERY AND IMPERIALISM

European Slave Trade, also known as the Transatlantic Slave Trade, undoubtedly was a tragic epoch in African history. It depleted Africa's population, weakening it while simultaneously enriching and empowering the West. Certainly, for Europeans to have succeeded in trafficking and trading on African bodies they utilized some Africans. The majority of the African masses were victims of this capitalist venture. The African collaborators' role in this heinous immorality must be understood and contextualized. Their roles were that of tools at the hands of a technician or engineer. The latter is the subject utilizing an object to control or operate on another object. An engineer initiates a plan, outlines and plots it, and then employs tools (an object) to help him accomplish his goals. The engineer, certainly and rightly, takes all the glory when the project succeeds. All the benefits accruable also go to the subject, not the object. The benefits that go to objects are minimal and are only redeemable with the former's permission. Objects are usually dispensable, but subjects are not. Thus, for Europeans to exploit Africa's human resources they utilized few Africans in the advancement of their goals. The same principle was applied to the plantation in the Americas whereby select minority was used to spy on and control the majority.

Second World War history is flush with unpopular stories of few Jewish collaborators with the Nazis toward the extermination of their people. Individuals such as Ans van Dijk, Abraham Gancwajch, Karol Hochberg, and Jakub Lejkin among numerous others, were alleged to have collaborated one way or the other with the Nazis.[18] The tragic story of the Jewish Holocaust is not centered around them nor is it portrayed in the context of Jewish people doing it to one another. Rather, the narrative takes into account who the enemy was and the fact that for the oppressor to succeed he always uses willing tools among the oppressed. Where there is none readily available, he creates one through multiple means of coercion. In today's judicial system, sometimes prosecutors use divide and conquer to convict one member of a family and set the other one free or give them a lesser sentence.

European Slavery not only separated Africans physically, the narrative of it further divides the latter thereby sustaining the separation. It is typical of historians interested in African history to toe this line of separation. Unfortunately, what it does is to justify the separation and build an identity based on oppression rather than on history, culture, and interconnectedness. For instance, why does the African Diasporan history start with Slavery? Why is the enslavement of African people not studied in comparison to the enslavement of the continent termed differently—imperialism? Simply put, Europe firstly took human resources initially to work as human machines for them in the Americas. The profits derived therefrom transformed Europe and its outlets. It led to the European Industrial Revolution, which in turn led to the need for material resources to lubricate the machines; be processed in the industries. Thus, imperialism served that need, leading to the enslavement of the people left on the continent and the seizure of the land and everything therein.[19]

African history had always been human history, not of government, or that of the bourgeois. Therefore, it is continuous and should not depend or be limited by geography or nationality. To fully grasp the history of slavery, the root of it must be explored which is European imperialism. Without it, there would not have been any need for the traffic on African bodies across the Atlantic. Eric Williams eloquently and articulately elaborated on this by indicating that the basis for European industrialization and the Industrial Revolution was the enslavement of African people which was born by imperialism.[20]

On the continent of Africa, the damages of firstly, the Arab slave trade and later European, is enormous and is well documented. After depleting the population of the continent and bastardizing its resources for four hundred years, Europeans who had started the trade had to stop to accomplish the second phase of slavery. This second phase meant that they needed to turn the entire continent into a plantation, the people into tenants, peasants, or "slaves" in their own land. Elsewhere on the continent, the same model of trafficking, buying, and selling of Africans was replicated inside Africa. For instance, in South Africa, European descendants turn Africans into beasts of burden in Cape Town and adjoining areas. They also bought and sold Africans in auctions as was the case in the Western Hemisphere.[21]

Imperialism is essentially slavery—slavery with another name. It is a form of indirect slavery as typified by the British Indirect rule system. The scheme involved administering and controlling people through their rulers or individuals appointed by the colonizers to act on their behalf. Like in the plantations of the Americas, the British, in particular, allowed private corporations to administer their colonies. In West Africa, they had the Royal Niger Company; India, East Indian Company, in the U.S., Virginia Company. The goal of these corporations, like in the modern times, was to make an astronomic profit and the best way to maximize it was to follow the template Adam Smith had outlined as enumerated by William:

> Labor, that is, must be constant and must work, or be made to work, in cooperation. In such colonies the rugged individualism of the Massachusetts farmer, practising his intensive agriculture and wringing by the sweat of his brow niggardly returns from a grudging soil, must yield to the disciplined gang of the big capitalist practising extensive agriculture and producing on a large scale. Without this compulsion, the laborer would otherwise exercise his natural inclination to work his own land and toil on his own account.[22]

Even when the British government revoked the charters of its private governments, the enslavement of peoples of Africa continued in a different form by a different entity, the same result. Under Indirect Rule, operation of government at grassroots, including law enforcement, was left for Africans with the British acting as the behind the scenes supervisors and controllers. The Courts were usually administered by the British. The rationale behind the system was: 1) it was cheaper to manage because it would have cost more to appoint British officers at every level. Also, they paid African appointed agents lower wages; 2) The system gives the illusion of self-rule to the colonized as the faces of local authorities look familiar; 3) Unfortunately, the face of oppression was African rather than European.[23] The brutal colonial army, police, and other arms of governmental oppression was black. But the face of justice in the court and policy design in governance, which is rarely seen, was European. It was a perfect system of oppression that used the oppressed to oppress, which was a reversal of the order in the American plantation system. Nonetheless, on those plantations and on many occasions, the enslavers used the enslaved to torture perceived recalcitrant African people to achieve the same desired goal of divide and conquer.

Before the advent of European colonialism, Africa had the highest proportion of individually owned land and properties. Unfortunately, imperialism reversed that and invented a dual system that put an overwhelming percentage of the land at the control of the European authority. The implication was that millions of Africans who had naturally worked for themselves now had to work for the former for a wage, in some cases on their ancestral lands. European capitalism, according to Rodney, meant that the capitalist—who controls the land/resources, often through coercion and venality—is responsible for the physical survival of the worker via "a living-wage."[24] This position is underscored by Home contending:

> Africa (at least sub-Saharan Africa) has the highest proportion of tribal[sic]/communal land, as distinguished from private and public/state land, of any continent. This can be attributed to a combination of geography, history and population distribution, and was reinforced by a history of external colonial rule, which created a dual system of land tenure that restrained private property rights in the tribal/communal land areas.[25]

Although some of the words such as "tribal" are quite pejorative, the weight of his argument is undeniable and factual. The implication was that politically, culturally, and economically, Europeans controlled the continent for their aggrandizement. At the same time turned the remnants on the continent, who survived formal slavery into other forms of "slave." Like in the diaspora, Africans at home were required to call Europeans (colonial) "masters," while on the other hand regardless of how old you were as long as you were African, you were a boy to the egotistical imperialists.

The ideology of imperialism and slavery is the same. The oppressor was the same, the oppressed the same. The difference between the continental and diaspora Africans' oppression is unmeasurable. But one has to acknowledge the fact that those in the diaspora faced trafficking across the Atlantic, were branded, routinely tortured, overworked, and more routinely raped on the plantation. While, they were also forcefully stripped of their ethnic names, languages, religions, and values, some of those on the continent due to the discreet nature of slavery and imperialism on the continent willingly gave up their identities to embrace European ones. Elkins's pivotal research has, on the other hand, thrown more light on the nature of British imperialism in East Africa, especially Kenya. Her painstaking research thoroughly documents the torturous and murderous nature of British colonial rule in Kenya in the former's desperation to douse the flame of revolution and maintain firm economic and social control. The research also underscores the fact that Europeans turned Africa into a giant plantation and enslaved the people on their own land forcing them to work as gangs.[26]

CELEBRATION OF INDEPENDENCE DAY AND EMANCIPATION

If the enslavement of Africa via slavery and imperialism was immoral, then it is time to rethink emancipation and independence-day celebration. How does it sound if an individual's car was forcibly taken or stolen, and after toiling to recover it, he then celebrates like he just bought a new car even though the condition of the property has deteriorated? While that celebration might be justified at first, the individual is best served to seek justice rather than wallow in euphoria. If there is any day that deserves commemoration, it was the original date, not the latter one. In the case of African nations, the independence-day celebration deletes the people's prior history and assumes that a nation-state is born after Europeans had made a mark. Certainly, most of the African countries were purely European creation, out of multiple existing nations, or they did so by splitting nations for administrative and exploitative reasons.

Celebrating independence day justifies imperialism, which at the same time undermines the efforts of the African people's ancestors to resist the forceful takeover of their patrimony. A wrongfully convicted person when eventually released should be happy on the one hand that he has regained his freedom, angry on the other that his freedom was unjustly taken. Thus, independence day, rather than being a period of celebration, should be one of sober and somber reflection and demand for justice for all the wrongs unleashed on the continent and its people around the world.

Why is it termed "independence" rather than freedom? The former stands for a condition of being without outside control or a condition of not being supported. It incorrectly interprets the relationship between the colonizer and the colonized as that of dependency. Thus, this notion stems from western paternalistic thought, which was also prevalent on the plantations of the Americas. On the plantations, Europeans claimed to be the father of all. Thus, the primary role of a father is to provide, protect, and defend. A father's role does not include, rape, torture, overworking his children, and so on. A father cannot socially and logically be a father to someone older than him. All these inconsistencies show that the paternalism theory was a smokescreen for the reality of slavocracy. Therefore, interpreting the colonial power dynamics in the dependence versus independence paradigm ignores the facts of imperialism and slavery. It presents imperialism as a favor to the colonized, who was dependent on the "mother-country" but has now grown old enough to be weaned. Like in the case of the diasporan plantations, it is as disingenuous as it is excruciating.

The same applies to the commemoration of emancipation although it is no longer prevalent. It should be a day that calls for a reflection, a somber one, on the history of African people. It should be a day that African peoples' ancestors should be honored through education on the true history of African people, their accomplishments, trials, and importantly, victories despite the odds. Emancipation-day celebrations should be a period of reflection on the fact that slavery, like its sister imperialism, was unjust and immoral. Therefore, emancipation and independence days should be days to demand justice or some forms of reparations like everyone else.

BIRTHDAY CELEBRATIONS FOR THE DEAD?

Another relevant point is the celebration of birthdays for the dead. It is completely un-African as it is unnatural. Life has two stages: birth and death. After someone's birth, every year the living felicitates with him/her. After his death, he has gone to the second stage. Therefore, what should be commemorated henceforth is his death, via a memorial. It is during a memorial service for the dead that his deeds and accomplishments, and in some situations, circumstances of the death, are contextualized. Thus, the interested public tap into that metaphysical energy for positive development. Birthday celebrations for the dead is akin to telling a visitor welcome on his way out of your house. It sounds sarcastic, because when the visitor initially came, you said "welcome." On his way out, it should be "goodbye," not welcome again. Thus, birthday for the living; memorial for the dead on their anniversary.

Unfortunately, in the diaspora and on the continent, African people now celebrate birthdays for their dead heroes. Marcus Garvey, Malcolm X, and Martin Luther King, Jr. are all misguidedly remembered on their birthdays even when they have passed on to the second stage. On the continent, the same Eurocentric trend prevails as Nnamdi Azikiwe, Chukwuemeka Odumegwu Ojukwu, Nelson Mandela, and Kwame Nkrumah among others are inappropriately remembered and celebrated on their birthdays.

NOTES

1. Pascal Blanchard, *et al.*, eds., *Human Zoos: Science and Spectacle in the Colonial Age* (Liverpool: Liverpool University Press, 2008), 30.
2. Paul Landau and Deborah Kaspin, *Images and Empires: Visuality in Colonial and Postcolonial Africa* (Berkeley: University of California Press, 2002), 2.
3. Blanchard, 6.
4. Landau, 2.
5. Edward Said, *Orientalism* (New York: Vintage Books, 1978), 14.
6. Jan Nederveen Pieterse, *White on Black: Images of Africa and Blacks in Western Popular Culture* (New Haven: Yale University Press, 1992), 90–92.
7. Z. S. Strother, "Display of the Hottentot Venus" in *Africans on Stage: Studies in Ethnological Show Business. Bernth Lindfers*, ed. (Bloomington: Indiana University Press, 1999), 1–3.
8. Anne McClintock, *Imperial Leather: Race, Gender and Sexuality in the Colonial Contest* (New York: Routledge, 1995), 1–3.
9. Ibid.

10. "The Birth of a Nation" was a racist movie released in 1915. Its central theme was that African American men are predators who rape and violate blonde helpless Caucasian women. Thus, the movie was instrumental in the reborn of the Ku Klux Klan whose main goal was to terrorize and brutalize African Americans. "The Birth of Nation" was played in the United States' White House as well as across U.S. cities.

11. U.B. Phillips, *American Negro Slavery* (Gutenberg's Edition, 2004), 6.

12. Ibid., 7.

13. See, U.B. Phillips, "The Economic Cost of Slaveholding in the Cotton Belt," *Political Science Quarterly*, 20 (2) (1905): 257–75; U.B. Phillips, "The Origin and Growth of the Southern Black Belts," *American Historical Review*, 11 (4) (1906): 798–816; U. B. Phillips, "The Slave Labor Problem in the Charleston District," *Political Science Quarterly*, 22 (3): 416–39.

14. Dan Macguill, "Did Florida State Rep. Kimberly Daniels Once Say, 'I Thank God for Slavery'?" *Snopes*, last modified January 2, 2019, https://www.snopes.com/fact-check/kimberly-daniels-thank-god-slavery/ (accessed March 17, 2020).

15. "Kimberly Daniels Thanks God For Slavery," *Youtube*, https://www.youtube.com/watch?v=CKCSUbJceeUandfeature=emb_logo (accessed March 17, 2020).

16. "Kimberly Daniels Candidate for City Council at Large Group 1," *News4Jax*, last modified March 12, 2015, https://www.news4jax.com/news/2015/03/12/kimberly-daniels/ (accessed March 17, 2020).

17. "This Video Will Shock South African People - American Politics," *Youtube*, https://www.youtube.com/watch?v=17m8OnHC7dQ (accessed March 17, 2020).

18. See, Marian Apfelbaum, *Two Flags: Return to the Warsaw Ghetto*, (Jerusalem, Israel: Gefen Publishing House, 2007);Daniel Boffey, "Who betrayed Anne Frank? Book Claims to Shed New Light on Mystery," *The Guardian*, May 25th, 2018. https://www.theguardian.com/world/2018/may/25/who-betrayed-anne-frank-book-claims-to-shed-new-light-on-mystery (accessed March 17, 2020); Lawrence Baron,*Projecting the Holocaust into the Present: The Changing Focus of Contemporary Holocaust Cinema* (Lanham, MD: Rowmanand & Littlefield, 2005), 83.

19. See, Eric Williams, *Capitalism and Slavery* (Chapel Hill, NC: The University of North Carolina Press, 1944); Walter Rodney, *How Europe Underdeveloped Africa* (Washington, DC: Howard University Press, 1982), 75–78; 82–83.

20. Ibid.

21. "To Be Sold and Let: On Monday 18th of May. 1829," *South African History Online*, last modified August 27, 2019, https://www.sahistory.org.za/sites/default/files/article_pics/2_1_slave_poster_big percent5B1 percent5D.gif (accessed March 17, 2020).

22. Williams, 2.

23. Emily Lynn Osborn, "'Circle of Iron': African Colonial Employees and the Interpretation of Colonial Rule in French West Africa," *Journal of African History*, 44, no. 1 (2003): 29–50; Anthony I. Nwabughuogu," The Role of Propaganda in the Development of Indirect Rule in Nigeria, 1890–1929," *The International Journal of African Historical Studies*, 14, no. 1 (1981): 65–92; Lakshmi Iyer," Direct versus Indirect Colonial Rule in India: Long-Term Consequences," *The Review of Economics and Statistics*, 92, no. 4 (November 2010): 693–713.

24. Rodney, 150.

25. Robert Home, "'Culturally Unsuited to Property Rights?': Colonial Land Laws and African Societies," *Journal of Law and Society*, 40, no. 3 (September, 2013): 404.

26. See Caroline Elkins, *Imperial Reckoning: The Untold Story of Britain's Gulag in Kenya* (New York: Henry Holt and Company, 2005).

Chapter Three

Popular Oppression in Entertainment and Public Places

Racism, no doubt, is a form of an oppressive ideological construct designed to impugn and invalidate the humanity of the victims. It is a form of oppression that targets victims and criminalizes them based on their biological features not necessarily culture. As Miller and Garran succinctly enumerate, it is socially constructed to oppress on one hand and employed as a justification for dehumanizing the victim on the other.[1] Often, racists misleadingly infer explicitly or implicitly that their victims are genetically inferior, but it is the former's attitudes and policies that confine victims to inferior social conditions. A crucial operational tool of this ideology is the stereotype. Simply put, a stereotype is an oversimplified image or notion of a type of person or thing. The creator intends to apply a universal vice as a particular, as prevalent among a vulnerable group. In doing so, he perjures, exaggerates, mocks, and present the same as fact through repetition. This damaging tool has been applied against women, the poor, and especially against African people intergenerationally.[2]

EUROPEAN CONSTRUCTION OF AFRICAN PEOPLE

From the onset of European enlightenment, they began to discard the biblical notion of human creation by God while simultaneously making a case for evolutionism. Evolution theory, with its central theme of natural selection, offered the Europeans perfect excuse to project non-Europeans as inferiors while accentuating the former as the fittest in the game of survival. This theory served to boost the European quest for material possessions around the world, resulting in their global domination through imperialism and slavery.

African descendants naturally employed multiple means to defend their humanity, dignity, and patrimony in the wake of these assaults. They have challenged the onslaught on the African bodies and lands through various means ranging from individual to community physical resistance against the European human traffickers and their indigenous enablers' encroachments. The struggle to throw off colonialism continued even after the establishment of European rules and came in the form of armed resistance as well as confrontation via the media. The independence movements that emerged typified this during which many African nations united under various auspices to demand home and self-rule. The post-colonial Africa also saw many African scholars charging the West with manipulating and dictating to their governments through neo-colonialism. While the narratives of physical enslavement and colonization of Africa and its people have been challenged, cultural annexation and conquest of the latter have not been exhaustively confronted.

Thus, this chapter centers on various forms of misrepresentation and exploitation of Africa by Europeans, the meaning and significance of the evolved stereotypes, as well as the functions they served the creators. Undoubtedly, politicoeconomic and cultural imperialism were not by any means charitable, they came with a cost to the colonized and the enslaved, but to the enslaver and colonizer, it was a rewarding enterprise. Borrowing Pieterse's theory of known and the unknown world will certainly aid to decipher how and why Europeans did these for several centuries. The Europeans of the eighteenth and the nineteenth centuries, accordingly, conceived of the world in a binary paradigm—the known and the unknown, the civilized and the uncivilized. This notion still prevails in the twenty-first century as the overt applications of this paradigm have given way to covert usages—the developed and developing nations, mob/mafia for Caucasians and gangs for the "savages," ethnic for Europeans and "tribe" for others. The "known" world represented European nations and cities, while the "unknown" referred to those areas that supposedly mystified them; that were non-western, unexploited, and "untamed." The "unknown" worlds, to them, have "jungles," the known have bushes, forests, and countrysides. "Jungles" are supposedly dangerous, while the western bushes are not but are there to be utilized leisurely. The "unknown" peoples of the world were classified in "tribes," their rulers called "chiefs," while the "civilized" "known" world's groups were ethnic, with kings, emperors, leaders, Prime Ministers, and Presidents. These "unknowns" were supposed to bedreaded because they were untamed, and wild beings are often dangerous. While they could be fearsome, they were paradoxically and simultaneously loved because they were exotic treasures with material values to the "civilized" Europeans. Pre-colonial Africa, like elsewhere, fits the above definition, hence justifying the need to annex and "tame" it. Further, the "unknown" world's people were constructed to be childlike needing European tutelage to mature into rational adulthood. Unfortunately, they could not grow mentally because of inherent and genetic inferiority.

With the above racist ideology, Europeans set out on paper to "civilize" the "uncivilized." In reality, however, it was about material and immaterial exploitation. While the material exploitation enriched Europe and their extensions or satellites, immaterial exploitation served to justify the former. They carved out for themselves imaginary images and ideas about the continent and the entire "unknown" world, developed such ideas into arts, literature, and eventually turned them into political policies that led to and justified the partition and conquest of Africa.

In the European arts and literature, this oppressive ideology set the tone as they constructed Africans to occupy the periphery of human social evolution while reserving the top for themselves. This served to desensitize the European masses on the humanity of the Africans while at the same time casting the imperial mission as noble. The stereotyped Africa which abounded in drawings, paintings, cartoons, and books about the continent over several generations became archetypes and formed the backbone of European and American policy thrusts on the continent and its people in the diaspora.

This stereotypical display of Africa also served commercial purposes as some of the artworks and literature including postcards depicting the land as feminine, awaiting European men's penetration, were sold in different parts of the globe. Some postcards that demonized the continent were also exported back to Africa and sold. In some of the images, they depicted half-naked women tagging them as "savage women" and insinuating that they were unvirtuous, unlike Caucasian women. Many of the pictures on the postcards have Africans barefooted even when dressed in western apparel, a suggestion that Africans were inherently inferior despite attempts to "civilize" them. These served to contrast Africa's past with its colonial present; contrasted African dressing styles with the western by juxtaposing the two. A critical assessment of these images reveals that the photos were not accidental but incidentally staged to justify the ideology of white supremacy.[3]

These carefully orchestrated images and inscribed literature were not only mendacious, the photographers also invaded the privacies of the African victims to satisfy the commercial and the lustful needs of European masculinity as well as serve as cheap sources of entertainment. Africans were objectified as well as displayed as trophies. Some Africans were captured barefooted and some even when dressed were juxtaposed with undressed others. Some were portrayed in kneeling positions, others bowed or lay prostrate while the supposedly superior European stood uprightand majestically. Instead of stating their names, some of these postcard captions de-individualized the African, naming only the ethnicity and inferring that that was the representation of the latter.

The concept of the unknown, which can be substituted with the "other," has also been used to identify the "us" (the hegemonic power); it has helped the Europeans in asserting their identity. The implication is that Europeans did not have a clearly defined identity nor the boundary of their civility, but by identifying what they were not, the boundaries of what constituted Caucasian emerged. The irony and contradictions inherent in this myth are that the Europeans by misrepresenting the "other" they denied the latter agency and identity, exploited them commercially while using the same concept to forge a cultural unity. In their search for identity, the Europeans developed the theory of racial hierarchy which placed them at the pinnacle of the pyramid and the "savages" and the entire "unknown" world below. Hence, white, like black, which is literally a color was employed to obscure and serve in the stead of group identity, while black did the same for Africans. Group names often locate and tie members to geography, history, and culture. But when replaced with color identity becomes pejorative.[4] It is not surprising that every racial group has successfully removed color as a mark of group identification except Caucasians and Africans. Europeans assigned white to themselves to signify purity and imposed black on African people to codify the latter's imposed inferiority.

Meanwhile, the imperative of deconstructing this form of ideological and cultural racism has been emphasized. Pieterse contends that such ungracious portrayals of Africans and other races in the past and present underlines the prevailing power dynamics between the two. And to fully grasp the predispositions of the originators of these racist ideologies and tropes and their functions in the present, these theories need to problematized and contextualized to have any chance of decolonizing the minds and culture of the African and the continent.[5]

Some of the nineteenth and early twentieth-century European cartographers and artists did not visit Africa but developed their hypotheses based on myths and secondary accounts of others. In one example, an unidentified French artist derisively portrayed what he termed the Klimmende people, their culture, and reality. One can imagine how such depictions misinformed large audiences in France, building on what they thought they already knew. The artist did not consider the fact that culture is not static but dynamic and relative as every culture serves the needs of the people who evolved it. Unfortunately, this art, like others, was created to exploit the African victims, commercially to enrich the artist, and ideologically to fortify and justify European imperialism.

AFRICANS ON DISPLAY

The history of European exhibition has its roots in the dehumanization of the downtrodden—from the display of the so-called freaks to the exhibition of Africans in zoos across the western world, the culture has thrived and mutated to its present form of innocuous public entertainment. The reality is that whatever the upper-class Europeans have done to the "other," they have, to some extent, done to their own people, the most vulnerable among them. Exhibitions, especially as it existed in the nineteenth century and the first half of twentieth century western nations, served mostly as a hobby or leisure event to the upper class and some of the working-class white men. Such inhuman shows, while dehumanizing to the victim and whatever group he/she represented, entertained the bourgeois, galvanizing them in their quest to flamboyantly and extravagantly display their wealth.[6]

To this end, the negative and false portrayal of Africans took the place of the freak shows. Secondly, it helped garner support in favor of the quest for colonies. Thus, culture intersected with politics to fortify the main underlying motive for imperialism—economics. At first, it served to elicit the European public's support for imperialism; in the latter part of the nineteenth century, however, it served to justify it. In collaboration with the private sectors, these western nations organized exhibition shows in the second half of the nineteenth century and onwards to demonstrate the superiority of their culture, while parading the vanquished as exotic trophies of victory.[7]

Racist exhibitions also helped western nations to homogenize by articulating what constituted a "savage" culture versus a "civilized" one. The result is predictable—westerners constructed whiteness and its culture as superior while non-whites, especially the darker ones were presented as inferior. By displaying Africans alongside animals in zoos with cages, the European exhibitionists attempted to use that to reinforce and underscore the racist thoughts in literature. The displayed African people served as a source of entertainment to white spectators from the former's entrapment; the cage representing the boundary between the known and the unknown, the civilized and the savage world. Although many of the concerts of the so-called savages were stage-managed, the organizers presented the stereotypes therein as archetypes. These carefully managed misrepresentations and cultural dehumanizations reinforced the racist notions in literature, combining to convince the gullible European about his place in social evolution and human hierarchy. To further humiliate their African captives, some of the spectators threw food items at the encaged Africans, reminiscent of monkeys in zoos.

The literal definition of the savage in the seventeenth-century English dictionary as a person living in the lowest state of development served to reinforce the binary paradigm. Since "savages" were the lowest in the social hierarchy, these constructions and portrayals placed Europeans at the top of the human pyramid.[8] To further this divide, African women were displayed to prove that the Caucasian woman is the standard of femininity both in physique and "innocence." To contrast her with the "other," African women like Saartjie Baartman were displayed almost naked on stage the same way modern-day museum's exhibits are showcased. The goal of these mendacious and devious displays was to prove and reassure white men that theirs is better. The implicit point they tried to drive home was that the Khoi Khoi and indeed African women were sexually undesirable with their bigger physique and curves. That such curves meant paraphilia and promiscuity. One wonders why Caucasian men of the nineteenth century needed such assurances. Perhaps, it was the case of preparing and refocusing their minds on European women before they embarked on the imperial mission to Africa. To further embellish the fallacies already prevailing in Europe about Africa, some African ethnicities like the Khoi Khoi were said to be the lowest or the worst of the "savage" groups. Europeans asserted that the Khoi Khoi, had no human language, but make clicking sounds akin to wild animals.[9] This sort of racist stereotype served to dehumanize the African on one hand and served to desensitize the European, on the humanity of the African, on the other.

These shows underscore the essence and functions of stereotypes, which are to exaggerate to amuse, denigrate to mock, and to demean the victim to entertain gullible spectators.The minstrelsy business in the United States, similarly, caricatured people of African descent exploiting them for the economic gains of various exhibition show owners and organizers. The African anatomical physique came under constant censure as well as the perceived "black culture," or "slave culture." With the popularization of commercial magazines and invention electronic media in the twentieth century, the stereotyping business was advanced. While western media continued to construct the African woman as undesirable as mammies and obese and dirty European colonizers continued to sexually exploit African women; exploitation that was prevalent on the plantations of America. While the media misleadingly presents the image of obese black women to represent their undesirability, the exploiters exploited younger, fitter African women.[10]

Some of the artists of the era employed the biblical narrative of the creation of the Earth and humans to construct their ideal Africa. They painted Africans to represent Adam and Eve who were frozen out in antiquity. Thus, that the African race was anachronistic, did not evolve like the Caucasians, and therefore lived in a state of nature devoid of sophistication and rationality. Other social phenomena such as, homosexuality, that prevailed in Europe were exported to Africa to denigrate, demean, and then bolster the former's ego.[11]

CRITIQUING THE *NATIONAL GEOGRAPHIC* MAGAZINE

The National Geographic magazine misleadingly presents itself as a scholarly, scientific, and somewhat government-endorsed journal/periodical. Like the public history sector, it serves to foster the binary worldview of the West—a narrative that categorizes the world racially and culturally between the superior and the inferior.[12] Lutz and Collins offer the most compelling critique of the magazine in *Reading National Geographic*. The authors aver that the magazine frames itself as somewhat academic, but unorthodoxically utilizes illustrative photographs, instead of historical or scientific facts, as the sources and inspirations behind its stories.[13] By so doing, the magazine constructs the other by employing the same nineteenth-century tropes that work to demean, demonize, and exaggerate—a racist paradigm that reproduces and embellishes fiction as factual.

Meanwhile, evidence of the editors' use of pictures as sources or proofs abounds in every episode past and present. The pictures, rather than serve to complement a given story, function to inform and, fundamentally, entertain the audience by depicting dramatic scenes that reinforce white supremacy as did the minstrel shows and human zoos of the nineteenth and twenty-first centuries. It must be stated, not all the stories on African people's past and present were overtly racist or stereotypical. Some of them contain humanizing messages that strike on cultural relativity and shared humanity. However, most stories on Africa and its people around the world have racist and stereotypical undertones.[14]

An evaluation of the magazine's contents between the decades of the 1930s and the 1960s reveals the consistency in their biased depiction of Africans. It also reveals a less overt negative depiction over time. These two decades are noteworthy in that the former was the era of European consolidation of imperialism in Africa and the beginning decade of World War II, while the latter was in the era of the Human Rights Movement in America as well as the decade of decolonization in Africa. In "The Mandate of Cameroun" by Vandercook, which centers on the country's "poverty" and "backwardness" as well as the changes colonialism was making on the country, a picture captioned, "He draws Haunting Music from Primitive Harp Strings" captures an African musician playing his harp,[15] entertaining his audience as a normal artist does. At the same time, the article carefully chose to portray the African in a negative light, dismissing the music as "haunting," and contrasting the artist's musical instrument with that possessed by westerners. The result of such contrast was damning as always leading to the use of words like "primitive" in presenting the African to the writer's audience. On one hand, the author humanized the entertainer as normal, on the other he attempted to maintain a racial boundary between the "superior" and the "inferior."

In Meyer's article, the story is similarly racist and condescending. Titled, "Foxes Fortell the Future in Mali's Dogon Country," the author focuses on a sorcerer, Foxes, whom the Dogon community of Mali ostensibly relied on for prognostication. In doing that, she explicitly collectivized on the Dogons, depicting them as anachronistic and superstitious, a narrative that would have served as a source of contrast and amusement to her European audience. The front page has two African girls with traditional pots of waters on their heads, ostensibly going to fetch water while half-naked and barefooted.[16] By showing them in these modes and placing the picture in the front page of the article, the magazine aimed to stimulate its predominantly white male audience's sexual fantasies, which was paradigmatically consistent with Lutz and Collins's contention that the magazine serves the interest of its clientele just like any other business enterprise.

National Geographic, which was founded in the 1880s during the height of western imperialism and racism, helped the latter to assert its identity by ensuring that racist notions of the "other" were preserved, refined, and presented to different generations of American and western audiences as factual. It constructed the "unknown" as "savages" and therefore different from "us," the West. Vandercook's article, for instance, embodied this paradigm of contrast, between nature and science, brute (African) physicality and white intellect, antiquity versus modernity, chronology versus anachronism and civility versus barbarity among others. In most pictures, the audience's attention is drawn to the materialistic contrast between Europe and Africa. In other cases, Africans were orchestrated as unwilling or unfit for modernity. The captions also helped to direct the audience to these disparities when they seemed obscure. In one of such, two Africans were pictured; one dressed in a baggy looking trouser with a clowny hat, the other wore a short, but both were without shoes and gazing aimlessly in a field in Doula, Cameroun.[17] By being fully dressed, the picture while serving as a sarcastic testimony of progress indicated to the Caucasian audience the efforts of the West in bearing the brunt of the "white man's burden;" it paradoxically justified the misleading narrative that the African was "uncivilizable."

Conversely, Lutz and Collins rightly pinpointed another major theme that shaped the magazine's discourse—the white masculine supremacy ideology.[18] Going by the fact that the audience was largely Caucasian male, it is not surprising that the medium outlet catered to its reliable patrons and sympathized with them in their delusion and grief over the perceived threat of women in the workforce, which they thought would weaken the place of men at home and in the society. Although there was no evidence that such fears were founded, the magazine, like other western literature attempted to stoke the embers of fear. Most of the pictures and texts in the two articles, between the 1930s and 1960s, consistently portrayed women aesthetically on the one hand and passively on the other situating them at home, taking care of their babies or doing some menial jobs, to reflect and in compliance with the concept of domesticity. Typically, two African women were pictured in Vandercook's article in front of their home seemingly preparing a meal for their family at the same time smiling for the camera. Their smile and function explained it all—that they were performing their normal and statutory duties at home and were happy to do so.[19] Men, on the other hand, were portrayed as adventurous, hard workers and perhaps the engine of the society. Most African men in the pictures were happily engaged in physical endeavors such as in entertainment, hard labor (some were depicted carrying white visitors on their shoulders across a river), or fetching for their families' daily bread.[20] This masculinity discourse reflects the National Geographic's effort to respond to the needs and fears of its constituency, otherwise, it would have rendered itself irrelevant.[21]

Despite the magazine's efforts to maintain a scholarly, scientific public image, and to appear nonprofit in principles, the events in the American society and around the globe, shaped its content and focus at home and abroad. In Africa, the 1930s were periods of consolidation and strengthening of the European colonial rules, hence Vandercook's article attention to the mandate of Cameroun, which had tossed from the Germans to the French and British. The magazine did not emphasize on the impending doom in Europe (World War II), nor the bitter Great Depression—a position that reflects the magazine's idealistic and progressive worldview of the West. In the 1960s, while the issue in America was human rights, in Africa it was decolonization. Accordingly, Meyer's focused on the future of Mali under African rulers and undeniably exhibited implicit nostalgia for the departing French colonizers. This, no doubt, accounted for the writer and (who doubled as) the photographer's treatment of the people as potentially resorting to their normal "barbaric" lifestyles because of the departure of Europeans. Another article that explains this was the one that pictured a group of Malian men butchering meat. Although there was no accompanying caption, this picture, in the context of the article, painted these Malians as scavengers or even cannibals. Without captions, the magazine left its audience to ponder what these men were doing, what type of meat, or even worse, whether that could have been human flesh?[22] It followed the same playbook of colonial literature that portrayed the colonized or enslaved as evil savages when they resisted oppression or when imperialism loses its foothold but portrayed the victims of oppression in a good light when they conform to the established order.[23]

Colonial literature, undoubtedly, attempted to convey a coherent message that followed the same stereotypical misrepresentations, inspiring adventurism in the west, while bastardizing the colonized.[24] The writing and editorial style of the National Geographic is complex and unconventional. In some instances, its captions and accompanying pictures reflect the narrative the writer is inviting the audience to share.[25] But in numerous instances, the narratives are multifaceted. The writers and editors, though, might highlight one aspect of the message, but by orchestrating the scene to be profoundly dramatic, they invite readers to arrive at varied interpretations all of which serve the entertainment interest and goal of the magazine. While the narratives in a given article might differ in meaning, they do not necessarily contradict each other in the grand narrative. In the picture captioned, "Jungle Presses in on the Iron Horse's Path," the picture depicted a train "penetrating" the interior of Africa and speeding past forests. Through the caption and text, the article utilized the paradigm of contrast, ostensibly between the "dark" African past and the "glorious" colonial present, and between technology and nature, with the train representing civilization while the pictured forest represented Africa, to advance a consistent trope. However, the vagueness left the audience room to draw the own inferences within the broad binary paradigmatic framework.[26]

In the same vein, the article, "River Transport in Cameroun" described two Cameroonians carrying a white visitor across a shallow river. While the caption clearly dealt with lack of adequate infrastructure and possibly the need thereof, the other message is clear, that whites are superior racially in the social pyramid and therefore should be served by their enslaved Africans.[27] The fact that the Caucasian man was fully dressed in shoes while the Cameroonians were not, underscores the point about the duplicitous and multifacetedness of their narratives.

Paradoxically, the National Geographic with its penchant for embedded stereotyping of the African as dangerous, primitive, and childlike, also attempts to portray the latter as content with servitude. Most people captured in the two articles under study here were visibly smiling or portrayed as happy. Lutz and Collins eloquently analyze this practice positing that it is part of the magazine's idealistic conceptualization of the world—a peaceful world that abhors violence or where it is marginal. Capturing Africans perpetually smiling (in their best mood), the magazine refines the slavery-era stereotype of African people being happily enslaved.[28] They further imply that African people, unlike Europeans, live a simple unsophisticated lifestyle, content with three basic amenities of life: food, shelter, and sex, all of which do not portend to cultural and material progress, but basic natural needs of both humans and animals.

The National Geographic continues even in the twenty-first century to advance stereotypical themes that foster the negative perception of Africa and African people in the eyes of many of its white middle-class audiences across the world. It is, as noted, an unscientific, unscholarly, and a profit-driven private enterprise that strives to satisfy the needs of its audience at the same time attempting to shape their perception of non-western nations in general. The goal of the magazine, like that of western museums and minstrelsy shows, was to continue to sustain the binary ideology at the same time reinventing itself to serve the cultural and ideological fantasies of its customers.[29]

BALTIMORE MUSEUM OF ARTS—A CRITICAL EVALUATION

The BMA museum houses exhibitions from nearly every continent of the world, which it purports to be a balanced representation of these nations, races, and ethnicities' arts. During the course of the study of the museum, between 2010 and 2013 there were no significant or noticeable changes in the museum's exhibition and display forms as well as narratives. The museum's exhibits seem innocuous and a true representation of all groups represented. However, a thorough deconstruction of how these objects were positioned, captioned, and placed indicates that the racist construction and display of the "other" continues into the twenty-first century.

Traces and legacies of these European negative sociocultural constructions, in which they placed themselves at the pinnacle and Africans at the bottom of the racial hierarchy, abound in the museum's exhibits and a comparative analysis of the African and European exhibits buttresses this point. Firstly, about four continents' (the so-called savage) arts were squeezed together in a rectangular room that looked like a hallway on the first floor: that of Africans, Asians, and North and South America. The cramped nature of this room suggested that the arts were of less value to the curators, and it is consistent with the nineteenth- and twentieth-century European depiction and treatment of the "other."[30] Crucially, on the second floor, European arts were displayed and methodically organized in contrast with the chaotic mess downstairs. It was fascinating to discover that the former's arts did not only have the luxury of being displayed singularly denied the "other," they have several rooms and spaces. The chaotic scene that the curators at the BMA created for the so-called ethnic arts reflects the consistent tropes seen in literature and culture of the nineteenth- and twentieth-century West—a narrative that cast non-Caucasian races as "exotic," "barbaric," and potentially dangerous, hence the need for the West's supervision.[31] The displays on the first floor were deliberately cluttered without a noticeable pattern unlike on the second floor where European arts were grouped stylistically and chronologically.

Another worrisome encounter was that most of the "unknown" world's arts on the first floor seem less sophisticated in comparison. They appear like works of dirty amateurs in contrast to the western arts. Such works like that of an Italian, Raphael, whose painting was captioned: "Emilia Pia da Montelfefltre" illuminates this and contrasts sharply with the "savage" arts, which have no name of the creators nor date of creation but were inscribed for instance as; "Seated Male Figure: Pre-Columbian, Mexico, Ixtlan (first century AD)." It raises a crucial question; how were these arts acquired? What is the full acquisition history? These questions were not answered by the curators when confronted. Many arts of the "other" came from one or two donors such as Alan Wurtzburger who is Caucasian. Did the latter buy them from the creators? If so, what was the logic behind the acquisition of these types of objects? The state and poor aesthetics of the arts, as well as their display pattern, served to bolster the paradigm of the inferiority of the "other." Most western arts serve to show progress, civilization, and cultural sophistication. None showed any negativity in European history or culture. Thus, the BMA fosters the Eurocentric narrative of progressive history and culture like the National Geographic. Both carefully ignored any negative themes relating to wars or diseases in furtherance of this discourse.

Another worrisome thought about the "ethnic exhibits" is the issue of identity. While European arts were elaborately labeled with the names of artists like Raphael and Picasso among others, dates of creation, country of origin and some other relevant information that contextualizes each art, the "ethnic exhibitions" were treated with disdain. Most, if not all, had no names of the creators and no specific dates of production. One might be tempted to rise in defense of the curators by contending that it is possible that the "ethnic arts" did not have this information because the societies where they came from were non-literate at the time of acquisition. If this was so, then the response is, why would some European arts be tagged with "artist unknown," "acquisition date unknown," when these data are unavailable? Certainly, these omissions were not accidental when it comes to the "other." The narrative is demonstrative as it is consistent—that it does not matter to identify the individual makers of the ethnic arts, but rather, tag the art collectively as Igbo or Benin art.[32] It is reminiscent of the stripping of the African people's identity during the course of European trade on Africans.

Typically, African exhibits at the BMA, like that of the Indigenous Americans, seem to project functional rather than aesthetic themes.[33] The manners of their displays are akin to the display of a war trophy. Littering the gallery at the "ethnic exhibition" corner were hunting, cooking, and many objects captioned, for instance, as for "rituals" in ceremonies. Although in some cases an "ethnic" object's aesthetic value was implied, their utility values were consistently overemphasized, which therefore blunted their exquisiteness. In the western division, however, paintings and other forms of arts displayed did not stimulate functionality question because the curators assumed that the public could identify and relate with them, but those of the "other" needed to be defined, their values enumerated because the "others'" cultures are supposedly basic and fundamentally primordial and survivalist.

In one instance, a sculptural figure of a man was captioned, "Seated Male Figure: Pre-Columbian, Mexico, lxtlan (first century AD). It was made of clay and polychrome and was acquired from its former owner, Alan Wurtzburger in 1960. A further perusal of the caption reveals the functional elements of the object, which are that it represented a male warrior "chief" and that the markings in the object's face and its nose, as well as ear clippings, were as a result of mutilations from "ritual self-sacrifice." This illuminates the pattern of conscious construction of the so-called savage as wild, exotic, and ritualisticby the so-called experts who in this case were the western curators rather than the originators of the arts.[34] In the same vein, a religious work captioned, "Goddess with a Tasseled Headdress: Pre-Columbian, Mexico (1369-1520)" was described as an illustration of the state of Aztec women of the time. The kneeling position of the object was fascinatingly tagged as "the proper pose for Aztec women..." Her oval face and calm gaze were touted as "representing the ideal Aztec girl, an image appropriate as a symbol of purity and preciousness of water." While the functional uses of these two exhibits were mentioned, the curators consciously desensitized their audience on aesthetics.

The same could be said of a "Dance Mask with Superstructure (D'mba)," which is a Guinean artwork of the late nineteenth century, made of wood and copper alloy tacks. The dance mask's aesthetics were highlighted; it was described as "finely braided and as an idealization of mature female body and vitality." This phrase is reminiscent of the nineteenth century sexualization of African female bodies discussed previously.[35] Its function was also highlighted as utilized by young men to dance at weddings, funerals, and agricultural festivals.

"Roof top Figure" was similarly ascribed as an artifact found in a Congo "chief's" house, a house where he performed rituals to protect his lineage from calamities. The fact that this object, which occupies a prominent position at the center of the "ethnic exhibition" section, was not dated, the creator was not identified, nor were there suggestions that all or any of this information was unavailable, stands in contrast to the curators' treatment of European arts. Also troubling is the fact that the object was kept in a cage-like glass. One wonders why. Based on the curators' evaluation of each art's worth, Picasso's, Raphael's, and other western arts were worth more than any other collections in their possession, yet they were not protected in a glass case but displayed openly that the public could be able to touch them. The inference here, therefore, is that this object is "fetish" and potentially dangerous and visitors need to be protected from it, hence the boundary as represented by the glass between the two worlds. This can also be related to how the U.S. police treat African people on the street—as dangerous, as criminals, and that the public must be protected from them.

The fact that these so-called expert curators and collectors interpreted the cultures and works of societies they do not understand and appreciate raises the question of why the need for foreign exhibits if the misrepresentations are going to continue? Since it seems inevitable that giant museums like the

BMA must have "exotic" "ethnic" arts to give the impression of diversity and inclusivity then, they should, as a matter of policy, hire representatives from the societies where these objects were obtained from to help in curating them. The same standard should apply to all exhibits, so that the public history sector does not miseducate the public.

CONSTRUCTION OF AFRICAN PEOPLE IN ELECTRONIC MEDIA IN THE MODERN ERA

Since the invention of the electronic media, the aforementioned paradigm of the racist and stereotypical depiction of Africa-descended people continued to this day. Like the minstrel shows and human zoos of the nineteenth century evolved and metamorphosed, stereotypes in electronic media has done so too and manifests in TV shows, cartoons, and commercials recently in subliminal ways. It was common for Europeans and Euro-Americans to use stereotypical images of Africans, engraved in merchandise, to entertain the former while selling the same to the rest of the population including their often credulous African victims. These products on the continent, in America, and elsewhere still bear these racist images and the products are still consumed by the same people these corporations demean. One of the notorious items that had always had a stereotyped "black woman" in it was the Aunt Jemima pancake syrup. Traditionally, the makers of the product had an image of an overweight African American woman with a bandana on her head. She had always worn a perpetual smile, signaling her commitment and contentment with being a servant for a Caucasian family. Since the 1980s, the makers of the product have changed that image to that of a younger African American woman, unfortunately with permed or "relaxed" hair.[36]

On the continent, the same attitude and exploitation prevailed and still prevails. One of those surviving products that continues to denigrate the continent of Africa, its people, and culture is Peak Milk. The dairy company, based in Amersfoort, Netherlands, continues to accentuate the Eurocentric and racist binary worldview that divides the world between the civilized and the uncivilized. A careful examination of the image on the product unravels this—one boat, near the coast of Africa and a modern ship approaching Africa from afar. The African men on the ship, who wore just underwear, as depicted, are standing and paddling the boat while an Arab Muslim is sited in the middle.[37] The inference is that Africa prior to the advent of European imperialism was backward. That technologically, it was antiquated, hence the coming of the Europeans brought "light" to a "dark continent." The Arabs who had been exploiting Africa, materially and through human trafficking, long before the coming of Europeans are portrayed as amateur imperialists and enslavers. By depicting Africans as laborers, the latter are excruciatingly painted as perfect "slaves," a beast of burden for both Europeans and Arabs. Unfortunately, this product and many others like it are still consumed daily in Africa and beyond with the racist images conspicuously intact.

On TV, the public is inundated with tons of ads many of which contain stereotypical themes against nearly every demography except wealthy Caucasian men. In a State Farm Insurance ad titled, "Girls Shopping State Farm TV Commercial," two ladies, one Caucasian, one Asian, walked into a shop. The former is shrewd as she had State Farm Insurance, which saved her money meaning she had enough to buy the bag that they both desire. The Asian, disappointed, calls on her spurious insurance to send her money. A Caucasian man appears with a fishing rod and a dollar tied to it. He dangles it toward the Asian lady teasing and taunting her "you got to be quicker than that..."[38] Dissecting this commercial, one can perceive the general portrayal of women as materialistic, who spend on impulse, and the fact that white women are a step ahead of their Asian counterparts in sagacity. On the older Caucasian man, he is used to illustrate the perceived status quo in corporate America whereby most institutions, businesses, and corporations are owned and controlled by that demography. While you work for them, they go fishing, hunting, or camping, using their monies to control your time and life choices. Anthony, the State Farm agent, is completely portrayed as a passive African American who is simply happy to have a job rather than own a franchise.

"The 2015 Cadillac Escalade Commercial" shows ancient Egypt as completely Caucasian as no African is depicted. European royalties are shown waving to enthused crowds at every step of the way as they are carried by men. Then in India, darker-skinned people are shown, to reflect the racial composition of India, and a man happily rode on an Indian elephant. Early modern Europe is also shown with the royalty riding on a horse carriage and enthusiastic crowd waves and cheers them. Lastly, an African couple in a 2015 Escalade is shown on their way to a hotel. No cheers, the only thing close to a royal service was the velocity with which a Caucasian hotel staff attended to them.[39]

This commercial misrepresents reality in multiple ways. By placing Europeans in Africa, the inference is that the Egyptian civilization was built by Europeans rather than indigenous Africans. It builds on the centuries-old hypothesis that displaced African people in civilizational discourse. The commercial, certainly, portrays African people as consumers, consumers of knowledge and products of European descendants. Civilization builders are ingenious, hardworking, sagacious, and smart. They research, produce, and innovate. A consumer, however, does not need any of these attributes to consume, as even wild animals are good consumers in their own ways.

The "World Cup South Africa 2010 Commercial," which ran as a promotional ad for the then-upcoming senior World Cup in South Africa, the first ever on the continent, denigrates the region and its people rather than showcase the beauty of the host nation. Every promotional content, for every sporting event held in Europe, America, and elsewhere always emphasized the beauty of the land, the hospitality of the people, and in some cases tourist attractions. In this case, however, few images of soccer players are shown mostly from previous World Cups. In the background are multiple wild animals roaming about including cheetahs, lions, and so on. The color of the background is also bleak—dark brownish, yellowish, and reddish tinge, that points toward barrenness and desertification.[40]

Despondently, what was missing is greenery as green represents life, the abundance of it. Brightness is also lacking except when they portray soccer pitch. These combine to reinforce the age-old construction of Africa as "dark," "wild," "dangerous," and home to "savages." By showing more animals than humans, the creators foster the racist metaphor that pairs African people with animals as was the case with Ota Benga, in the Bronx New York zoo.[41] Unfortunately, these depictions work to steer Africans in the diaspora away from their ancestral land. Unlike other races, African Americans are less likely to choose Africa as their favorite vacation spot. They prefer other places including Europe over their heritage because of the sustained demonization of their ancestral land.

In the "State Farm Commercial Robbed Hoopers," the dysfunctional black family stereotype is emphasized. On the surface, the ad could be fun especially if one is a basketball fan, familiar with all the black male characters on display. DeAndre Jordan played the role of the "mama" of the house who is desperately searching for her rings while screaming, "We got robbed." Jordan's supposed husband/boyfriend, Chris Paul counters that the former has no rings. The supposed grandfather to Damian Lillard, Kevin Garnett, kissed his ring in support of Paul uttering, "Sure you don't." The Caucasian State Farm agent intervenes as the stereotypical white savior to offer a solution to the unfolding drama.[42]

This ad is extremely racist because a black man was feminized as was the case during the height of minstrel shows as well as Jim Crow. Jordan is not only feminized; he wears a blonde wig—a symbol of perfect femininity from the prism of whiteness. Sadly, on the continent, there is a growing trend of men emasculating themselves in the name of comedy by dressing up in female costumes and acting in feminine manners.[43] Although one may argue that the ring debate relates to Jordan's inability to win an NBA championship, the setting is home and ring at home symbolizes marriage. Thus, the inference is that African American couples do not commit to marriages. Garnett is utilized to depict the stereotypical African man who makes a baby with a "baby mama," but does not take responsibility in caring for the child, let alone his grandchild. He is shown kicking the baby's walker while complaining about the stench of his diaper. Another racist trope portrayed is the man-child stereotype. Historically, Europeans have hypothesized that African people were physically strong but mentally weak. That they have the minds of children, therefore needing constant supervision and tutelage of the white man. Another curious point in the ad is why the "mama" of the house is conspicuously taller than the supposed man of the house. In European culture, height means might. In a few commercials involving African people, there are few noticeable height imbalances. For instance, in "Young Couple State Farm Insurance Commercial (2011)," the first man shown was conspicuously shorter than his partner as well as the Caucasian lady and State Farm agent that came to resolve the situation.[44] This height reversal implies and insinuates that in African American homes the woman is the authority of the house, while the man is dispensably subservient.

"Love Hurts" is a Pepsi Max commercial that ran during the NFL Superbowl in 2011. It stereotypically portrays a dysfunctional African family where the balance of power, again favors the woman. The woman virtually controls her man, abuses him physically and emotionally that the man is terrified of her. In her bid to stop his unhealthy eating habits, she kicks him, puts a bar of soap in his mouth, and slams his face in a pie—things that usually get parents in trouble when done to a child. In a park, the man is relieved to know that his mentor-wife or trainer-partner approves of Pepsi Max as a healthy drink. The only time he smiles genuinely is when a blonde, skinny, athletic Caucasian lady came close and sat beside him. As the man and the athletic jogger exchanged smiles, the black woman enviously threw a can of Pepsi at the other lady in a bid to hit her partner as usual. Rather than take responsibility and help the victim, they took to their heels.[45]

The title of the ad is as problematic as the content. It contains multiple racist notions that have been used by whites to dehumanize and oppress African people. The fact that the ad created a fictional dysfunctional black home, where the woman is placed at the top authority-wise and the man relegated, portrays role reversal stereotype. The woman is used to advance the prevailing racist notion of the aggressive and dominant "black matriarch," who runs the show while the man is constructed to illustrate an imagined passivity among "black" men at home. Certainly, this ad paints an unreal image of a pacified, physically strong but mentally weak, and childlike African man—tropes that are consistent with the racist notions of the nineteenth and first half of the twentieth century.

The fact that an athletically fit Caucasian woman is depicted contrasts with the heavy build of the projected black woman. As was the case during the other phases of racism discussed in this chapter, the African woman was displayed as undesirable, unattractive to contrast with the physique of the Caucasian lady. This was the essence of the display of the body of Baartman in various cities of Europe. Also worrisome is the stereotype of an insecure, low self-esteemed African American woman who feels inferior to a blonde Caucasian lady. The fact that the former is cast to be aggressive and violent is a recurrent stereotype against both black men and women. This aggression, the video implies, made the man unease and admire the white woman—a supposed symbol of the perfect woman. This scene evokes the image and memory of the racist historic movie "The Birth of a Nation" by D. W. Griffith in 1915 that portrayed black men as aggressive savages who prey on blonde Caucasian women, a symbol of white men's pride.

The "2015 Volkswagen Tiguan Prom Night" TV commercial in the same vein, portrays a somewhat dysfunctional African household by showing just a single dad taking his daughter and a Caucasian boy to the prom. Along the way, he notices that his daughter and the guest are about to get romantic. Rather than boldly make his stand, because of lack of confidence and esteem, he relies on his wheels by doing sharp turns that work to interrupt the burgeoning romance. Once they reached the location of the prom, and as the two left the car, the father was still in his car watching his daughter's buttocks being grabbed by the white boy. Again, his car rescued him as he used his horn to force him to stop.[46]

The stereotypes in this commercial are apparent as it is concerning. The first is the persistent portrayal of one form of dysfunctionality or another in African families. It is rare to see an ad that depicts an African American nuclear family: with husband, wife, and children acting normal. In this case, the single-parent stereotype is the first. The second is the portrayal of the African man as weak-minded and lacking in parental authority and control perhaps due to the dereliction of fatherly duties at home. The commentator crucially mentions at last that this is the car "that puts you in control," as the man again uses his horn to control the salacious grab of his daughter, to further buttress the stereotypical point. The fact that the ad portrays the African American girl as a foible and "loose" exhumes the historically racist notion of African people being deviants and readily available, unlike the "typical" Caucasian girl. A girl that respects her father as well as has self-worth would not let a boy grab her behind in front of her dad. Thus, in the commercial, she did not make any effort to correct or chastise the boy; indicating that her father's honor, her dignity are all inconsequential. Added to the above is the implicit suggestion that she is a perfect sexual object.

Similarly, the "Demo Farxiga" commercial, an ad about a diabetes drug somehow turns to denigrate African femininity. It shows a heavy built African American woman, working out with a Caucasian man. Certainly, the goal of every physical and mental exercise is to get stronger, to stretch the muscles. As the man trains the woman on boxing, she certainly looks appreciative. At the end of every training session, the Caucasian goes back home to his family where he has a wife, children, a house, and even a dog. On the other hand, the newly empowered African woman is shown in her loneliness basking in her power, "I am doing this for me," while the man with his family at the dinner table says, "I am doing this for my family."[47]

The contrast is clear and not even implicit. The ad is consistent in stereotypically painting an imaginary view of African people, their relationships, and their goals. Thus, it constructed an image of a single African American woman, who is typically empowered by a Caucasian man, but in spite of her power and strength, she is lonely and possibly miserable in a self-centered goal of being strong and not using the strength to benefit her partner or community. This theme is similar to the image created in the Pepsi Max ad where the woman is constructed to be very strong, aggressive, and combative. Unfortunately, her strength is not complementary but destructive.

Regrettably, racism and oppression of African people have metamorphosed and continues to manifest in multiple guises that the oppressed often fail to identify it when it occurs. The worrisome part is that as was the case during European slavery, African people act as tools in their own destruction. Some TV shows work to foster these stereotypes, advance them and even naturalize them in the minds of the audience. Naïve theatrical presentations like "The Diary of Mad Black Woman," and "Madea," among others serve to perpetuate the ignoble notion of the African woman, in particular, being what has been said of her—loud, aggressive, bossy, and recalcitrant. It is quite tragic. The producer of the aforementioned shows, Tyler Perry, who has been successful in movie production, has the unfortunate habit of accentuating one form of stereotype about African people or the other. The most damaging of all is the consistent stereotyped themes of the "crazy black woman," the "angry black woman," the "aggressive black woman," and sometimes sexually deviant black people. These despicable themes abound in movies such as "Why did I Get Married" and "Why did I Get Married Too." The dangerous part of this syndrome is that it turns the stereotypes into archetypes.

NOTES

1. Joshua Miller and Anne Marie Garran, *Racism in the United States: Implications for the Helping Professions* (second edition) (New York: Springer Publishing Company, 2017), 15.
2. For more on stereotypes that target African people see, Janks Morton and Ivory A. Toldson, *Black People Don't Read: The Definitive Guide to Dismantling Stereotypes and Negative Statistical Claims About Black Americans* (Scotts Valley, CA: CreateSpace Independent Publishing Platform, 2012).
3. Paul S. Landau and Deborah Kaspin, *Images and Empires: Visuality in Colonial and Postcolonial Africa* (Los Angeles: University of California Press, 2002) 2–5.
4. Ibid., 4–5.
5. Jan N. Pieterse, *White on Black: Images of Africa and Blacks in Western Popular Culture* (New Haven: Yale University Press, 1992), 36.
6. For more on the history of Freak Shows see, Nadja Durbach, *Spectacle of Deformity: Freak Shows and Modern British Culture* (Berkeley, CA: University of California Press, 2009);

Anna Kerchy and Andrea Zittlau, *Exploring the Cultural History of Continental European Freak Shows and 'enfreakment'* (Newcastle, UK: Cambridge Scholars Publishing, 2012).

7. Raymond Corbey, "Ethnographic Showcases, 1870-1930," *Cultural Anthropology* 8, no. 3 (1993): 338–69.

8. Z.S. Strother, "Display of the Body Hottentot" in Bernth Lindfers, ed. *Africans on Stage: Studies in Ethnological Show Business* (Bloomington: Indiana University Press, 1999), 7.

9. Ibid., 4.

10. Sander L.Gilman, "Black Bodies: Toward an Iconography of Female Sexuality in Late Nineteenth-Century Art, Medicine, and Literature" in Henry Louis Gates, Jr. ed. *"Race," Writing, and Difference* (Chicago: University of Chicago Press, 1986), 223.

11. Ibid., 228.

12. Hal Foster, "The "Primitive" Unconscious of Modern Art," 1985, 1.

13. Catherine Lutz and Jane Collins, *Reading National Geographic* (Chicago: University of Chicago Press, 1993), 1–5.

14. Pamela Meyer, "Foxes Foretell the Future in Mali's Dogon Country" *National Geographic* (1969): 440.

15. John Vandercook, "The Mandate of Cameroun: A Vast African Territory Ruled by Petty Sultans Under French Sway" *National Geographic* (1931): 250.

16. Meyer, 1.

17. Vandercook, 227.

18. Lutz and Collins, 8.

19. Vandercook, 229.

20. Meyer, 438–41.

21. Lutz and Collins, 8.

22. Meyer, 439.

23. Rider Haggard, *King Solomon's Mines* (New York: Penguin Books, 2007), 1–6.

24. Patrick Brantlinger, *Rule of Darkness: British Literature and Imperialism, 1830–1988* (Ithaca: Cornell University Press, 1988), 227–29.

25. Lutz and Collins, 276–77.

26. Vandercook, 227.

27. Ibid., 231.

28. Lutz and Collins, 95–97.

29. Paul Landau and Debora Kaspin, eds. *Images and Empires: Visuality in Colonial and Postcolonial Africa* (Berkeley: University of California Press, 2002), 2–3.

30. Edward W. Said, *Orientalism* (New York: Vintage Books, 1978), 1–2.

31. Marianna Torgovnick, *Gone Primitive: Savages Intellects, Modern Lives* (Chicago: The University of Chicago Press, 1990), 75–76.

32. Paul S. Landau and Deborah D. Kaspin, *Images and Empires: Visuality in Colonial and Postcolonial Africa* (Berkeley: University of California Press, 2002), 19, 22.

33. Pascal Blanchard, *et al*, eds. *Human Zoos: Science and Spectacle in the Age of Colonial Empire* (Liverpool: Liverpool University Press, 2008), 4.

34. Torgovnick, 4.

35. Z.S. Strother, "Display of the Hottentot" in Bernth Lindfers, ed. *Africans on Stage: Studies in Ethnological Show Business* (Bloomington: Indiana University Press, 1999), 1–2.

36. "Two Minute History | Aunt Jemima," *Youtube*, https://www.youtube.com/watch?v=grkgS4y5_1c(accessed January 17, 2020).

37. *Peakmilk*, https://www.peakmilk.com.ng/ (accessed January 17, 2020).

38. "Girls Shopping State Farm TV Commercial," *Youtube*, https://www.youtube.com/watch?v=BFhP6f02Euw(accessed January 17, 2020).

39. "The 2015 Cadillac Escalade Commercial," *Youtube*, https://www.youtube.com/watch?v=3im23e4Z-gY(accessed January 17, 2020).

40. "World Cup South Africa 2010 Commercial," *Youtube*, https://www.youtube.com/watch?v=G9hHyZiHZNs(accessed January 17, 2020).

41. See, Phillips Verner Bradford, *Ota Benga: The Pygmy in the Zoo* (New York: St Martin's Press, 1992).

42. "State Farm Commercial Robbed Hoopers," *Youtube*, https://www.youtube.com/watch?v=DDGjASZToyM,(accessed January 17, 2020).
43. "Woman-Like MrIbu 2 - John Okafor Nigerian Movies 2017 | African Movies | Nigerian Movies,"*Youtube*, https://www.youtube.com/watch?v=NSHbLLZLlp0(accessed January 17, 2020).
44. "Young Couple State Farm Insurance Commercial (2011)," *Youtube*, https://www.youtube.com/watch?v=VA14cagdtwo,(accessed January 17, 2020).
45. "Love Hurts,"*Youtube*, https://www.youtube.com/watch?v=Y09z8lwOEYA,(accessed January 17, 2020).
46. "2015 Volkswagen Tiguan Prom Night TV Commercial," *Youtube*, https://www.youtube.com/watch?v=0Lu765vTn8U,(accessed January 17, 2020).
47. "Demo Farxiga,"*Youtube*,https://www.youtube.com/watch?v=i5uDfLs4Yy4,(accessed January 17, 2020).

Chapter Four

The New Jim Crow and Neocolonialism

New Jim Crow and Neocolonialism are modern forms of oppressive regimes that are bedeviling African people in the diaspora and on the continent. They share a lot of similarities in origin, nature, and operation. Unfortunately, scholars approach these phenomena separately like they do with other oppressive systems such as slavery, imperialism, and emancipation and independence. Such a segregated paradigm follows the same oppressive regime in that African people's problems are perceived and analyzed in the context of differences rather than oneness, continuum, and Pan-Africanism. These two regimes succeeded the previous orders. They function to give the illusion of freedom, justice, and equality, whereas in reality they replicate and perpetuate the old orders.

America's Jim Crow laws have its origins in the North, where most states abolished slavery in the first quarter of the nineteenth century, while simultaneously enacting racist laws, known as black codes, that dehumanized free African people. The plantation South did not need Jim Crow laws at that time because they had slavocracy. The northern hypocrisy is unveiled when one considers the fact that while these white liberals chastised their southern counterparts for slavery, they denied African people their human rights and dignity via laws and customs. The northern social clime made it possible for incessant extra-judicial and public killing of blacks by white mobs, while the South valued not the life but the labor that black lives provided. Certainly, the South did not need to execute their dehumanized "chattels" because it was counterproductive. The North had nothing to lose, they had a lot to gain by exterminating blacks through lynching, terrorism, or deportation to Africa. The advantage lay in the fact that African people provided real job competition for ordinary Caucasian men with the former's practical skills and experiences acquired through slavery. Thus, this factor provided the northern mobs and some abolitionists with a perfect excuse to try to exterminate the northern African population through executions and deportations. It is noteworthy to add that the American Colonization Society (ACS) was primarily interested in deporting not enslaved Africans in the South, but free ones in the North.

However, the emancipation of the enslaved meant that the South joined the North in this "game" of extermination and took it to a whole new level. They organized themselves forming different racist and white supremacist organizations like the Ku Klux Klan (KKK), to mete out terror and assaults methodically and systematically on their African victims. The North was culpable in this. During the Civil War, European Americans in the north were war fatigued by 1862. It was easier for the South to defend their home turf than for the North, who were unfamiliar with the terrain, to attack. African Americans' participation in the war was decisive in giving the Union victory. By leaving the plantations following Abraham Lincoln's Emancipation Proclamation, the southern resistance was severely broken. It meant that the backbone of their economy was irrecoverably shattered. Without money for weapons, foods, and supplies, the Confederate strategy became about hanging on as much as they could. African Americans' entrance into the Union's army also supplemented the dwindling white population, especially on the Union's side.

The northern culpability and betrayal can be seen in the Compromise of 1877 when the northern and southern whites reconciled. That reconciliation meant that power was returned to the former rebel class, the planters, at the expense of beleaguered African people. It meant that the little economic, political, and other social progress that blacks made since Reconstruction, starting in 1865, was summarily reversed. The liberal North watched while the conservative South executed the worst acts of terrorism, dehumanization, rape, and bastardization.

THE NEW JIM CROW

The northern historic attitude toward racial oppression is a reflection of the nature and niceties of the New Jim Crow. Their attitude is akin to observing a crime without reporting itor passively assisting a criminal to accomplish his vice and feigning innocence or moral high ground. This method is apparent in every field where oppression manifests. The attitude is usually of pretense, that there is fairness, equity, and justice.

Mitchell Alexander's seminal research is a masterpiece in social justice discourse. Accordingly, slavery did not end with the emancipations of 1863 and 1865 and the passage of the 13th Amendment, it was rebranded, refurbished, and reinvented in a disguised form. Also, the old Jim Crow was replaced by a new one. Thus, while the old one did not pretend about oppression, the new one did. Whereas the old one did not cover its tracks, the new one did, which unfortunately leaves the victims with doubts, doubts of self-worth, their humanity, competence, and about the causation and sources of their oppression. During the old order, explicit laws forbade African descendants from exercising their political franchise. Laws such as "The Grandfather Clause," literacy tests, and poll taxes, among others, were enacted to deny African Americans their voting rights. Added to these explicit racist laws was the overt and flagrant physical terrorization of blacks who were able to defy these odds to try to vote. It was a signal to either choose to survive for the day or die trying to thrive.[1]

In the past, during the old Jim Crow era, vagrancy laws meant that African people were incessantly harassed and terrorized on the streets of the South. In some instances, blacks were arrested for being unemployed, for walking on the street, or lynched for talking to a white person.[2] In the present, the U.S. police continue to intimidate, harass, torture, and kill black people for no justifiable reasons. The police often arrest African Americans for resisting arrest without recourse to probable suspicion as defined by the law. Probable suspicion in their interpretation and application, when it involves an African American victim, could mean being of African descent. Similar to how the "slave" hunters and Caucasian vigilante groups of the past viewed every African seen on the street as a potential fugitive "slave," those of the twentieth and twenty-first centuries treat African Americans as potential criminals.

While chattel slavery provided the European American upper class of the South with unlimited free labor, the modern form of slavery—the prison industrial complex does the same for many American corporations who utilize convict labor at extremely low costs to maximize profit. One wonders why the 13th Amendment made an exception in the supposed abolishment of slavery. The language of the law is explicit on what qualifies one as a modern-day slave: "Neither slavery nor involuntary servitude, except as a punishment for crime whereof the party shall have been duly convicted, shall exist within the United States, or any place subject to their jurisdiction." Therefore, one is enslaved if convicted of a crime.

Why then is the prison system popularly called "correctional facility" instead of punitive centers? The answer to this question follows the same paradigm of the New Jim Crow, of pretense, of hypocrisy, of covering its tracks. The fact is that once convicted and imprisoned, an individual loses his freedom, his civil rights as well as human rights. The person is placed in the conditions African people were positioned in America between 1619 and 1865. During slavery, the prison population in the U.S. was predominantly white, and the prison work was usually industrial. After emancipation, there was a switch around—the population became African, the work switched to agrarian.[3] The same work structure applies in both the old and new order—work as a gang or individually, be supervised by overseers on horsebacks, and earn enough to be alive to work the next day, the day after, until your term is done. The pain does not stop there, once released it is usually harder to adjust to the real world because one has been conditioned and is used to being enslaved. Being free becomes a challenge rather than the other way around. Besides, a convict, like the African American under slavocracy, has lost all his human and civil rights including his voting right. He also has a criminal record as a badge of shame, which means that freedom is paradoxically prison. With criminal records, one is unable to gain meaningful employment or qualify for many public programs. Everything he or she does or could potentially do pushes him back to prison. The more he frequents prison, the longer he stays on each sentence.

It is worth reiterating that in modern times, covert laws, policies, and attitudes accomplish the same goals while covering the tracks not just in the criminal justice, but in every sphere of American social fabric. This vexatious syndrome is also discernible in social institutions like education at all levels. This scheme prevails in the academy in multiple guises. During old Jim Crow, there were explicit codes that ensured that educational institutions were exclusive to Caucasians. Following Reconstruction, and as compensation for blacks' heroics during the war, Historically Black Colleges and Universities (HBCUs) were henceforth created in the former confederate territories and in some northern states that also had slavocracy before the Civil War. Old Jim Crow meant that segregation laws were put in place. These laws on their surfaces stated that there should be separate, but equal institutions for both Europeans and Africans. In practice, the former's institutions were funded exorbitantly more than the latter's own.

The element of hypocrisy in those laws is apparent; they were duplicitous about funding and equality. However, the New Jim Crow does not acknowledge segregation at all. It strenuously hides it in policy, but in application separate and unequal is sustained at every level in both northern and southern states. The policymakers, who are the creators and sustainers of the New Jim Crow, use multiple tricks to perpetuate these racist policies. In New Jersey, for example, there was a lawsuit filed in 2018 challenging the New Jim Crow system of school funding which maintains the old segregated school district lines to ensure that white districts get more funds. According to an *NPR* report, the suit was significant as the filing marked the sixty-fourth anniversary of the Supreme Court ruling on *Brown* v. *Board of Education*. The ruling outlawed separate but equal policy, but policymakers in the U.S. have multiple ways of circumventing it as is the case in New Jersey and elsewhere. Thus, predominantly white school districts receive $23 billion more than other districts in the United States. A staggering twenty-one states fund majority Caucasian school districts a lot more; and these states include the most liberal and diverse in the country—New York, California, and New Jersey. On the continuation of the old order in the present, the report states,

> More than half of students in the U.S. go to segregated or "racially concentrated" schools, according to the report. Those are schools in which more than three-quarters of students are white, or more than three-quarters are nonwhite. Researchers found that high-poverty districts serving mostly students of color receive about $1,600 less per student than the national average. That's while school districts that are predominately white and poor receive about $130 less.[4]

Various states utilize what Asante describes as "Process Racism" in the dispensation of the New Jim Crow.[5] They bury their racism and biases in the law by, for instance, crafting laws that fund schools based on property taxes generated from each given district. Of course, communities with low-income houses will generate less revenue, which then translates to poor funding, poor infrastructure, and less motivated teachers who are paid less for working more, and the result is students that are not college-ready nor intellectually skillful enough to function at an optimum level. A Washington Post article bemoans the situation:

> The funding gap is largely the result of the reliance on property taxes as a primary source of funding for schools. Communities in overwhelmingly white areas tend to be wealthier, and school districts' ability to raise money depends on the value of local property and the ability of residents to pay higher taxes. And while state budgets gave heavily nonwhite districts slightly more money per student than they gave overwhelmingly white districts, in many states it was not enough to erase the local gaps. "States have largely failed to keep up with the growing wealth disparities across their communities" . . . The funding disparities that result have been challenged in many states, frequently in court. Many states have worked to make formulas more equitable, with varying success.[6]

To cover their tracks, these government agents and politicians appear to try to rectify what they project as a "natural" problem by giving a little extra to those poorer districts. Before the laws had been put in place, the expected result was known. In other parts of the world, in Ghana and Nigeria, for instance, public institutions are funded equally from taxes and other funds available to the government rather than based on vexatious and convoluted school district take-as-you-pay systems. It is a smokescreen for separate but/ and (un)equal policy. At every level in these two African nations, government at all levels fund their schools equally and salaries are based on cadre rather than which district you work.[7] In Nigeria, where education is funded by all levels of government, teachers' payment is not tied to the property tax of a given district. The responsible government pays its tutorial staff based on an equal scale. This scale is determined by academic qualifications and experience. The same principle applies in terms of the provision of social amenities and infrastructure.[8]

In Kenya, the same non-segregationist funding formula prevails. Financing of education takes four major formulas. None of them is premised on a get-as-you-pay principle, but other considerations including particular needs of a district take precedence in policy formulation and funding.

BASIC FUNDING

There are three main types of state funding formulas: Student-based, calculated based on counts of students (generally and with particular characteristics); resource-based, calculated based on the cost of resources and inputs; and program-based, which provide limited-use funding for particular programs. Student-based formulas include a base amount, representing the cost of educating a student with no-special needs or disadvantages before further adjustments are made.

Local Revenue

In almost all states, the funding formula includes an expectation that school districts will raise a certain amount through local taxes, with the state providing the remainder. This expected local contribution may be based on a variety of factors, most often local property wealth. Typically, school districts raise this local share from property taxes, but in some states, school districts may impose other types of taxes as well.

Students Characteristics

Most state funding formulas take into consideration the costs necessary to educate children with additional needs. State funding formulas most commonly provide additional funding for English-language learners, students with disabilities, and students from low-income households. Some states may also provide additional resources for students in certain grade levels, or those in special programs, like gifted education and career and technical education.

District Characteristics

> Some state funding formulas consider the costs associated with the characteristics of the school districts and the communities they serve, apart from the costs associated with individual students. They may provide additional resources based on the concentration of students in a district from low-income house-

holds or based on the smallness or rurality of the district. States also vary in how they fund charter schools, if any.[9]

What the Kenyan educational funding formula indicates is a sensitivity and sensibility to the needs of Kenyans. Although they, like everywhere else, expect local tax from each district, it is not decisive in shaping the funding future of the schools in the district. In the U.S. system, the principal revenue comes from the district. The government provides or serves a supplementary source. In this case, the reverse is occurring. The system expects the districts to raise some amount through district taxes, but the bulk comes from their government. Further, this principle is cognizant of students' and districts' characteristics, which entails that the most vulnerable and the neediest get more attention or assistance. In the United States, the less help you need, financially, the more you get and the more assistance you need, the less support you get. This is unnatural as it is oppressive and inhumane. In families, it is common sense that parents tend to give extra attention to any of their children with any form of physical or mental challenge, they do not give less.

The tragic plight of HBCUs comes to mind. While the latter are handicapped in multiple areas, the funding and support systems always favored the Predominantly White Institutions (PWIs). Since inception, the historic role of the HBCUs has been to serve the underserved and provide an educational platform for academically disenfranchised African people in America. The PWIs' discriminations against the former are well documented. Thus, since the Reconstruction era, the idea of having a "separate but equal" opportunity for African Americans educationally and otherwise was spearheaded by northern liberals of the nineteenth century. Hence, the use of both state and federal resources to build separate schools for the formerly enslaved. Like other sectors, "separate but equal" meant separate and unequal in practice as the PWIs, which had obvious advantages in multiple areas continue to get more at the detriment of those that needed it more.

According to research published by the American Council on Education (ACE), HBCUs play a pivotal role in not only the American education sector but also on the economic front. They provide platforms for first-generation students who would have had no chance with the PWIs. The former awarded 17 percent of all bachelor's degrees obtained by African Americans between 1999 and 2019. But the problem lies in the dilemma they face. They depend heavily on government funds to be operational. They have limited sources of revenue generation, unlike their PWI counterparts, who usually have a strong and wealthy alumni base, make a ton of money from sports, and can afford to charge higher tuition without any decline in enrollment. The ACE listed the crux of the disparity as:

- Public HBCUs rely on federal, state, and local funding more heavily than their non-HBCU counterparts (54 percent of overall revenue vs. 38 percent).
- Private HBCUs are also more tuition-dependent than their non-HBCU counterparts (45 percent tuition-dependent compared with 37 percent tuition-dependent).
- Private gifts, grants, and contracts make up a smaller percentage of overall revenue for private HBCUs relative to their non-HBCU counterparts (17 percent vs. 25 percent).
- Both public and private HBCUs experienced the steepest declines in federal funding per full-time equivalent student between 2003 and 2015, with private HBCUs seeing a 42 percent reduction—the most substantial of all sectors.
- Within both public and private sectors, HBCU endowments lag behind those of non-HBCUs by at least 70 percent.[10]

The challenges facing HBCUs are mountainous. Because of the lack of prestige and financial resources, they cater to those who are academically less prepared for college and in many instances, have other socio-personal challenges. Coupled with this is the fact that facilities, learning environment, as well as research tools are not at the highest standards. Graduating students, therefore suffer for it. Chris Moses's experience sums up the result:

> Chris Moses, a graduate of HBCU Virginia State University, commented that while he had an enjoyable college experience, he felt that the university did not academically prepare him to the level of some of his peers. He said that while attending pre-med conferences with his fellow Biology Majors from PWIs, "They just knew things I didn't [learn]." Kyle reports similarly. When asked about Howard's administration and funding, he said both are "horrible."[11]

For professors at HBCUs, there is also less motivation in terms of pay, workload, and research resources. Various research shows that professors at PWIs tend to earn above national average compared to those at HBCUs who earn significantly below the national average. Instructional faculty average salary for Land Grant doctoral research institutions in the southeastern United States indicates that as of 2011, the average salary was over $70,000. In PWI, it was nearly $90,000, while for HBCU the average was just above $60,000.[12] Consequently, for both students and professors admiring PWIs becomes natural. It also means that both students and instructors at HBCUs are not optimally motivated; everything, by design, just works against you.

The standard teaching loads in HBCUs are 4/4—that is, four courses each in the Fall and Spring semesters. In PWIs, the load is less. It ranges from three to two per semester. Professors at PWIs also have to contend with fewer students in their classrooms, which is always beneficial to the students and the instructor. These variables are not contextualized when ranking institutions and analyzing academic successes or failures. According to research by the United Negro College Fund (UNCF):

> When we compare HBCUs and non-HBCUs, HBCUs underperformed non-HBCUs in 2009. The second-year retention rate for HBCUs was 9 percentage points lower than that of non-HBCUs, the six-year graduation rate was 21 points lower than that of non-HBCUs, the overall black graduation rate was 10 points lower than that of non-HBCUs, the black male graduation rate was 14 points lower than that of non-HBCUs, and the black female graduation rate was 9 points lower than that of non-HBCUs. . . . Rather than consider how institutional differences may account for these performance gaps, we might instead consider how differences among students may explain these disparities. We cannot assume that HBCUs and non-HBCUs are enrolling identical students. Indeed, HBCUs, as special-mission, minority-serving institutions (26 percent of which are open admission, compared with 14 percent of non-HBCUs), have from their very inception been concerned with enrolling, retaining and graduating populations of students not historically served by non-HBCUs. HBCU students, upon enrollment, can differ from non-HBCU students in important ways, many of which might impinge on their ability to see a college education through to a successful completion. . . . We must remember that HBCUs and the students they enroll historically have had to overcome numerous barriers, the most famous of which have been racial discrimination and segregation. As discussed, however, other barriers also exist, such as economic inequality and lessened academic and financial preparedness.[13]

The greatest irony and question of it all is, why are these types of institutions, belonging to different classes in terms of funding and in college sports, judged by the same academic standards? Why is it acceptable to judge HBCUs based on admission versus graduation rate, as well as retention rate when these are antithetical to the latter's present reality? These categories of assessment evidently, represent the manifestation of the New Jim Crow in the academy. Certainly, to survive, the HBCUs have to attract as many students as they could, which means lowering standards. Unfortunately, it leads to other problems such as interest. Some of the HBCU intakes lack college preparedness, have divided attention due to potential social problems in their lives, families, and even within the school environment. Some come to school to get the refund check and disappear. Others want to take some classes and then transfer to another school of their choosing. Judging everyone by the same rule looks fair on the surface, just like "separate but equal" did in the nineteenth century, but in practice, not everyone is on the same platform or has the same access to resources from inception. The foundational aspect of the problem is the fact HBCUs historically serve those that were tactically underserved at the pre-college levels leading to the perpetuation of the social cycle.

Educational success indices have to be re-examined because the current parameters are flawed and tilted in favor of Caucasian majority institutions. When an individual has all the support and platform he needs in life, he has an overwhelming success chance compared to another who has little or no chance. How do you measure their successes? So many intangible factors have to come in, many of which are immeasurable. In the case of HBCUs versus PWIs, success should not solely depend on retention and graduation. It should include resource allocation, the intellectual and social skill sets of students admitted within a given period, the workload of instructional and non-instructional staff, their pay rates as well as the infrastructure on the ground such as libraries and research centers. When all these are accounted for, one will notice that the so-called underperforming schools are epitomes of academic excellence, despite the odds. One will appreciate HBCUs as miracle centers rather than dumping grounds.

NEOCOLONIALISM

Dr. Kwame Nkrumah's pioneering research and thought on Neocolonialism is as groundbreaking as Alexander's on New Jim Crow. The two seminal works not only complement each other, but they are also dealing with the same problem methodologically and thematically differently. While *The New Jim Crow* exposes the newly disguised forms of oppression in the diaspora, Nkrumah's *Neocolonialism* does the same by exposing the veiled form of imperialism that gives the illusion of freedom, democracy, and self-rule. In both instances, the victims are often oblivious of the root of their problems, not knowing they are externally instigated, hatched, and executed internally through proxies at home:

> The neo-colonialism of today represents imperialism in its final and perhaps its most dangerous stage. In the past it was possible to convert a country upon which a neo-colonial regime had been imposed—Egypt in the nineteenth century is an example—into a colonial territory. Today this process is no longer feasible. Old-fashioned colonialism is by no means entirely abolished. It still constitutes an African problem, but it is everywhere on the retreat. Once a territory has become nominally independent it is no longer possible, as it was in the last century, to reverse the process. Existing colonies may linger on, but no new colonies will be created. In place of colonialism as the main instrument of imperialism we have today neo-colonialism. The essence of neo-colonialism is that the State which is subject to it is, in theory, independent and has all the outward trappings of international sovereignty. In reality its economic system and thus its political policy is directed from outside. The methods and form of this direction can take various shapes. For example, in an extreme case the troops of the imperial power may garrison the territory of the neo-colonial State and control the government of it. More often, however, neo-colonialist

control is exercised through economic or monetary means. The neo-colonial State may be obliged to take the manufactured products of the imperialist power to the exclusion of competing products from elsewhere.[14]

With these succinct words, Nkrumah eloquently described the nature, reality, and operational menace of neocolonialism in Africa and around the world. To him, Neocolonialism works behind the scenes to control victim nations using western spy agencies to overthrow non-compliant nationalist leaders and replacing them with conservative conformists who are willing to dance to the tone of the neocolonialists. In other instances, they use unpayable loans to mortgage the future of a target country thereby having access to its natural resources. The end game is to have disguised control of former colonies. Thus, the old order—visible and physical imperialism, is substituted by the invisible new form giving the west deniability and somewhat alibi in their exploitation of the neocolony.

Neocolonialism, seemingly, was perfected even during the colonial era. In Nigeria, for example, the British created a country, not a nation going by the characteristics of nationhood and nationalism. The infrastructure the British constructed was carefully built to aid effective colonization, control, and exploitation of resources. Thus, the railway lines, for instance, ran from north to south in two directions. One connected the North to the South via the Southwest and emptied on the Lagos port. The other from north to the southeast port of Port Harcourt. None ran from east to west to integrate the country horizontally. These rail lines made the evacuation of agricultural products reach the port faster. The East-West line, from the colonial perspective, would have amounted to economic waste. The political structure was also sectionalized so that each region had its own separate government. There was rarely a uniform system at any level, except in the army or a few other inevitable institutions. When political parties were allowed to be formed, it followed the same ethnic cum regional lines: National Council of Nigeria and Cameroon (NCNC) with its base in the East; Action Group (AG), based in the West; and Northern Peoples Party (NPC) in the North.

The debate for independence also followed the same pattern. The North, predominantly Muslims, feared domination by the South after independence and thus trusted the British more than their African supposed brethren and compatriots. Thus, it opposed independence several times in the early 1950s, arguing that Nigeria was not due for independence or self-rule. Earlier in 1947, Obafemi Awolowo, a British-educated Western Nigerian leader and nationalist, published a book titled, *Path to Nigeria Freedom*, he declared thus:

> Nigeria is not a nation, it is a mere geographical expression. There are no "Nigerians" in the same sense as there are "English" or "Welsh" or "French."

> The word Nigeria is merely a distinctive appellation to distinguish those who live within the boundaries of Nigeria from those who do not.[15]

Tafawa Balewa, who became Nigeria's first post-independence leader said in the same year, "Since the amalgamation of Southern and Northern provinces in 1914, Nigeria has existed as one country only on paper.... It is still far from being united. Nigeria's unity is only a British intention for the country." The British governor of Nigeria, Sir Arthur Richards, toed the same line of thought when he confessed that:

> It is only the accident of British suzerainty which had made Nigeria one country. It is still far from being one country or one nation socially or even economically . . . socially and politically there are deep differences between the major tribal groups. They do not speak the same language and they have highly divergent customs and ways of life and they represent different stages of culture.[16]

When the BBC interviewed the former premier of the northern region, Ahmadu Bello, he suggested that he loved the British and preferred them to other Nigerians, especially the Igbo of southeastern. Accordingly:

> Well the Igbos are more or less the type of people whose desire is mainly to dominate everybody. If they go to a village or a town, they want to monopolize everything in that area. If you put them in a labor camp as a laborer within a year they will try to emerge as head man of the camp, and so on. Well, in the past our people were not alive to their responsibilities. Because you can see from our northernization policy, that in 1952 when I came here, there weren't 10 northerners in the civil service. I tried to have it northernized and now all the important posts are being held by northerners . . . what is, is a northerner first, if you can't get a northerner, then we take an expatriate like yourself on contract. If we can't then we can employ another Nigerian but on contract too. This is going to be permanent, I should say, as far as I can foresee because it will be rather dangerous to see the number of boys who are now turning from all our learning institutions, turning out having no work to do. I am sure whichever government of the day it might it will feel rather embarrassed. It might even lead to bloodshed. . . . Well it might but . . . I mean how many northerners are employed in the east or in the west. The answer is no! And if there are there maybe 10 laborers employed only in the two regions.[17]

From the foregoing, one can perceive the tension in colonial and neocolonial Nigeria. The foundation for discord was laid by the British, who had no interest in building a real nation, nor working with the natural ethnic borders. It is not surprising that the Scottish people want to separate from Britain. It is also not shocking that the people of Cataluña of Spain are clamoring for independence; neither was it surprising when eastern Europe Balkanized. The common denominator in all these nationalistic aspirations is homogeneity—it is the decisive ingredient in nationalism. England is homogenous, hence there is no known clamor for dismemberment. Many Scottish people, apparently, feel disenchanted about their union in the kingdom and want out. Thus, the root of Nigeria's problem, and indeed, many African countries, are directly traceable to the Berlin Conference where Africa was arrogantly apportioned based on European interests.

Like Euro-Americans did in the diaspora, the British enforced a form of intra-African as well as Africa versus Europe segregation or Jim Crowish policy at all levels of governance and society. The fact that they gave Africans at home the short end of the stick not news. They crafted societies based on racial and ethnic hierarchies with Europeans at the top and Africans at the bottom on one hand, and a dichotomized cum segregated cities for Africans on the other. Thus, it was a conscious effort to ensure that there was no uniform culture for the people of those countries created, which provided grounds for mistrust, ethnic violence, nepotism, and instability. In Nigeria, for example, in every city, the British reserved certain portions for the indigenes and another for non-indigenes. Thus, in the North where you have predominantly Hausa Muslim people, the British codified a system of segregation that officially apportioned *Sabon Gari* (strangers' quarters), for non-indegenes. Those dichotomies still stand to date and can be seen in various northern Nigerian cities such as Kano and Kaduna among others. Post-independent Nigeria follows and maintains that same segregation. In the southern states and cities, such a segregated residential structure is also still in place.[18]

The British also introduced classist segregation. They erected residential quarters for Europeans, the Government Reserved Area (GRA), which will form the fulcrum of the Neocolonial residential quarters for the African elites desperate to emulate the colonizers. The GRAs of the past and present always had the best infrastructure and social amenities. Sadly, various states and Nigeria's federal government have blindly followed that segregationist, elitist, and Eurocentric paradigm in residential planning. They continue to build new GRAs and always try to make it stand out from the rest of other districts. Like the colonialists who built a smaller house (Boys Quarters) at the back of the big "master's" house for their Nigerian "boys" (servants), the Nigerian elites follow the same pattern with a little modification. They erect the "Boys Quarters" in front so that the latter serves as both servant and pawn in an event of a security breach.[19]

These forms of segregation means that corrupt politicians have a safe-haven away from the prying eyes of the masses. It also meant that Nigerians hardly perceive their commonalities, because their differences are more apparent than their commonalities. Perhaps, the apparent common area of interest that cut across ethnicity and class is sports, especially soccer.

With the benefit of hindsight, one could decipher why the British, like other Europeans, created countries rather than forge nations. There were nations before Europeans came with their imperialism, they just collapsed those nations and forced them into various conglomerates of their fancies, that suited their imperialist interests. Neocolonial Nigeria, like elsewhere in the Congo, was riddled with conflicts and instability, predictably leading to coups and counter-coups and genocides. Eventually, it all boiled down to a brutal civil war that lasted thirty months.

Recent events have thrown more lights on the nature, scope, and reach of neocolonialism in Africa. Currency, apparently, is one of the tools of neocolonial control. France, which created a unified currency, CFA, for its fourteen former African colonies still requires them to use it to this day as the medium of exchange and legal tender. Each country is also required to keep their foreign reserves in the French central bank. These sorts of neocolonial policies have led to protests against the puppet African leaders who are the "blackfaces" of Neocolonialism. In 2017, Senegalese and Beninese peoples of West Africa rose in righteous protest against these sorts of injustice. It led to the arrest and incarceration of many, including activist Kemi Seba. The latter was charged with the burning of 5,000 CFA notes in protest of such flagrant neocolonial imposition. In a BBC report in August 2017:

> On Friday 25 August police officers descended on a residence in Dakar with an arrest warrant for probably one of the most controversial black activists in the Francophone world. A week earlier, at a demonstration, Kemi Seba, whose real name is Stellio Gilles Robert Capochichi, in a symbolic public protest against the CFA, burnt a 5,000 CFA bank note. The CFA is used in 12 francophone African countries as well as Guinea Bissau and Equatorial Guinea. The BCEAO, which prints the notes for West Africa, took issue with the public destruction of what it considered its property. The bank sought court action and Mr Seba was arrested on the charge of destroying property, which could have landed him in jail for up to five years if he were found guilty. The AFP news agency reports that he was acquitted on a technicality. Senegal's penal code punishes the destruction of banknotes rather than a single bank note. Mr Seba is part of a growing movement chorus calling for the CFA to be dropped.[20]

In the same vein, Luigi Di Maio, Italian deputy Prime Minister has also chided France's president, Emmanuel Macron, for the latter's exploitation and milking of its former colonies, leading to impoverishment in Africa and copiousness in France. Maio accused France of being at the root of desperate African emigration to Europe. According to him, "Mr. Macron 'first lectures us, then continues to finance public debt with the money with which he exploits Africa.'"[21] Some critiques of France have also alleged that many of the former French colonies are required to pay colonial taxes to France.[22] Thus, these fourteen countries of Africa that use the CFA contribute $500 billion annually to France. Sadly, France does not use that currency but utilizes the Euro as a medium of exchange.

The recent termination of the appointment of the African Union (AU) ambassador to the United States, Dr. Arikana Chihombori-Quao reinforces Nkrumah's prognosis. The chair of AU, Moussa Faki Mahamat, summarily dismissed the diplomat for exposing the enslaver versus the enslaved relationship between the West and Africa, especially between France and its former colonies. In her own words,

> We were ahead of them in our civilization. They set out, to destroy us; and Berlin Conference put the nail on the coffin. So they gave Djibouti the same sovereignty as the United States. They gave Burundi the same sovereignty as China. They gave Togo . . . you see the EU realizes individual little countries, they can't survive on the world stage. So they came together as European Union. Now picture this now, so they cut Africa in this tiny little countries. Small economies that could never survive on their own, but gave them the same sovereignty as the big boys. So, that way, when the little bit countries go to the world stage for the purposes of development and discussing trade . . . they are wannabe boxers who are being thrown intoa heavy weight boxing ring every day. How do you put China in the same boxing ring with Eswatini. Eswatini has 1.2 million people, China has 1.4 billion people. And you put them on the same stage to go at it to negotiate. . . . When Eswatini is thrown in the same boxing ring with China and Eswatini collapses before Eswatini gets on the stage, the world says Eswatini, what's wrong with you? Why can't you take care of your people? China comes in and says, give me all your gold or else! And if Eswatini does not agree, they just go next door to Lesotho and give Lesotho an extra dollar. And if Lesotho doesn't take it they just jump on to Togo. . . . It was all by design. 1884 . . . in addition to chopping us up, they also set out to make the African believe that everything African was bad and undesirable and everything western particularly French and British was more desirable. We call that the legacy of colonization. . . . They . . . set on working on the slaves make them think everything about them, forget about everything about Africa. Where you come from is a terrible place, diseased and dying people, constantly at war with themselves, uncivilized. . . . We call that the legacy of slavery . . . a 135 years later, a system that was put in place to see that Africa and her children are forever defeated that Africa is forever exploited remains in place today, alive and well . . . Why isn't Africa moving forward? Why does Africa continue to be taken advantage of? . . . Until Africa comes together, as a continent speaking with one voice, one continent, one people, nothing! And I repeat nothing is gonna change! . . . we must speak with one voice.[23]

Dr. Chihombori-Quao further outlines the perpetual colonization pact that the French coerced the 14 African nations to sign, a document that heralded Neocolonialism. They include over eight points that puncture and ridicule Africans' sovereignty as a whole: (1) deposit 85 percent of your bank reserve with the French Central Bank under the control of the French minister of finance. The French are allowed to take the 85 percent from each of the 14 countries that signed the pact and invest in the French stock market. The dividends belong to France, not the depositors. Annually, France makes trillions of dollars from this scheme, generating $300 billion out of every $14 billion it took from these African nations. (2) To withdraw from the deposit, African countries have to seek permission from France. If the French authorities approve the request, it comes in the form of a loan. The interest, interestingly, goes to France. Each country could be permitted to take up to 20 percent of their total deposit, not more. (3) The French have access to all the minerals and natural resources in those African nations, the former also has the first right of refusal. (4) France controls the currency, CFA, and prints it exclusively. (5) The language of instruction and business in these countries is French. (6) These countries agree to allow French military presence in their countries; each country's military to be trained by the French army; all the military equipment must be purchased from France. (7) None of the signatory countries is allowed to enter into a military alliance with their African neighbors; in the event of war, allegiance is to France. (8) France is authorized to invade any of the signatory countries without notice if the former feels that its interest is threatened or at risk.[24]

Many African people both on the continent and in the diaspora have come to the defense of Dr. Chihombori-Quao calling for her reinstatement. The African Diaspora Congress in requesting the AU to reverse course contends that she spoke facts and that the retribution, which was influenced by the European governments, was vindictive. Dr. Apollos Nwauwa, the leader of the group argued that many people at the top echelons of the AU were not happy because she was bold and honest in her presentation. The online petition to get the AU to rescind the decision garnered over 61,000 as of October 31, 2019. The petition against her removal reads, "Why was she dismissed, or better, who benefits from her removal? Were African heads of states and governments consulted? Who called the shot? Or is Africa, and peoples of African descent, still facing the debilitating effects of modern colonialism or neocolonialism?" In defense of AU, the chair's spokesperson, Ebba Kalondo, claims that her three-year tenure has run its course. The fact is that the AU is not bold enough to admit its toothlessness. Dr. Chihombori-Quao was appointed in 2017, according to CNN, and relieved of her duties in the fall of 2019, that is not three years. Former Ghanaian President Jerry Rawlings was among those who have condemned the African Union's decision. Rawlings said in a tweet, "The diplomat shared her views on the detrimental impact of France's influence in Africa, and termination of her appointment was coming from 'French-controlled colonized minds.'"[25] One wonders why her statements were offensive to the AU hierarchy since she defended the continent against exploitation.

There is no doubt that Mr. Moussa Mahamat was influenced by the French and their western backbones to relieve the ambassador of her duties. It further reinforces the points she and numerous others, including Nkrumah, made on the devastating and regressing effects of Neocolonialism on Africa. Also glaring is the fact that the syndrome works by proxy, unlike the old regime.

RESULTS

New Jim Crow and its counterpart on the continent, Neocolonialism, have impacted African people in multiple and innumerable ways. The ongoing police killings and brutality, resulting in the emergence of various movements like the Black Lives Matter, is a case in point. The Old Jim Crow was a terrible experience for African people in America. It was so brutal that millions of blacks sought to get out of the southern United States just to live another day. Millions left the South and migrated to different cities in the northeast, northwest, Midwest, and elsewhere. In the urban North, they faced a different type of Jim Crow. Different in form, strategic in attack and color, but ultimately the same result of deprivation and dehumanization. While the Ku Klux Klan brazenly killed African people in the South even after the second half of the twentieth century, in the North the police routinely brutalized and killed the former, also openly. While there were no consequences for the KKK murders, it was essentially the same for the unjust murders of African men and women in the North at the hands of these Caucasian police officers.

On the continent, the syndrome of Neocolonialism has left Africa impoverished despite abundant material and human resources. As they say, one man's meat is another's poison. Therefore, one person's disadvantage is another's advantage, unfortunately. In response to these, millions of Africans, the wealthy and the poor, annually try to find ways to escape the unbearable socioeconomic realities in their countries. Thousands cross the treacherous Sahara Desert and the Mediterranean on their way to Europe.[26]

Each year, thousands of West Africans die in the Sahara Desert due to fatigue, starvation, or dehydration in a desperate bid to escape oppressive systems at home. This desire to emigrate has opened up opportunities for an illegal network of transporters and their agents. These agents who often advertise their businesses sound compelling to the unsuspecting victims. They usually promise their clients that certain amounts in local currency or U.S. dollars would be enough to take them to Europe. Many intending migrants are oblivious of what lay ahead. They often do not know that their journeys to Europe could be on foot, via a hot sandy desert, stretching thousands of miles until or if they reached the Mediterranean coast.

The illegal human smugglers are very organized at every stage of the journey, but also very dubious. The agents who initiate the deal charge their victims a certain amount and then connect him or her to others, who will then transport them from point to point. At the end of each epoch, the intending migrant is transferred to another vehicle if they are in good financial standing. At every stage, there is a roll call to ascertain who paid up to that stage of the journey and who did not. Whoever did not is usually abandoned in the desert to their fate. Many die after abandonment. According to former victims, abandonment is very rampant. Many agents overcharge their clients but underpay to the transporting agents and network. One does not know this until you are told that your fare has expired and then abandoned. The few who managed to hold enough dollars on their pockets are allowed to continue the journey. Those abandoned walk aimlessly to their death. Along the route, corpses litter the whole trail.[27]

Many who managed to make it to Libya's coastal cities face another level of danger at the hands of the Islamic terrorists and slave traders who hunt, buy, and sell their fellow humans in the twenty-first century. Before the U.S. invasion of Libya, the country was calm and acted as an oasis for the migrants. Now, it has become one of the most perilous spots on the journey to Europe. In the case of Andrew (alias), a Nigerian, he paid the middleman the agreed amount that should take him to Europe. Unfortunately, the middleman or agent did not pay the smugglers the full amount, which led to the termination of his journey in Libya. Still, the smugglers wanted the full amount paid, thus they chained every duped victim and tortured them to call their families to send the remaining balance in U.S. dollars. In Andrew's case, the smugglers demanded $2,500 instead of the $750 he had agreed with the first agent he paid in Nigeria. Anyone who could not pay up in time is sold to the human traffickers on the infamous "Libya slave market" that emerged following the U.S. bombing of the country.[28]

THE COMPROMISED "TALENTED TENTH"

Contemporary African leaders, seemingly, work as willing tools to help advance the cause of Neocolonialism. There have been allegations and insinuations that leaders like Patrice Lumumba, Thomas Sankara, and Kwame Nkrumah, among others, were either assassinated or deposed because they refused to dance to the tune played by Neocolonialism. The majority of African leaders, however, seem happy to follow the rule. These leaders, while preaching patriotism at home, execute policies that are clearly against their national interests, politically, culturally, and economically. How does one justify stashing away money from his country's wealth in European banks? Some of these political leaders preach national patriotism in their countries but act unpatriotically by undergoing medical treatments in Europe and America and doing the same for their family members. Rather than invest in healthcare, research, and education the so-called "Talented Tenth" prefers to send their children to western countries for education. Rather than stimulate industrialization, they continue to allow Africa to be the dumping ground of European and Chinese merchandise. Thus, African people hopelessly remain consumers rather than producers.

In the diaspora, the "Talented Tenth" demonstrates the same self-centered, self-serving attitude. Those in politics always encourage African Americans to come out and vote in every election. The only problem is that these people, mostly Democrats, do not account for the previous vote that the mass of African people gave the Democratic Party. There should be probity and accountability in the electoral process especially between black politicians and the masses. Some of these political machines put their party interests ahead of their race or constituency. While other demographies, like the gays, Latinos, and even white women get concessions from the Democratic Party, the latter habitually ignore African American problems. The reason for this is not far-fetched. The African American vote is easy! It is locked in. There is no need to ask or work for it. But other constituencies are not guaranteed. The Latino vote swings from party to party, therefore, each party tries to reach out to them with their programs. During elections, Democratic black elite working within the liberal agenda help remind black people about the racist Republicans rather than the specific agenda of the party for African American people.

The relationship between African Americans and the Democratic Party is akin to a peculiar marriage. This marriage is anomalous because one party invested heavily in it, but the other did not and therefore has no commitment. In such a dynamic, one person pulls all the weight, while the other becomes redundant and lethargic. Democrats treat blacks like a partner in the relationship, who is vulnerable, who has no option and as a result, is taken for granted. She not only has no option; she cannot leave the union because that is not in her calculus. There is no point talking about a person (Republicans) who is not part of the metaphorical marriage. You do not have any expectations from someone you have no relationship with or love for.

Regrettably, the African "Talented Tenth" both at home and abroad have connived with oppressive forces to ensure that New Jim Crow and Neocolonialism are firmly cemented. The defenseless are put in a position of helplessness and hopelessness. To worsen the situation, they are made to defend the strong (the black bourgeois), which is a paradox. How could the defenseless defend the strong? It defies conventional wisdom. African American masses often defend their political elites with all their strength in voting for them, verbally justifying their actions, and even providing misguided excuses as to why these elites could not inspire or execute any programs for them.

The relationship dynamic is flawed. Flawed because it lacks reciprocity and symbiosis. It is analogous to the individual fighting for his god. Between an individual and a spirit who is supposedly stronger? The spirit is and has a responsibility to protect the mortals not the other way round. The only way this incompatibility is sustained is through further miseducation, leading to both mental slavery and colonial mentality.

NOTES

1. Michelle Alexander, *The New Jim Crow: Mass Incarceration in the Age of Colorblindness* (New York: The New Press, 2010), 1–4.
2. Ibid., 31.
3. Thomas Aiello, *Jim Crow's Last Stand: Nonunanimous Criminal Verdicts in Louisiana* (Baton Rouge: Louisiana State University Press, 2015), 10.
4. Clare Lombardo, "Why White School Districts Have So Much More Money," *NPR*, February 26, 2019, https://www.npr.org/2019/02/26/696794821/why-white-school-districts-have-so-much-more-money (accessed March 17, 2020).
5. Molefi Kete Asante, *Afrocentricity* (Trenton, NJ: Africa World Press, Inc., 1988), 35.
6. Laura Meckler, "Report Finds $23 Billion racial Funding Gap for Schools," *Washington Post*, February 26, 2019, https://www.washingtonpost.com/local/education/report-finds-23-billion-racial-funding-gap-for-schools/2019/02/25/d562b704-3915-11e9-a06c-3ec8ed509d15_story.html (accessed March 17, 2020).
7. Peter Okebukola, *Towards Innovative Models for Funding Higher Education in Africa* (Accra, Ghana: Association of African Universities, 2015); Chinedum Nwoko and Hyacinth Ichoku, *Assessment of Public Finance Management in Anambra State, Using PEFA—Performance Management Framework*, Consultant Report, 2007.
8. M. A. Adelabu, "Teacher Motivation and Incentives in Nigeria," (2005), 14–20.
9. "Key Elements of Funding," *FundEd: State Education Funding Policies for all 50 States*, last modified November 21, 2019, http://funded.edbuild.org/ (accessed March 17, 2020).
10. "ACE Brief Illustrates HBCU Funding Inequities," *ACE*, last modified January 22, 2019, https://www.acenet.edu/News-Room/Pages/ACE-Brief-Illustrates-HBCU-Funding-Inequities.aspx (accessed March 17, 2020).
11. Jalen Banks, "Community or Funding: How American Universities Are Failing Black Students," *Berkeley Political Review*, March 18, 2018, https://bpr.berkeley.edu/2018/03/18/community-or-funding-how-american-universities-are-failing-black-students/ (accessed March 17, 2020).
12. Minerva Brauss, Xi Lin, and Barbara Baker, *A Gender Comparison of HBCUs and PWIs in the Southeast* (Women's Leadership Institute, 2016), 18.
13. David A. R. Richards and Janet T. Awokoya, "Understanding HBCU Retention and Completion," *UNCF-Frederick D. Patterson Research Institute*, (2012), 11.
14. Kwame Nkrumah, *Neocolonialism: the Last Stage of Imperialism* (London: Thomas Nelson and Sons, Limited, 1965), ix.
15. Ray Ekpu, "Geographical expression: So What?" *The Guardian*, August 15, 2017, https://guardian.ng/opinion/geographical-expression-so-what/ (accessed March 17, 2020).
16. Ibid.
17. "Ahmadu Bello on Igbos," *Youtube*, https://www.youtube.com/watch?v=5_odAy4rVz8 (accessed March 17, 2020).
18. See Thomas S. Gale, "Segregation in British West Africa (La Ségrégation En Afrique Occidentale Britannique)," *Cahiers D'Études Africaines* 20, no. 80 (1980): 495–507; Maryam Salihu Muhammad, Rozilah Kasim, and David Martin, "A Review of Residential Segregation and Its Consequences in Nigeria," *Mediterranean Journal of Social Sciences* 6, no 2 (March, 2015): 376–84.

19. Lee Wengraf, "Legacies of Colonialism in Africa: Imperialism, Dependence, and Development," *International Socialist Review*, 103, https://isreview.org/issue/103/legacies-colonialism-africa(accessed March 17, 2020). Bayo Amole, "The Boys Quarters: An Enduring Colonial Legacy in Nigeria," in *Socio-Environmental Metamorphoses: Proceedings 12th International Conference of the IAPS. IAPS* (Halkidiki, Greece: Aristotle University Press, 1992), https://iaps.architexturez.net/doc/oai-iaps-id-iaps-12-1992-1-008 (accessed March 17, 2020).

20. Lamine Konkobo, "African Protests Over the CFA 'Colonial Currency,'" *BBC*, August 30, 2017, https://www.bbc.com/news/world-africa-41094094 (accessed March 17, 2020).

21. Megan Specia, "The African Currency at the Center of a European Dispute," *The New York Times*, January 22, 2019, https://www.nytimes.com/2019/01/22/world/africa/africa-cfa-franc-currency.html (accessed March 17, 2020).

22. "'Colonial tax' or important currency stability? Debate rages over CFA Franc," *Africa Check*, September 6th, 2019, https://africacheck.org/fbcheck/colonial-tax-or-important-currency-stability-debate-rages-over-cfa-franc/ (accessed March 17, 2020).

23. "AU Ambassador To The U.S. Offers Masterful History Lesson Dissecting The Legacy Of Colonization," *Youtube*, https://www.youtube.com/watch?v=jOTEs2UHego (accessed March 17, 2020).

24. Ibid.

25. Bukola Adebayo, "AU Faces Backlash after Terminating Ambassador's Appointment," *CNN*, October 16, 2019, https://www.cnn.com/2019/10/16/africa/petition-over-sacking-of-au-ambassador/index.html (accessed March 17, 2020).

26. John Campbell, "African Migration Across the Sahara Is Down," *Council on Foreign Relations*, January 23, 2019, https://www.cfr.org/blog/african-migration-across-sahara-down (accessed March 17, 2020).

27. Lisa Schlein, "Thousands of African Migrants Die Crossing Sahara Desert," *VOA NEWS*, December 23, 2018, https://www.voanews.com/africa/thousands-african-migrants-die-crossing-sahara-desert (accessed March 17, 2020).

28. Yomi Kazeem, "The Harrowing, Step-by-step Story of a Migrant's Journey to Europe," *Quartz Africa*, October 25, 2018 ,https://qz.com/africa/1341221/the-harrowing-step-by-step-story-of-a-migrants-journey-to-europe/ (accessed March 17, 2020).

Chapter Five

Swimming Against the Tide

The turn of the twentieth century saw European consolidation of colonialism on the continent of Africa from Cairo to Cape Town and from Dakar to Mombasa, it also witnessed the intensification of both Jim Crow and New Jim Crow in America. On the other hand, the century saw African people, led by the diasporans, spearhead the crusade for justice and redemption for victims of these regimes. Marcus Garvey was pivotal in this with his timely arrival from Britain. He had hoped to team up with the foremost practical Black Nationalist, Booker T. Washington. Unfortunately, the latter died before the meeting could take place in 1915. Garvey, through his eloquence and articulation organized and inspired African people to wake up from their slumber, work together, connect with their ancestral land, and fight physical and mental oppression. Hence, Garvey's thoughts and organization provided the basis and the fulcrum for Pan-Africanism.

Of course, like African history, the history of Pan-Africanism is a continuum—a continuity from the thoughts of nineteenth century intellectuals like David Walker and many others. Walker conceived of Africa and its people beyond the artificial national boundaries, he saw beneath Europeanized cultural differences to strive to pave a homogenous path for Africa-descended people. In his *Appeal*, he sought to remind the enslaved Africans about the pivotal accomplishments of their ancestors and urged them to work to emancipate themselves from chattel slavery. Walker was sagacious to appreciate the fact that slavery of his era was of two kinds, the physical and that of the mind. The premise of his *Appeal* was for the mind to be liberated first; that if the mind is freed, the body would inevitably follow the former.[1]

By the turn of the twentieth century, Garvey built on this paradigm to urge the victims of Jim Crow and imperialism to emancipate their minds from the invisible scourge of oppression. In one of such eloquent arguments, he submitted that "The power that holds Africa is not Divine. The power that holds Africa is human, and it is recognized that whatsoever man has done, man can [un]do." Garvey also prophetically declared that Africa and indeed its people shall be free, they just have to recognize their lack of freedom and work to liberate themselves and their homeland. He acknowledged not knowing exactly when, but that the result will be African unity; "no one knows when the hour of Africa's Redemption cometh. It is in the wind. It is coming. One day, like a storm, it will be here. When that day comes, all Africa will stand together."[2]

Garvey, severally, admonished and urged the African man and his mind to wake up. Accordingly, "Wake up Ethiopia! Wake up Africa! Let us work towards the one glorious end of a free, redeemed and mighty nation. Let Africa be a bright star among the constellation of nations." The only person that needs such a loud call is a person who is truly asleep metaphorically and otherwise. And like Walker, he saw the need to emancipate African people through proper education as "[it] is the medium by which a people are prepared for the creation of their own particular civilization, and the advancement and glory of their own race."[3] Throughout his stay and mission in the United States, Garvey worked to unite African people, inspired them to strive to be independent business owners rather than dependent employees, and attacked the disease of mental slavery.

In the second half of the century, many African people continued to disseminate this message of the emancipation of the mind from mental oppression both in the diaspora and on the continent. On the continent, Pan-Africanist and freedom fighter, Fela Anikulapo Kuti led the campaign against colonial mentality, a.k.a. "colo-mental." In the diaspora, another Pan-Africanist, reggae legend Bob Marley led the movement through his lyrics. In his ultra-classic titled, "Redemption Song," Marley clearly was echoing and answering the calls to duty, the call of Pan-Africanism, and the calls Garvey made in the 1910s and 1920s:

> Old pirates, yes, they rob I
> Sold I to the merchant ships
> Minutes after they took I

One can deduce the metaphorical reference to European slavery as well as how they outwitted each other in the game of human trafficking and piracy. Marley and indeed Reggae singers' lyrics wax spiritual. He contended that the Almighty God has given him victory and delivered him from his enemies. The essence of that was to inspire millions of African people around the globe to have hope of being victorious. Without anticipation of victory, one has lost a battle before it began. Thus, redemption is the reward that awaited those who persevered to fight for freedom and endured to the very end.

> Emancipate yourselves from mental slavery

None but ourselves can free our minds! . . . [4]

From the foregoing, Marley was extremely conscious of oppression, not just the menace of it on the body and material possessions, but the one that devastates the mind. He wittily and figuratively described and identified the oppressor as "Old Pirates," the devastation he has caused over the centuries and then urged the oppressed to emancipate himself from that invisible disease of the mind. Like Garvey, Marley contended that it is the victim of mental oppression alone who feels the pain, who knows where it pinches, and who could find a solution through emancipation and therefore redemption. Without an active mind ruling the body, the body is as good as dead walking. But the paradox lies in the fact that a victim of mental slavery is akin to a mentally ill patient. The latter do not usually seek help from health institutions and practitioners because he is unaware of his invisible health conditions. It is usually his relatives and the concerned public that seek help on his behalf. The legend also lamented about the physical harm oppression has caused and is causing; the assassination of African cultural and political leaders on the continent and in the diaspora.

On the continent, Lucky Dube echoed the same line in his "Reggae is Strong Album." He lamented that efforts have been made severally to kill not just reggae, but also its "prophets" through methodical assassinations. According to him, you can kill the "prophets," change the rhythm or the style of playing reggae, but never can one kill the message, which is the essence of reggae. Interestingly, Dube and Marley had sometimes different code names for oppression and the oppressor. Marley's was "Old Pirates," while Dube's was "Bald Heads." Both used the word "Babylon," also for the same phenomenon.[5] In another, "Back to My Roots," Dube reiterated the Pan-Africanist paradigm of unity, connectivity, and solidarity concluding that he was going back to his roots. Unfortunately, Dube was assassinated by unknown persons in 2007 in South Africa, his home country.[6]

Fela Kuti's song, "Colo-mentality" or "colo-mental" released in 1977, rhymes perfectly as the continental version of the diasporan syndrome of slave mentality. These artists, like their counterparts in the academia, have diagnosed the African problem as more mental than bodily, more invisible than it is visible, and proffered the solution of mental emancipation and redemption. Like Garvey, Malcolm X, Marley, and Dube, Kuti designed his message to reach the commoners, to appeal to them instead of the disengaged elites who are somewhat part of the oppressing class. Thus, to ensure that his audience got his message unadulterated as well as the nuances therein, Kuti used broken English in his songs, including in the "Colo-mentality" one:

> He be say you be colonial man
> You don be slave man before . . .

Kuti bemoaned the fact that the African elites functioned as agents of oppression and have stoutly refused to emancipate themselves from the scourge of colo-mental. He sided with the mass of African people placing them as victims who were eager to be liberated from the shackles of oppression. The elites are comfortable with Neocolonialism: "Them don release you now . . . But you never release yourself."[7]

The singer attacked not just European New Colonialism, but also its accomplices, the African elites who make policies that favor their "masters." Kuti lamented, arguing that it is unconscionable to favor Europeans, their culture, and values at the expense of Africa. He diagnosed, problematized, and offered a solution, which was emancipation from the syndrome of colonial mentality. His critique of the African elites and their roles as accomplices to oppression is relatable to Malcolm X's scathing critique of the "House Negro" who looks down rather than up. He looks down to mock his fellow Africans rather than look up toward freedom.[8]

SLAVE AND COLONIAL MENTALITY

In Names

Names, throughout history, have been a powerful tool in every group's identity and a signifier of distinctiveness. They also serve to connect individuals to their families, lineages, and it personalizes an individual. In Africa, names connect people to their direct families, communities, and ethnicities. An individual without a name is socially unable to function as a human. Animals, as far as humans are concerned, do not always have names except the ones we impose on them.

Unfortunately, during the European Slave Trade, one of the most tragic things they did to African people in the diaspora was to delete their ancestral names, and of course, rid them of other elements of their cultures thus reducing them to the level of animals. To assert European control and ownership, they renamed these Africans, which functioned to relegate the latter to a level of lower beings. One of the first things that happen when one buys a pet is to name or rename the animal, signaling ownership, control, and marking it as one's property. With their original names, enslaved African people and their descendants would have found it easier to reconnect back to their roots, because names are distinctive.

After emancipation in 1865, many African people in the United States struggled with a sense of identity at an individual level or as a race. Some renamed themselves with names like Freeman, majority retained the names of their former enslavers. This choice, sadly, reconnected them to their recent oppressive past—a past they were so eager to get out of physically, but not mentally. In today's America, it is fascinating that there are probably more

African Washingtons, Johnsons, Jones, and Smiths than there are Caucasians. By the turn of the twentieth century, especially during the second half with the explosion of African consciousness and revolutions, many African people began to embrace their ancestry. Without a viable way of reconnecting with one's original families and communities, bolder African Americans began to change not just their first names from European ones to African and African themed names, they changed their last names as well. Notable among this group, were Kwame Toure, formerly called Stokely Carmichael and Molefi Kete Asante among others. Others in the Nation of Islam chose to use "X" as their last names signifying that the true names were missing or stripped. Clarence 13X and Malcolm X were notable personalities who toed this line. The latter eventually changed to El-Hajj Malik El-Shabazz, when he converted to Sunni Islam shortly before his assassination.

On the continent, future African leaders like Kwame Nkrumah and Nnamdi Azikiwe, who were educated at an HBCU, were inspired by this conscious movement to remove any un-African names in their identities. Azikiwe's middle name was Benjamin, he eventually expunged it and preferred to be known by his full Igbo name, Owele Nnamdi Azikiwe.

In the same vein, colonized Africa was also commodified like the enslaved African people in the diaspora were. It is well documented that the decisive factor that inspired European slavery and imperialism was economic the factor. As the latter trafficked and traded Africans in the diaspora, they branded them as properties. When they came to the continent, having profited enormously from trafficking on African bodies, they partitioned the land in Berlin, based on their individual countries' interests. The carving up and branding of Africa depict and illustrate this commodification. For example, the European age-old economic and commercial interests in Ghana were humans and gold, hence the misnomer Gold Coast. The French's interest in Cote d'Ivoire was similar principally ivory and human, hence Ivory Coast (Cote d'Ivoire in French). The original names or indigenous ones did not matter to the colonizers. As they did to African people, the countries they created bore the names imposed by the creators. Rivers and other natural resources and landscapes were not spared either. Almost all the major rivers of Africa bear a name imposed by Europeans—Niger, Orange, including lakes such as Lake Victoria among others.

Like Africans in the diaspora, Africans at home were conditioned to admire and desire to follow the values and culture of the West. This factor explains why most African nations, despite "independence," retained and continues to retain their slave names. Some of those names are pejorative and have no connections to the indigenous peoples. The Arabs did the same where and when they had influences in Africa. Nubia, today, has been undignified and is now Sudan—a name that means "land of blacks" in Arabic. Zulu Empire has now been rechristened, the Republic of South Africa.

Cameroon got its name from a Portuguese person in the fifteenth century who saw the Wouri River and called it Rio dos Camarões (shrimp river), for the abundance of shrimp in it. The name was validated by the Germans who colonized the country centuries later, and the British and the French who later split it for themselves following the former's defeat during the First World War.[9] Sierra Leone is another African nation who got its name from material resources it has, signifying the material values that Europeans attached to the land. Another Portuguese called the mountainous parts of Sierra Leone, Sierra Lyoa or Serra Lyoa (lion mountains), that it looked like the lion's teeth. There are conflicting accounts among Sierra Leonian historians about which of the Portuguese gave their country its name, instead of what indigenous name should they call their country, a step toward freedom.[10]

The conflict over the origins of many African names is limitless. Nigeria and Niger Republic, clearly, got their names from the Niger River, which spans multiple West African countries. Undoubtedly, Nigeria's name was formulated by Lord Lugard's then-girlfriend Miss Flora Shaw, who wrote an article in the 1890s and also suggested it to her lover, Lugard who was the imperial governor representing the British crown. Nigeria, accordingly, came from the Latin word *nigreos* (noun) for black, adjective of which is *niger*.[11] There is no consensus on what Miss Shaw utilized to coin the phrase "Nigeria." Some have suggested it was a combination of *bother* "*niger*" and area, hence Nigeria. The N-word has been problematic since the slavery era as it is a form of racial epithet used against African people. In old Latin, *niger* means pejorative things such as ill-omened, pitch-black, and unlucky among others.

The origin of the N-word is telling and explains why it was employed as a tool of verbal oppression by Europeans and still serves that purpose to those who still use it discreetly or otherwise. Incomprehensibly, the oppressed have embraced it, rebranded it, and internalized it as a term of endearment. The question to those who defend its usage in whatever guise and form is: is it possible to wash and refine feces or excrement and then consume it? If that question is absurd, so too is an intangible substance such as the N-word. If African people in the 1960s rejected "Negro" as a group name and identifier, how could one justify this one that is even more sinister? The difference between the "accepted" N-word and the rejected one is in the last two letters of the prohibitive word and the last of the "approved" one. While the forbidden version ends with "er" the "accepted" one ends with "a." Both have the same racist origins and were imposed to demean, dehumanize, and to oppress. Undoubtedly, the spread of these obnoxious terms stems from America's music industry, which is overwhelmingly outside the control of African people. Although rappers are African people, the record label owners, who control the lyrics, are not.

To appreciate the damage of the N-word with "er" or "a," one has to look at the European Jews. These people know who their oppressors were and are, and they fight them and their tools of oppression. The European Jews not only condemn Nazism, but they also reject and rebuke anything connected with it be it a tangible and intangible artifact. The swastika and the Nazi salute are vehemently considered racist, offensive, and reprehensible. They do not try to embrace, embellish, and somehow refine any of these because whatever that was offensive to their ancestors is and should be offensive to the present generation. The B-word falls in line with the N-word as it is as degrading to women as it is misogynistic. Literally, it means a female dog, who stereotypically have babies frequently. And this proclivity implies that the female dog is promiscuous. These terms are allegorical, a blatant animalistic comparison that should not have any place in the mainstream anything, be it in the music or movie industry. These words, among others, were used to destroy the psyches of African people on the plantation. How could they be permissible and endearing in the twenty-first century? Or is it a case of regression?

Meanwhile, it is worth reiterating that the 1960s was a decade of consciousness throughout the African world—a decade where African people began to demand justice, freedom from tacit and overt oppression. On the continent, as many countries became "independent," which grammatically is not freedom; they largely chose to retain their colonially imposed names. This decision seems to justify imperialism. But not all nations toed this line of reasoning. Kwame Nkrumah's Ghana was one of those that perceptively chose a name that has a bearing on its people's history and culture.

In Nigeria till date, vestiges of colonial legacy and mentality abound at every level. This is apparent in the names of towns and cities. During the colonial era and after, various ethnic nationalists worked to reclaim what was left of their cultural heritage. In the Igbo areas of Southeast Nigeria, a series of conferences were held to harmonize and centralize the written aspect of the language. By 1961, Dr. S. E. Onwu Committee met at W. T. C., Enugu to produce an acceptable orthography. Their recommendation was later accepted and began to be implemented from 1972. Despite their efforts, the Igbo leaders failed to emancipate the language completely from its unfavorable leaning toward the western morphology, spellings, and linguistics. Although the 36 alphabets that were designed served the interest of the Igbo language, in the spelling of individual and town names, there is still an inclination to making it easier for the white man to understand and be able to enunciate, rather than stand on the principles of linguistic autonomy:

The Igbo Alphabet:
A B CH D E F G
GB GH GW H I Ị J
K KP KW L M N Ñ

NW NY O Ọ P R S SH
T U Ụ V W Y Z[12]

Based on design and conception, each consonant and vowel is pronounced exactly as they phonetically appear. This principle applies to word formation as well. Unlike in the English language where there is an inconsistency between the pronunciation of letters and their forms in words. For instance, the consonant "X" is often vocalized as "Z" in many instances and as "X" in others. Some typical examples are "xylophone" and "Alexander." Other instances abound such as with the letter "C" which alternate between the "s-sound" and actual "c-sound." Thus, you have "ceiling" and "cyclone," on one hand "car" and "cat" on the other. In the Igbo language, however, the consistency is apparent. There is no "C" consonant, but instead, there is the consonant "CH" as in "child." The latter can be found in words like "*chi*," or "Chukwu" and are vocalized exactly as they are spelled. Vowels follow the same linguistic pattern as there is a difference between for instance "O" and "Ọ." Using an English word to illustrate this, an example of the former will be found in "open," while the "O" in "Oscar" represents the former.[13]

The ethnic name, Igbo was initially written and vocalized by the British as "Ibo." This aberration had to be dialectically challenged and corrected to the right form, Igbo. The earlier wrong spelling, evidently, stems from the English language not having the "GB" consonant sound in its alphabet. Rather than accommodate it, thereby admit deficiency, the British colonizers made Ndigbo bend to them as has always been the case in other spheres. Another double consonant letter such as the GW can be found in some western terms, especially those that originated from Southern Europe like Guadalupe, Guardiola, or LaGuardia.

Meanwhile, in application, individuals due to proclivity to leaning or bending over toward their colonizers by westernizing their African values, inexplicably misspell their names and that of their towns, perhaps to make it easier for the former. Multiple examples are found in the names of the following towns in Igboland: Awka, Amawbia, Awgu, Enugu, Nawgu, Awgbu, and Onitsha; the list is endless. Conforming to the articulated standard, Awka should be "ỌKA," Amawbia becomes "AMAỌBIA," Enugu should be "ENUGWU," and Onitsha, "ỌNICHA."

Individual names follow the same flawed pattern of unintelligible misspellings. Thus, it is often common to find contemporary Igbo names ending with consonants in an apparent attempt to bend over. This is patently antithetical to the principle of language autonomy. Names such as "Ejiofor," "Okafor," "Orji," "Ibeh," "Okoyeh," and "Ezeh" are some of the examples of this linguistic debasement.

Others, especially those in the diaspora, either spell their names incorrectly or are too ashamed of their African names, as a result, they let others anglicize it. Evidence of this abound in the United States and in Europe where a lot of African people of Nigerian heritage let their names be mispronounced and therefore lose its flavor and meaning. Some of these include Dele Alli, a prolific soccer player for Tottenham FC of London. English commentators and his fellow players pronounce his first name as "DELI" instead of "DÉLÉ." Jordan Ibe, who plays for AFC Bournemouth lets his name be abused like Dele. Commentators call him "AIBE," an anglicized form; the right pronunciation is "ÍBÉ," closer to "EBAY" than to "AIBE." In the United States, instances of this abound in both the NFL and the NBA. Players like George Iloka, of Dallas Cowboys, allows commentators and fans as well as teammates to call him "IALOKA." The victim tragically also pronounces his name as such. Iloka literally means enmity abound or is everywhere, while Ibe stands for family or kindred. Who can tell what "AIBE," or "AILOKA" stands for?

Not all African or diaspora-born African athletes lack self-esteem. Players like Kelechi Iheanacho, who plays for Leicester City FC, proudly spells his name correctly. To ensure that European commentators do not call him "AIHANACHO" or something of that nature, he spells it phonetically for them in his jersey. Thus, his Leicester City jersey bears "IHEANACHO." Contrast the attitudes of Iloka, Ibe, and so on to that of other European players, especially those from eastern Europe, whose names are as likely to be mispronounced by western match day commentators, you find a staggering difference in confidence and esteem level. Christian Pulisic "Captain America," who plays for Chelsea FC, clearly told some commentators that he prefers to be called the anglicized version of the name, hence "PULISICK" rather than "PULISICH." He has the confidence to be called what his family calls their name. That is boldness. That is audacity and self-confidence lacking in many African people's lives. In the same vein, Mateo Kovačić, Pulisic's Chelsea teammate writes out his name to avoid potential abuse or mispronunciation. Thus, everyone, the commentators, players, and fans know and call him "KOVACHICH" instead of "KOVASICK."

Even in the twenty-first century, many African American fraternal and sorority organizations call themselves Greek or identify themselves and their groups in Greek letters. Sadly, most do not necessarily know the meanings of these words and letters, nor why they have to use them. Of what use is it for an African man or woman on the continent or in the diaspora to claim they are anything other than proud African. How does it sound for an Asian to say he is an African or vice versa? These are supposedly the educated ones, the "Talented Tenth" and the future ones who engage in this kind of charade that is as embarrassing as it is confusing. Would it not be natural for African American organizations to have African letters and words, proclaim themselves Africans than to call themselves Greeks and utilize Greek letters that they mostly do not understand?

In Beauty Standard

African people both at home and in the diaspora share this phenomenon, undoubtedly in their perception of what constitutes beauty. However, the traits and manifestations of the syndrome differ in some instances. In the sphere of the standard of beauty, the symptom of slave mentality has blurred African people's sense of judgment that they tend to try to swim against the current in a bid to appear exquisite and be validated by the Eurocentric society. Slavery and imperialism meant that the victim's essences and uniqueness were demonized, caricatured, causing the latter to overtime seek to imitate the oppressor consciously and unconsciously. Words such as "kinky," "nappy," and "dread" among others have been used by Europeans to mock Africans and their nature. It is not surprising that African women were compelled to use a bandana to cover their supposedly "ugly" hair. Those who grew their hair naturally into locks were called dreadful, hence "dreadlocks." African body complexion was also attacked with words like "black," "dark," or "darkies." Certainly, these opprobrious languages had a profound effect on the victims as they caused low self esteem and low self worth. In response to these unprecedented attacks and mental colonization, African people began to reorder their standard of beauty to fit and suit the Europeans' preferences. One of the earliest attempts at altering African hair texture came with the invention of the hot comb. This tool, mechanically, works to straighten the African curls to resemble that of the colonizer and make it appealing and acceptable to the latter.

Thus, African beauty standards were forever altered. The original rationale was to please the Europeans. Over time, it has become normalized that if an African woman is wearing a natural look, she is perceived as abnormal or somewhat deviant. Indeed, this is a clear case of both slave and colonial mentality in the cultural realm. A slave is literally a person who does not have the independence of mind or body. Someone else controls him, he does not have to be mentally strong; he is required to be physically strong. In this case, a culture that destructively imitates another at its detriment, a culture that is absolutely harmful especially when one applies the chemical called "relaxer," is a slave culture.

Since the twentieth century, wigs have become popular among African people around the world. It is not only used to cover the natural hair; it fakes the wearer and presents the individual in a form he or she is not. Seemingly, the wig took the place of the bandana. They both serve the same function, the function of covering one's nature. The former is just an upgrade on the latter which serves to cover nature and presents the wearer in a Europeanized and enslaved cultural state. Can anyone in their right mind wear a mask to a first date or any date for that matter unless the individual is a clown? African

Figure 5.1. A Nigerian lawyer in his full regalia. *Nnaemeka Ezeamalukwue.*

people wearing wigs appear comical; they hide their identities in those costumes that infuriates as much as it is embarrassing.

Undoubtedly, slavery and imperialism imposed these impossible beauty standards on African people. Apparently, emancipation and "independence" did not lead to the independence of thought and action. When the United States asserted its "independence" from Britain, the former, despite the bulk of its Caucasian being Anglo-Saxon, moved to assert cultural, political, and economic distinctiveness. These can be seen in the political system it evolved and also in linguistics. While the British priced tea, white Americans preferred coffee; while the British had a monarchy, America evolved a presidential system, and while the British love soccer, white America adores baseball and "football."

Nevertheless, Africa, which has less or zero commonality with the colonizing British, largely chose to retain most of the legacy of the latter. This implicitly justifies the forceful takeover of Africa. It pitches the post-independent African against his ancestors who resisted slavery and imperialism until he could no longer do so. This syndrome of colonial mentality can be

Figure 5.2.   A Nigerian lawyer. *Nnaemeka Ezeamalukwue.*

perceived at every level of governance in most African countries. In Nigeria, for example, judges and lawyers wear wigs and gowns, a derivative from the colonialists. While these attires probably serve cultural and aesthetic needs in Britain, in tropical Africa they constitute a nuisance. They serve as an embarrassment and punctuate the miseducation of the so-called "Talented Tenth." They serve to illustrate what Garvey, Malcolm X, Marley, and Kuti among others have urged the African to do—to emancipate himself from mental slavery.

Similar to problems in hair styling is the skin complexion. As Europeans have historically attacked the African complexion, the victims responded varyingly by devising means of lightening their skin tones to bring it closer to that of their oppressors. Thus, various skin bleaching chemicals masquerading as lotions or creams have been invented to be used to bleach away what the victims believe were undesirables in their bodies. This syndrome has subsided substantially in the United States, but on the continent and in the Caribbean, it is still exploding and metamorphosing with alacrity.

Figure 5.3. A mannequin in Enugu, Nigeria. *Nnaemeka Ezeamalukwue.*

Morally speaking, how could these types of behavior be justified? Someone who is a Christian, for instance, indulging in the chemical or artificial alteration of any part of their body, is actually telling his creator that "you have not done a great job on my body . . . therefore, I can do a better job." Most monotheistic and even polytheistic religions in the world commend and appreciate the handwork of the Creator. Doing otherwise constitutes an audacious challenge to the relationship dynamic between the Creator and the creature. The created is trying to supplant the former by acting as a "recreator." These kinds of cultural and bodily abuse informed the vociferous messages of Pan-Africanists for African people to embrace their bodies. A person that is in good health does not usually take medications. Garvey's message about emancipation from mental slavery and the Black Power era mantra of "Black is Beautiful" were all geared toward tackling this naturalized scourge of self-hate. The messages served as drugs for the sick. Miseducation leads to self-hating attitudes causing African people on the continent to relate desirable things to Europeans and their skin-tone while connecting the undesirable substances to themselves. Figures 5.1 through 5.7 illustrate this real-

Figure 5.4. A mannequin in Enugu, Nigeria. *Nnaemeka Ezeamalukwue.*

ity. Even mannequins used in boutiques, as well as celestial bodies, are created to mimic Europeans.

In South Africa for instance, the menace has reached an astronomic proportion as in other parts of the continent. A University of Cape Town research indicates that one in three blacks use chemical creams, a.k.a bleaching cream to lighten their skin. The report confirms already-known health hazards associated with such practices, including skin cancer and other types of skin diseases. This interdisciplinary study was led by Dr. Susan Levine, senior lecturer in the School of African and Gender Studies, Anthropology and Linguistics and Dr. Lester Davids, senior lecturer in Human Biology. Levine avers that the chemical creams contain a "mixture of compounds including mercury, corticosteroids and hydroquinone (HQ) to enhance the bleaching effect. Despite legislation that bans the use of HQ in concentrations of more than 2 percent in the USA, creams in Africa are being found containing up to 15 percent." The report, perspicaciously "Dying to be white," further states that,

> High concentrations of HQ accumulate over time and can lead to severe, irreparable damage to skin through a condition called exogenous ochronosis

Figure 5.5. Madonna statue at a catholic church in Enugu, Nigeria. *Nnaemeka Ezeamalukwue.*

(EO). There were 756 reported cases of EO in Africa recorded in 2007, of which 2.6 percent were found in Senegal, 15 percent in Nigeria and a staggering 82.4 percent in South Africa . . . "We believe that our interdisciplinary approach will allow us to alter perceptions regarding the use and abuse of skin lighteners, as well as to highlight the persistence of racial aesthetics of beauty . . . "[14]

In the same vein, another report indicates that on average, 70 percent of African women on the continent use one form of skin lightener or the other, which has prompted actions in Cote d'Ivoire leading to a nationwide ban on such substances. Certainly, there is an upsurge in this self-hate induced culture. In the 1960s, 60 percent of urban-dwelling African women reported using some forms of bleaching cream. A recent report indicates that among many city dwellers, such creams have become fourth-most commonly sought-after household products after soap, tea, and milk. Nigeria leads the rest of Africa in craving for these chemicals with 75 percent, while between 52 and 67 percent of women use it in Senegal.[15]

Figure 5.6. A statue of an unidentified catholic saint. *Nnaemeka Ezeamalukwue.*

Based on a BBC report, the story of a South African musician, Nomasonto "Mshoza" Mnisi, is a tragic one. The 36-year-old claims that her new light skin makes her prettier, more confident, and therefore happier. But other South Africans, who are proud of their natural selves, have criticized her, calling on her to rethink and retrace her steps. In her defense, she claims that it is a personal choice as much as breast implants and other forms of cosmetic surgeries are. Doubling down, Mnisi added, "I've been black and dark-skinned for many years, I wanted to see the other side. I wanted to see what it would be like to be white and I'm happy." The cost of her transformation is extravagant:

> Over the past couple of years Ms. Mnisi has had several treatments. Each session can cost around 5,000 rand (£360; $590), she tells the BBC. Unlike many in the country, she uses high-end products which are believed to be safer than the creams sold on the black market but they are by no means risk-free, doctors say.[16]

While some African men and women fall prey to this colonial/slave mentality syndrome, the syndrome has its tentacles all over the African world in

Figure 5.7. A mannequin in Enugu, Nigeria. *Nnaemeka Ezeamalukwue.*

multiple forms and guises. These individuals, having been brainwashed or miseducated, perceive whiteness and European standards and values as the Eldorado even at the cost of their health. Although the bleaching epidemic is not the biggest issue of slave mentality in the United States, there are other areas where the diasporan Africans manifest this symptom too.

Universally, African people continue to be bedeviled by the quest to embrace fake/artificial beauty at the expense of the original. It is less comical but very embarrassing to see African women fighting each other on national TV shows and the internet. The first area of attack is the hair, to try to expose each other's fakeness. It serves to entertain other races while reminding African people that nothing unnatural can compare to natural in all ramifications, especially when it comes to dealing with human anatomy. Like in the past, some white commentators and TV personalities have on some occasions been caught making jest of African women's hair. Bill O'Reilly, the former *FOX News Talk* show host was caught denigrating a black Congresswoman, Maxine Waters calling her hair, " . . . a James Brown wig," a clear reminder to her that her hair was not natural. This insulting remark is akin to how the enslavers denigrated African people and their bodies on the plantation with racist words.[17]

Other African Americans in expressing the harmful effects of changing ones' natural texture or complexion have rebranded relaxer—"creamy crack." The insinuation is that like crack cocaine, fake hair and relaxer is addictive. Like an addict, individual victims often take risks just to satisfy their quest for a feel. Some denigrate the inside of their bodies, eating unhealthy foods, just to have enough for fake hair products. A remarkable incident occurred in Tulsa, Oklahoma, a few years ago at an Asian-owned beauty shop. At the shop, identified in a YouTube video as "Jun's Beauty Supply," an Asian man was said to have mercilessly punched and brutalized a young African American woman customer, resulting in a bloody nose and hospitalization. "Locals say this store owner has a history of violence against black female customers." African American men came out in solidarity with their women, to protest against the human rights violation, as they protested and convinced these women not to shop there because of the undignified treatment they receive from the shop owner. When the shop owner realized that African people have united in a protest, he announced a 50 percent discount on all products. Something remarkable happened next. 100 percent of the African women that had joined the men in protest left and rushed into the shop. The line was so long that many stood outside. Some of the ladies turned against the men who came to protect and support them.[18] This story epitomizes mental slavery. It causes one to ponder on the addictive similarity between fake hair products and crack cocaine. No wonder some call "relaxer" "creamy crack." Certainly "creamy crack" is quite addictive, so addictive that one values it above her dignity and essence.

There have been concerted efforts in the diaspora, mostly, to counteract the negativity associated with being African and having natural African features. Since the times of Marcus Garvey, who beckoned on African people to, "take the kinks out of your mind . . . instead of out of your hair." Thus, being African is not the problem; the problem is having a destructive mindset that is self-destructive. The founder and leader of the Universal Negro Improvement Association (UNIA) always refused advertisements from bleaching cream and hair straightening companies, with the UNIA newspapers reaching about 200,000 people per week. The Black Power Movement of the 1960s also advanced that self-love theme, preaching "Afro styles," "Black is Beautiful," and "Right On," among other inspirational mantras.[19]

Since the turn of the twentieth century, efforts have intensified to counteract and provide a lasting antidote to the syndrome of self-hate manifesting in bodily care. In Cuba, some African Cubans are preserving their natural hair and passing down such positivity to their youngsters. Irma Castañeda, for instance, maintains her natural hair as well as that of her toddler daughter. According to a news report by The Final Call,

> In the Balcón Arimao barrio in the largely Black municipality of La Lisa, on the west side of Havana, Ms. Castañeda and nine other women have launched an effort to improve self-esteem, teaching hairdressing techniques and traditional cosmetics recipes for Black skin, because they are not available in stores . . . "We want to break the stereotype that we Black women are less beautiful, without trying to look like White models," added Ms. Castañeda, an educator by profession and promoter of the project Rizos (Spanish for "Curls").[20]

Some institutions in the United States still discriminate against African people with natural hair, calling it "unprofessional," a clear indication of the stronghold of oppression. How can one be professional when they are fake or unnatural? As African descendants continue to fight for justice in every sphere, there are some legislations underway to outlaw such obnoxious discriminations. In California, Democratic State Senator Holly Mitchell proposed Senate Bill 188, the CROWN (Creating a Respectful and Open Workplace for Natural Hair) Act to outlaw such racism. The bill passed unanimously, 37-0, in April 2019. According to *The Final Call*,

> Until very recently, a Google image search for "unprofessional" hair styles yielded only pictures of Black women with their natural hair or wearing braids or twists, said Sen. Mitchell before the vote. "Although disheartening, this fact was not very surprising. Eurocentric standards of beauty have established the very underpinnings of what was acceptable and attractive in the media, in academic settings and in the workplace," Sen. Mitchell stated. "She said that even though Blacks were no longer excluded from the work place, their features and mannerisms remained unacceptable and "unprofessional."[21]

In Education

Paradoxically, the syndrome of slave and colonial mentality is preponderant in various academic institutions within and outside the continent of Africa. The academy is supposed to be at the forefront of intellectual empowerment, but unfortunately, the "Talented Tenth" who had been charged with liberating the rest seems to have abandoned their task to indulge in self-adoration or in some cases is helplessly bedeviled by the same disease it was called to treat.

The number of HBCUs that do not have an African American or Africana studies program is astounding. One would think that this should be a matter of priority—life or death—going by their acronym, HBCU (historically black colleges and universities). Elite ones like Howard University, Morgan State University, and Morehouse College do have some forms of Africana programs. However, Morgan State only offers that as an option at masters and doctoral levels. More infuriating is the fact that the latter does not offer one course on African people's history as a requirement at those upper levels.

The implied message from the department to graduate students is that your history, your story, and your values are not so important to be a prerequisite at this level. Everything else matters more than yours. The question is, why does the institution proudly call itself an HBCU?[22]

Also worrisome is the fact that the institution's history program has a non-official policy of not hiring any of its graduates from its graduate program at the time of writing. The counsel to graduates is always to try your luck elsewhere. That they prefer their graduates to test the waters outside. Unfortunately, the import is that the faculty does not trust its "products" and therefore their techniques. PWIs like Yale, Harvard, and Columbia Universities pride themselves in their ability to employ their best.

At Virginia State University (VSU), the swim against the tide is more apparent. The history department has only one African American on the tenure track. The rest is Caucasian and other races. The philosophy program within the department has no African presence at all.[23] The reality is that VSU is predominantly and historically African American on paper and at the student level. The demography of the history department's student population and the school, in general, does not reflect in the faculty composition nor does it reflect in the courses offered. They offer very few courses on African people's history; none is a requirement. Also disturbing is the fact that they do not offer any general education class on African Diasporan or African American history. This begs the question, how would thousands of students who come to HBCUs to have the "black experience" get it? Is the experience just on style rather than on substance?

At Grambling State University, the same trend prevails. There is only one African American history class at the undergraduate level, and two African history courses; none are required, and no African American course is offered at the graduate level. There is no African diasporan course at the General Education level. Instead, they offer Western civilization and two sections of world history at the survey level. The same implicit suggestion to their overwhelming African American students applies—that their experiences and history do not count much or enough to be made part of the prerequisite or to be offered at the General Education level.[24]

On the continent, the mentality is the same although with some variations. The largest black nation in the world, Nigeria recently banned history at all levels except at tertiary institutions.[25] Yes, that is true. History was banned in 2007 and it is only recently, as late as 2018, that the debate began over reinstating it.[26] In an article by *The Abuja Inquirer*, the tabloid laments this decision, tracing its origins to 1969:

> In Nigeria however, the Federal Government officially expunged history from its basic school curriculum in 2007 and relegated it as an elective, instead of a core subject at senior secondary level, thus widening a generational gap on

students' mental development. The attack on history actually started after the 1969 National Curriculum Conference, which resulted in the adoption of a National Policy on Education, and subsequent adoption of a 6-3-3-4 system of education. The ensuing years after the conference saw a gradual decline on the teaching of history in Nigerian schools, resulting in the removal of the subject from the 2007 curriculum, which was implemented in 2009 and 2010. While the decision contradicts the national policy on education, which aligns history with subjects like literature in English and Geography at the Senior Secondary School level, government's quest for human capital development and eradication of poverty rendered the old curriculum which prioritised history defective. Consequently, a massive ripple effect has hit universities in the country as very few currently have dedicated departments of history, while some have merged the course with strategic studies, international studies or diplomatic studies. Apart from undoing such an established system, the surge in criminal activities and glaring lack of nationalistic spirit among young Nigerians, lays credence to the considerable damage the unpopular government policy has inflicted on the society.[27]

Another sad side of colonial mentality in Nigeria's academic system could be found in the fact that since independence, the English language had remained the language of business and official transactions. Thus, the lack of utility value attached to indigenous languages meant that they are fast becoming irrelevant and unfashionable. The British colonial policies and the subsequent post-colonial policies were responsible for this. During the colonial time, African languages were relegated, like everything of African value. They were either classified as vernacular or called dialects. At schools, speaking vernacular equaled noisemaking. Both were punishable offenses and continue to be to this day. Punishment for speaking your African language could range from suspensions, to fines, to manual labor.[28]

It is heartbreaking to know that many churches in Nigeria and parts of Africa are part of tools that destroy African languages. How can one fathom a situation where the English language is used to preach in a church where 98 percent or sometimes 100 percent of congregants speak and understand the language of the area? Pentecostal churches, unlike the Catholic and Anglican churches, are guilty of this.[29] These preachers' approaches seem to suggest that the more fluent one is in the language of the west, and the more powerful their prayer becomes. Surprisingly, some individuals like Kwabena Taiwo have justified the slow but gradual extermination of African languages in the alter of westernization and nation-building.[30] This sort of position is antithetical to common sense and nature, yet they are being put forward by some of the so-called educated Africans who are undoubtedly victims of miseducation.

In Ghana, the same sad trend prevailed and prevails. Ghanaian languages were not only pejoratively called vernacular, but students were also punished and mocked for doing so. Recounting his experience growing up in Ghana, a

U.S. resident of Ghanaian descent expressed sadness how they were often whipped and abused for speaking "vernacular" in school. In the United States, at school, he seemed fascinated that Latinos frequently spoke Spanish even in the presence of teachers. Reflecting, he frowned that what was supposed to be an endearing language, a pride to him turned out to become a "physiological trauma to me":

> Growing up in Ghana, we were not allowed to speak our native tongue anywhere around school. It was more of a taboo, at least in my eyes. The punishment was cane whipping. I never understood the idealogy of why English, which is a foreign language, had more power than our native language, and why it had such a negative connotation. However, I dared not ask why. It was a simple law without an explanation. My assumption was that it was probably a way to help us improve our English....Have you ever wondered why it was a taboo to speak our local language in school? Did it somehow make you look down upon your rich language or feel embarrassed when your parents spoke vernacular to you in public?[31]

The trend is growing rather than subsiding. The more fluent you are in the language of your colonizer, the smarter you seem, and the better you are appreciated. The middle and upper classes seem to fall victim to this syndrome than the lower class. Many children raised in Nigeria's urban cities such as Lagos, Abuja, Port Harcourt, and Calabar grow up speaking English and not their indigenous languages.[32] Many might understand a lot of words of the latter but cannot speak it coherently. The result is as adults, they are unable to transmit and inculcate what they do not have nor mastered. The problem is ideological, an ideology that accentuates everything European at the expense of Africa's.

Africa's supposed "Talented Tenth," seemingly, have abandoned the downtrodden to seek greener pastures elsewhere. On the continent, it is this class that, rather than invest in education and research, hospitals and healthcare, prefers to take care of their health and education of their children in the west. Some of the political class also prefer to stash away their loots in foreign banks thereby depriving their nations of the needed resources. Those in the education sector follow the same template. In Nigeria's research institutions, research that is published in a western journal or university press is more appreciated and valued than the local ones. One will not fail to ask, what problems are these researches attempting to solve? Are they local or foreign ones? Does charity still begin at home?

In the diaspora, especially the United States, the "Talented Tenth" has a similar mentality. They have absconded the inner-cities and black communities and ran to "nicer neighborhoods." As they flee, they take their resources and their "smart" children to the white communities and schools where they face a different kind of oppression they ran away from. In the same vein, the athletic teens also follow the lead of the "Talented Tenth" by seeking to play for PWIs rather than HBCUs. Their argument and rationalizations are always that the former have more money, better facilities, and offer more exposure for a potential draft.The counters to these are: if the "Talented Tenth" stayed back or lived back instead of trying to give back, the black communities would prosper. If the best stayed in African American institutions, HBCUs would dominate college sports and generate tremendous revenue for the schools and communities. If they stayed back, African American communities could not be seamlessly gentrified. With their resources and aura, gentrification would stand little or no chance. With their wealth, connections, and personalities, a lot of social vices would abate because the root of the problems in inner cities is lack of investment, lack of leadership, leading to hopelessness. Sadly, by keeping the best outside rather than inside, African people at home and in the diaspora seem to be aimlessly swimming against the tide.

NOTES

1. David Walker, *David Walker's Appeal to the Coloured Citizens of the World* (Eastford, CT: Martino Fine Books, 2015).
2. Marcus Garvey, *Emancipated From Mental Slavery: Selected Sayings of Marcus Garvey* (Cleveland, OH: Universal Negro Improvement Association, 2016), 6.
3. Amy Jacques-Garvey, ed., *Philosophy and Opinions of Marcus Garvey*, *The Journal of Pan African Studies* (2009 ebook), 6–7.
4. "Bob Marley 'Redemption Song'—Lyrics" *Youtube*, https://www.youtube.com/watch?v=h_a3hh5nRrY (accessed March 17, 2020); "Redemption Song Bob Marley and The Wailers," *Genius*, https://genius.com/Bob-marley-and-the-wailers-redemption-song-lyrics (accessed March 17, 2020).
5. "Lucky Dube - Reggae Strong (lyrics)"*Youtube*, https://www.youtube.com/watch?v=R0B6BhwpR3w (accessed March 17, 2020).
6. "Lucky Dube - Back To My Roots"*Youtube*, https://www.youtube.com/watch?v=AktF2MT9wF4 (accessed March 17, 2020).
7. "Colonial Mentality - Fela Kuti (1977)," *Youtube*, https://www.youtube.com/watch?v=9Q2F2TaRghE (accessed March 17, 2020); "Fela Kuti—Colonial Mentality," *Song Meanings*, https://songmeanings.com/songs/view/3530822107858727873/ (accessed March 17, 2020)
8. "Malcolm X - The House Negro and the Field Negro," *Youtube*, https://www.youtube.com/watch?v=7kf7fujM4ag (accessed March 17, 2020).
9. Ciku Kimeria, "The Most Unusual Ways Many African Countries Got their Names," *Quartz Africa*, October 6, 2019, https://qz.com/africa/1722919/how-many-african-countries-got-their-names/ (accessed March 17, 2020).
10. Ngozi Cole, "The Real Meaning Behind Sierra Leone's Beautiful Name," *Culture Tip*, last modified, September 3, 2018, https://theculturetrip.com/africa/sierra-leone/articles/the-real-meaning-behind-sierra-leones-beautiful-name/ (accessed March 17, 2020).
11. Omo Omoruyi, "The Origin of Nigeria: God Of Justice Not Associated with an Unjust Political Order. Appeal to President Obasanjo not to Rewrite Nigerian History (PART 1)," *Rework Nigeria*, January 19, 2010, http://reworknigeria.blogspot.com/2010_01_19_archive.html (accessed March 17, 2020).
12. "Igbo Alphabet," *Ezinaulo*, https://ezinaulo.com/igbo-lessons/pronunciation/igbo-alphabet/ (accessed March 17, 2020).

13. Christie Omego, "The Igbo Language Development: The Challenges of the Igbo Lexicographer," in *Convergence: English and Nigerian Languages: A Festschrift for Munzali A. Jibril*, edited by Ndimele Ozo-mekuri, 689–706. Port Harcourt: M and J Grand Orbit Communications, 2016. www.jstor.org/stable/j.ctvh8r1h7.59.

14. "Dying to be White," *University of Cape Town News*, September 10, 2014, https://www.news.uct.ac.za/article/-2014-09-10-dying-to-be-white (accessed March 17, 2020).

15. "It's Time for Africa to Take a Stand on Skin Lightening Creams," *University of Cape Town News*, January 14, 2016, https://www.news.uct.ac.za/article/-2016-01-14-its-time-for-africa-to-take-a-stand-on-skin-lightening-creams (accessed March 17, 2020).

16. Pumza Fihlani, "Africa: Where Black is not Really Beautiful," *BBC*, January 1, 2013. https://www.bbc.com/news/world-africa-20444798 (accessed March 17, 2020).

17. Charlene Muhammad, "The Constant Fight Against Disrespect Of The Black Female," *The Final Call*, April 6, 2017, http://www.finalcall.com/artman/publish/National_News_2/article_103592.shtml (accessed March 17, 2020).

18. "Asian Store Owner that Punched Black Woman in Face Give 50 percent Off Sale," Youtube, https://www.youtube.com/watch?v=xI-7mHrcWjA (accessed March 17, 2020).

19. Thandisizwe Chimurenga, "How Toxic is Black Hair Care?" *The Final Call*, February 8, 2012, http://www.finalcall.com/artman/publish/National_News_2/article_8598.shtml (accessed March 17, 2020).

20. Patricia Grogg, "Taking Efforts to Fight Prejudice in Cuba to the Barrios," *The Final Call*, December 9, 2013, http://www.finalcall.com/artman/publish/World_News_3/article_101032.shtml (accessed March 17, 2020).

21. Charlene Muhammad, "Legislation Protecting Natural Hair Styles Makes Progress," *The Last Call*, May 1, 2019, https://www.finalcall.com/artman/publish/National_News_2/Legislation-protecting-natural-hair-styles-makes-progress.shtml (accessed March 17, 2020).

22. "Graduate Programs in History—Seventh Edition 2019," *Morgan State University*, https://www.morgan.edu/college_of_liberal_arts/departments/history_geography_and_museum_studies/graduate_program_handbook.html (accessed March 17, 2020).

23. "College of Humanities and Social Science," *Virginia State University*, http://www.sola.vsu.edu/departments/history-and-philosophy/index.php (accessed March 17, 2020).

24. "Department of History," *Grambling State University*, https://www.gram.edu/academics/majors/arts-and-sciences/history/curriculum/ (accessed March 17, 2020).

25. Chigozie Obioma, "There Are No Successful Black Nations," August 9, 2016, *Foreign Policy*, https://foreignpolicy.com/2016/08/09/there-are-no-successful-black-nations-africa-diginty-racism-pan-africanism/ (accessed March 17, 2020).

26. "Stakeholders Condemn Removal of History from School Curriculum," *Daily Post*, October 26, 2015, https://dailypost.ng/2015/10/26/stakeholders-condemn-removal-of-history-from-school-curriculum/ (accessed March 17, 2020).

27. Emmanuel Ogbeche, "Removal of History from School Curriculum," *The Abuja Inquirer*, https://www.theabujainquirer.com/?page=920andget=920 (accessed March 17, 2020).

28. Timothy A. Awoniyi, "The Yoruba Language and the Formal School System: A Study of Colonial Language Policy in Nigeria, 1882–1952," *The International Journal of African Historical Studies* 8, no. 1 (1975): 63–80.

29. Esther Chikaodi Anyanwu, Queen Ugochi Njemanze, and Mark Chitulu Ononiwu, "English Usage Pattern in Nigerian Religious Settingsperspectives From Selected Worship Centers in Imo State," *Journal of Humanities and Social Science*, 21, no. 6 (June 2016): 1–6.

30. Kwabena Taiwo, "Indigenous African Languages are Dying Out and it's a Good Thing," *International Policy Digest*, June 6, 2018, https://intpolicydigest.org/2018/06/06/indigenous-african-languages-are-dying-out-and-it-s-a-good-thing/ (accessed March 17, 2020).

31. "Stop Speaking Vernacular in Class," *Orijin Culture*, http://www.orijinculture.com/community/stop-speaking-vernacular-class/ (accessed March 17, 2020).

32. Katrin Gänsler, "English Threatens Nigeria's Native Languages," *DW*, May 14, 2019, https://www.dw.com/en/english-threatens-nigerias-native-languages/a-48730346 (accessed March 17, 2020).

Chapter Six

Using Multiperspectivity Theory to Confront Monoperspectivity in the U.S. History Pedagogics

While watching a professional U.S. men's basketball game recently, I realized that I never saw anything wrong with the name of the league known as the National Basketball Association (NBA), until I saw a commercial about the forthcoming Women's National Basketball Association (WNBA) season. The question that followed was why WNBA and not MNBA? Why are men's events described in neutral, central terms while women are treated marginally as the "other?" Another relevant question is found in the media's financial and economic news reportage whereby the balance favors the capitalist producers, manufacturers, and the "big guys." When the ordinary Americans' perspectives and conditions are reported it is mostly in their ability or inability to feed into and sustain the former. Hence, the preponderance of reports on consumer spending, profits (for corporations), and sales, but very few or none on savings or the virtues of saving which favors the latter.[1]

This paradigm is not exclusive to TV programs and media reports but is commonly found in history, especially in U.S. history textbooks. The quickest way to determine if there is any commonality between these analogies and U.S. history is to examine the relevance of ethnic studies. Evidently, U.S. history thematically and paradigmatically treats everybody—but the well-to-do white men—as the other while presenting this hegemonic group as neutral or in racial terms as colorless. This quandary serves to reinforce and justify the power of this demography. Essentially, this paper, utilizing the multiperspectivity theory, contends that a balanced perspective of historical narratives is critical to nation-building in two ways—it helps us historians inspire our students to think critically rather than memorize and affirm every data; doing so also allows scholars to empower their students to be producers of knowledge rather than docile consumers and at the same time help create better citizens.

Multiperspectivity theory, as proposed by Peter Huhn, Wolf Schmid, and Jorg Schonert (eds.) and advanced by Marcus Hartner in their literary discourses, advocates the application of multiple narratives and viewpoints in storytelling. The implication is that rather than the conventional singularity of plotting a story from one narrative, authors are invited to challenge their audiences and stimulate their curiosity by simultaneously conveying two or more viewpoints in the same literary project.[2] Historians can emulate this innovative literary approach in historical writing. U.S. history can as well benefit immensely from it because of the multiracial and multicultural make-up of the nation from the onset.

The goal of this chapter is to inspire critical engagement through multi-perspectivity in historical research, writing, and teaching not just in the United States but around the world. Although U.S. history is the focus of this constructive critique, the aim is to use the United States as a test case for a global paradigmatic rethink. Thus, the work of these Germans is central to the theoretical framing of this chapter. This also means that their innovative literary method is interdisciplinarily introduced to history. This research employs the qualitative method to scrutinize a selection of U.S. history textbooks in use since the late 1980s to 2017. In doing this, these texts were critically examined and interrogated for accuracy and objectivity. The presentation of the findings is done using the textual analytical method.

Since the 1960s, following the social revolution called the modern Civil Rights Movement, various racial and ethnic groups in the United States have begun to seek redress and request for curricular change that would mirror their experiences to ensure social justice. These demands have changed the teaching and writing of U.S. history in fundamental ways making it not just more inclusive, but also more democratic and nationalistic. In spite of these accomplishments in curricular reform, problems persist in U.S. history—in content, analytical paradigm, and in the language of the texts. By merely adding some contents of the so-called "other" to the margins of U.S. history, these problems were haphazardly addressed, meaning that the core of U.S. history remains largely European male-oriented thematically, chronologically, and perspectively.

Thus, these marginalized "others" seek alternative means of telling their stories outside the core U.S. history, hence the proliferation of ethnic versions of U.S. history such as African American, Native American, American Women's history, and more, each with its own terms of reference.[3] This separatist approach was in response to academic segregation as was the founding of the HBCUs. Thus, separation becomes a countermeasure to intellectual exclusion. If the narrative is truly about U.S. history, the need for specialties in a thematic and perspective sense would dissipate. Increasingly, however, scholars have begun to address this apparent lack of social and historical democracy in teaching and research.[4]

Following the intellectual revolution that shadowed the Civil Rights Movement, scholars and advocates of multiculturalism have increasingly attacked U.S. history narrative and content as exclusive, sectional, and non-encompassing. Thus, authors and publishers have increasingly tried to introduce thematic innovations as well as tweaking the narrative a bit to reflect American varied cultural and racial origins. Some multiculturalists have acknowledged the progress made in survey texts in terms of inclusion of minority themes in the central narrative of U.S. history but call for a paradigmatic rethink.[5] Others continue to contend that the textbooks still treat non-white groups as outsiders like the NBA treats women.[6] Vickery, on the other hand, has moved beyond content to challenge the narrative's perspective—for not inspiring historical curiosity in students and for affirming the prevailing social order rather than repudiating it.[7]

In light of the above, U.S. history textbooks require a critical assessment thematically, perceptively, and linguistically. Certainly, the survey courses can serve as agents of Americanization if the textbook contents are democratized enough, if the tone and prism of analyses are inclusive, and if the diction is weeded of anachronisms that serve to justify and perpetuate the agonies of America's past.

CRITICAL APPRAISAL OF THE HEGEMONIC NARRATIVE

The standard practice for authors of the U.S. history survey textbooks is to delineate the United States history into neatly defined, periodized, and thematic structure: the first half of the survey is periodized from Pre-Columbian Contact to 1865 or 1877 (Emancipation or Reconstruction), while the second half starts from Emancipation or Reconstruction 1865 or 1877 to present. Despite some progress made in expanding the content, there are still many unaddressed issues especially concerning the conveyance of the narrative in areas of race, class, and gender, which authors like Hijiya, Lindenmeyer, and Anderson have painstakingly highlighted in their discourses.[8] Thus, a critical appraisal of survey textbooks published between 1990 and 2014 reveals that no fundamental or radical change occurred in the narrative tone of these texts.

Christopher Columbus

Born in 1451 in Genoa, Italy, Christopher Columbus was a politician, a merchant, a navigator, and much more. Like many of his contemporaries, he was ambitious, desperate to attain fame and accumulate wealth. Thus, he began to hatch a radical plan—a plan of reaching India westwardly rather than from the east to profit from the spice trade. Fortunately for him, the Spanish monarchy bought into the idea after some persuasion and sponsored his mission. Leaving Spain in August 1492 with three ships, he arrived at the Western Hemisphere in October and quickly began to establish Spanish colonies, thus ushering in a new epoch in world history.

There is no doubt that Christopher Columbus deserves a place in not just U.S. history but also in world history textbooks for his role in helping transform the world through interconnection. However, his exploits are often romanticized and presented from the prism of Europeans. This narrative misleadingly presents Columbus as a nobleman, a Christian whose aim was to explore, "discover," "civilize," and Christianize the heathen. Although this blatantly embellished narrative has subsided in the textbooks a bit since the 1980s, the subtlety of it still prevails not only in the texts but also in the American society at large.

Thomas Bender and Eric Foner, writing in 2006 and 2017 respectively, have critiqued the undue elevation of Columbus, but have continued to fall victim to the same praise-singing narrative. While the former acknowledges the need to start American history from the history of Indigenous Americans rather than the latter's encounter with Europeans, he fell prey to the same monoperspectivity by hailing the voyage as a connector and an eye-opener for the world.[9] Though that may be true, such a narrative hides the significance of such an eye-opening connection for African people and the Indigenous Americans. Foner, in the same vein, follows the same paradigm by focusing on the Columbian Exchange, highlighting it as transformational. He then seemingly blames the victims of Columbus for their deaths stating that "because of their long isolation, the inhabitants of North and South America had no immunity to the germs that also accompanied the colonizers."[10] This logic places Europe at the center of existential reality, the farther one is from that reality the more isolated he became.

To truly democratize and nationalize U.S. history beyond content, beyond the memorization of data as Stout invites us to do, critical assessment and perspective diversification is veritable.[11] To this end, when Columbus' expedition is analyzed from the prism of the people he met at the Bahamas in 1492, he takes a whole new character and form. He transforms from a man who discovered America as Levine, Brown, and Rosenzweig; Davidson, Delay, Heyman, Lytle, and Stoff; Davidson, Gienapp, Heryman, and Lytle maintain; or who saved the world via Columbian Exchange as Faragher, Czitrom, Buhle, and Armitage uphold; a pious Christian—as most 1990s texts will have it—to the anchor and facilitator of the destruction of the indigenous American culture, values, and lives according to Hoffer and Stueck.[12]

Critically examined, Columbus's exploits and attitude portrays an exploitative, murderous, ungrateful man who, "had no regard for the people he encountered on the islands in the Caribbean, and he did not appreciate their friendship toward him and his crew." Also noteworthy, according to Clarke, is the background of most of Columbus's crew—"criminals" and "thugs" who were released from prison for the journey because regular citizens would not agree to embark on such a dangerous and ambiguous journey (Clarke, 1998).[13]

History, like every story, has different sides and often depends on who is telling the story as well as whose point-of-view he is presenting. Balanced narratives about Columbus should expose students to a multiplicity of historical perspectives from where they can reach or draw their own conclusions. By not doing so, historians tell the story from the prism of the victor—Columbus and his contemporaries—and ignore the narrative from the perspective of the vanquished. The inability to expose students to multiple perspectives on this subject, like many others, misinforms the latter and disables their thought process. Highlighting multiple components and perspectives avail the students the opportunity to think for themselves.

By so doing, we create better citizens who can apply classroom lessons to their daily lives. Such a critical mindset would help students bring the past to present by, for instance, assessing the validity or necessity of a national holiday for Columbus in light of what they have learned. It would potentially make them see a contradiction in the fact that while some scholars have discarded the notion of "discovery" we still live in a society that still celebrates Columbus by having multiple towns, cities, and a country named in his honor.

Andrew Jackson

Andrew Jackson is another historical figure in American history that continues to receive his share of attention in U.S. history textbooks because of his role as a U.S. military officer, a politician, a reformer, and an ex-president. Born in March 1767, in the Waxhaw Settlement of the Carolinas, Jackson was above all a wealthy planter who enslaved African people on his plantation like his contemporaries. As a soldier, he won accolades for his role in The War of 1812 against Britain and their Indigenous Creek allies, earning him the persona of a national "hero" among white Americans. As a politician, he narrowly lost the presidential election of 1824 to John Quincy Adams, but defeated the latter in the next election, thus becoming the nation's seventh president. As a president, he was polarizing because of his fiscal and social policies. One of the policies that made his administration controversial was his war against the Bank of the United States. Jackson, as well as his supporters vehemently opposed the idea of a centralized banking system and as a result, let the bank's charter expire and vetoed attempts by Congress to recharter it. He was also largely perceived as a dictator who expanded the powers of the presidency unhesitantly utilizing presidential veto to advance his cause. He also introduced the patronage system, which allowed cronies to be rewarded with appointments after an election.

Increasingly, Jackson's place in history has come under scrutiny because of his inhumane social policies. Unlike in South Carolina where he mobilized the military for invasion because of disagreement over tariff, he remained aloof as Georgia violated federal laws by invading and taking over indigenous lands. When the U.S. Congress signed the "Indian Removal Act," he swiftly signed it into law, authorizing the uproot of indigenous populations from their ancestral land from the East Coast to present day Oklahoma, in what is now known as the Trail of Tears. The treaty, which ensured this translocation, was signed in 1835 by the Cherokee, and by 1838 about 15,000 people were forced to evacuate on foot, resulting in thousands of deaths.[14]

A critical assessment of textbooks in use since the 2000s reveals that Jackson is still portrayed as an American hero and not at all as a villain. His politics and personality continue to be associated with phrases like, "broad franchise," "embodiment of the people's will," "growth of democracy," "national hero."[15] On the surface, these assessments are objective, but a deeper probe reveals a lack of multiperspectivity.

However, from an academically balanced standpoint and perspective, they are not. These authors' depiction and affirmation of Jackson's brand of politics as encompassing "broad franchise" conspicuously ignores the fact that at the time, the United States had one-third of its population enslaved, while the same man worked to get rid of the indigenous.[16] Thus, by ignoring these realities, the authors misinform their students through perspective omission. Also, by portraying Jackson as a national hero, these authors misrepresent and impose one perspective as universal or national while ignoring the possibility that from the African and Indigenous American standpoint, he was a racist persecutor as well as an emasculator who enslaved the former and engineered the transfer of the latter's patrimony to invaders. Essentially, by guaranteeing the transfer of the indigenous lands to white men, Jackson can best be described as a white man's hero. This transfer not only empowered whites at the expense of the Indigenes, it meant that the slave empire was extended thus deepening African American enslavement.

The phrase "broad franchise" refers to his broadening and extending voting rights to white men while ignoring other demographics. How is this act broad rather than sectional and gross nepotism? The only way these historians can use those terms to refer to Jackson and his presidency would be if they can argue that African people, the Indigenous Americans, and even white women are not humans. This consistent ahistorical attitude from

American historians is akin to a tacit rationalization of the injustices of the past.

This justification in the classroom is reflective of the hegemonic consensus about a man as divisive and as oppressive as Andrew Jackson. A more objective assessment of Jackson allows students to critically evaluate his policies and the inhumane consequences of such in the lives of the victims. A good way to start would be to ask students hypothetically: If the indigenous people were able to tell their stories would they portray Jackson as a hero, a nationalist, a monster, or a villain? An empowered student could easily look at a twenty-dollar bill and discover that the portrait of the same Andrew Jackson he learned in school is found there. Therefore, with a critical mind, he could arrive at his own conclusion by determining whether Jackson deserves a place on the bill.

John Brown the Hero

John Brown, the abolitionist, was born in 1800 in Torrington, Connecticut, into a deeply religious family. His family has roots in Puritanism, and Brown himself at some point aspired to become a Christian minister, but his dream was cut short due to medical and financial problems. His marriage with Dianthe Lusk in 1820 produced a baby boy, John Jr., and many more; they moved to Pennsylvania where he managed to purchase 200 acres of land and set up a business. Prior to that, he had lived in Ohio and Massachusetts as a youth with his family. After the death of Dianthe in 1832, he married Mary Ann Day, with whom he had thirteen more children. His unapologetic stance against the inhumanity of slavery was firmly forged with his relocation to Massachusetts in 1846. It was in Springfield, MA, that he was captivated by the anti-slavery rhetoric of African American abolitionists including Frederick Douglass at the Sanford Street Free Church. Thus, he became a member of the church and got acquainted with Douglass (Connelly, 1900; Sanborn, *The Atlantic Online*).[17]

Frederick Douglass was massively impressed by the humanity and morality of Brown. According to a *PBS* article, he remarked of the latter, "Though a white gentleman, he is in sympathy with the black man and as deeply interested in our cause, as though his own soul had been pierced with the iron of slavery." On his virtue and selflessness, His lack of funds, however, did not keep him from supporting causes he believed in. He helped finance the publication of David Walker's Appeal and Henry Highland's 'Call to Rebellion' speech. He gave land to fugitive slaves. He and his wife agreed to raise a black youth as one of their own. He also participated in the Underground Railroad and, in 1851, helped establish the League of Gileadites, an organization that worked to protect escaped slaves from slave catchers (*PBS*). Douglass was inspired by such selflessness and especially the fact that the former was white and knowing that a lot of white abolitionists also espoused and exhibited racist notions and attitudes towards African Americans.[18]

John Brown's unquenchable appetite to destroy slavery, by all means, continued to intensify as years went by. It can also be perceived in his relationship with another African American unapologetic abolitionist, David Walker. The latter was born in North Carolina to an enslaved father and free mother, which meant that he was free. Relocation to Massachusetts offered him the opportunity to team up with like-minded abolitionists. It was there that he wrote and published his famous pamphlet in 1829, "Appeal to the Colored Citizens of the World." In this, Walker employed revolutionary rhetoric enjoining blacks to wake up and to destroy slavery from inside. Walker understood the fact that slavery served the economics of capitalism and that appealing to the beneficiaries would make no sense. Hence his focus on the victims of slavocracy. This appeal terrified white Americans of the South who moved swiftly to try to scuffle the pamphlet's circulation. It is worth reiterating that John Brown deserves credit for managing to sponsor this publication in spite of his financial difficulties; his business was on the verge of bankruptcy.[19] Thus, after the publication, the pamphlets were distributed to the enslaved in the South through sympathetic sailors. While the literature inspired hope among African Americans, white planters put a bounty on Walker offering $3,000 or $10,000 to anyone able to assassinate the author or bring him alive to the South respectively. Unfortunately, Walker died mysteriously a year later in his home.

Despite John Brown's apparent heroics, he has been consistently reduced to a footnote or obscurity by American historians. Even among white abolitionists, people like William Lloyd Garrison take higher pedestals than Brown, who paid the ultimate price in pursuit of justice and human rights. He not only lost his life in Virginia, but he also lost a handful of his sons who were part of the invasion of Harper's Ferry in an attempt to seize a federal armory so as to attack and destroy slavery, plantation by plantation. Rather than receive credit for being morally upright, history books ridicule Brown as a crazed old man, and they focus on his shortcomings such as his indebtedness. His religious beliefs have also been criticized; that his God was not the forgiving Jesus of the revivals but the vengeful one of the Old Testament.[20]

Clearly, by pejoratively depicting John Brown, these authors are projecting and advancing the perspective of the oppressive enslavers and their sympathizers. The alternative perspective here is the fact that John Brown is a hero and an upright man who gave all he had—his life, his family, and all his possessions—in pursuit of a noble cause which was the destruction of the inhuman slavery. This is the hallmark of heroism, and John Brown is a hero for not only African people, but for everyone who believes that all kinds of oppression—torture, rape, forced labor, child abuse, and extrajudicial killing—are wrong.

Emancipation of the Enslaved

There is no doubt in the fact that Abraham Lincoln signed and issued the Emancipation Proclamations. One took effect in January 1863, and the second one after the war had been won by the Union in 1865. Why then was the Proclamation issued in batches? Because the war was not about freedom for the enslaved, it was about another type of freedom from the Union's prism — economic freedom for poor Europeans many of whom recently immigrated to the United States. The nineteenth century saw a massive influx of Europeans into the Americas from Canada to the Caribbean down to Argentina. This massive immigration in the United States, for instance, affected political debates. Immigrants naturally prefer ethnically diverse urban centers, thus most settled in northern cities. The dominant political party in the north was the liberal Republican Party, which was amenable to these immigrants more than their Democratic counterparts in the South. The Republican and Democratic Parties had conflicting interests in political economy—the former sought to use the western and mid-western lands as resettlement reserves for these recent immigrants. Allowing slavery in these territories meant unemployment for many whites who lived there because the enslaved Africans did all the labor work for their enslavers. This calculation would be advantageous politically to the Republican-controlled North as it would help the party spread its reach and tentacles thereby having more potential Electoral College votes. The Democratic Party, controlled by "slavocrats" of the south, intended to expand the party's reach by seeking to extend slavery in those regions as well as thereby having both economic and political advantage over their rivals.

This clash of interest was the remote cause of the war, leading to other immediate causes such as the clashes in Kansas and Nebraska between the two factions and their supporters, the John Brown raid of Harper's Ferry, and the secession by southern states led by South Carolina. No doubt, the Union fought the war to reintegrate the south back into the Union. Every war policy, strategy, and tactics activated by Lincoln's government revolved around this goal.

At the onset, the Union's war tactic was to invade the Confederacy and crush them into submission. As the former later found out, it is easier for one to defend his home court than to attack someone else's. By 1862, war fatigue set in as casualties mounted on both sides. The southern desire to defend seemed to outlive the northern desire to attack, prompting a change of tactic. This change meant that the Union began to think of how to strategically weaken and break the Confederacy's resistance by all means necessary. Indeed, Lincoln decided that the best way to frustrate his adversary was to strangulate their economic stronghold—slavery. Thus, he drew up the first Emancipation Proclamation that offered freedom to enslaved Africans in the

Confederate territory. African people enslaved in Border States that were not part of the rebel states remained enslaved. This act blatantly proves that the document, the inspiration, and its intent was to win the war and bring the rebels back to the Union.

The cogent question is, did Lincoln emancipate Africans? As stated, he issued the emancipation document, but did he liberate the enslaved? Certainly, no. To appreciate this fact, one has to compare President Lincoln's actions to that of other executives, past or present. If a governor or president wants to grant clemency to inmates, he signs the document and a copy is transmitted to the prisons where the inmates are held. The prison officials, acting on it, release the eligible inmates. In the case of Lincoln, his document had no teeth in the Confederate territory. He had no means of executing his executive orders because the rebelling areas did not recognize his authority at that point. The document served the purpose of morale boosting to African people as they began to fight and flee by themselves. In all practical sense, the enslaved freed themselves, having been encouraged by the Emancipation Proclamation document and the promise of integration into the army. Many Africans died in the process of fleeing from the plantation to attempt to cross into the Union lines. By leaving the plantations, the economic backbone of the Confederacy was irrecoverably shattered. To sustain their war efforts, they needed weapons, food, and medical supplies. The source for all of these came from the enormous wealth generated by slavery. Lincoln's, and indeed the Union's, sole goal was to win the war. Lincoln himself said it several times before and during the war that he cared less about the freedom of Africans. He also stated at some point that he was willing to extend slavery to non-slave states as long as the Union remains united.

History, sadly gives a lot of credit to the bourgeoisie, even at the detriment of the heroic masses. War stories, persistently, focus on the actions and conducts of the few elites who do not always deserve all the accolades they get. The First and Second World Wars are flush with such narratives. The stories of various revolutions and movements follow the same top-to-bottom approach. If emancipation is critically reviewed with the theory of multiperspectivity, the historian's understanding and interpretation of it changes dramatically. While Lincoln signed the document, African people liberated themselves. The paper was a morale booster, an encouragement; it had no force of law nor was it backed by action.

LANGUAGE DECONSTRUCTION

The question of perspective could be advanced into questioning the phraseology of these textbooks. Between 1989 and 2017, very little has changed in terms of choice of words and phraseology of history textbooks. Many still use anachronistic and opprobrious terms in discussing America's past. These words not only demeaning, they also affirm the injustices of the past. Ironically, these historians condemn some of the inhumanity and oppressive policies but use terms that endorse those egregious crimes.

European Trade on Africans Instead of "Trans-Atlantic Trade"

An important subject-term worthy of critical evaluation is the "Trans-Atlantic Slave Trade," which was immoral traffic and trade by Europeans on African people as merchandise. The trade, which was initiated by the Portuguese saw nearly all the western European nations engage in it and make an astronomic profit from the mid-1400s to the mid-1800s. As Europeans conquered indigenous lands in the Western Hemisphere their appetite to enslave Africans and use them to cultivate the lands grew. Without the land, there would not have been any need for labor. Undoubtedly, the ideology of capitalism drove European interests their professed Christianity notwithstanding. Eric Williams' seminal and neo-classic work, *Capitalism and Slavery* conclusively demonstrated how this ideological impulse inspired the trade, enriched these European actors and their states, as well as funded the Western Industrial Revolution.[21]

Certainly, without Columbus stumbling on the hemisphere and the attendant European scramble and partition of it, the so-called "Trans-Atlantic Slave Trade" would not have occurred. But he did, and then the over four hundred years of trade on Africans that cost Africa millions of youth and depopulated the continent resulted. Why then do historians blame the victims of this inhuman trade on the latter? How do historians do this? They accomplish this through their narratives that absolve the Europeans of their culpability in this barbarity.

U.S. history textbooks, even in the present, term the trade as either "Trans-Atlantic Slave Trade" or more pejoratively "African Slave Trade." The problem with the former is that it is not descriptive enough. It defines and identifies the trade by its routes rather by the actors or actual subjects. It is also suggestive that people that live within the Atlantic world engaged in the trade. The trade represented an unbalanced "business" relation between Europe and Africa on one hand and the Western Hemisphere on the other. And everyone else was used as objects for the advancement of European commercial interests. "African Slave Trade" is even more insidious as it places the object of trade as the subject of the sentence/phrase while not mentioning the real subjects of the trade. Thus, the object of trade misleadingly becomes the subject of the sentence while the subject, the initiator, the beneficiary of the trade disappears and is absolved. To correct this abnormality, the subject has to be the subject, hence European Slave Trade or European Trade on African people. Both make sense grammatically and contextually as they identify the subject within the title. The latter does more by not only identifying the subject; it also places the object within its right place as a victim.

Another way of critically examining this inhuman trade is by exploring it from a human rights perspective. From this standpoint, this trade represents the largest human trafficking in history in terms of volume, period, and distance. This perspective uses morality rather than legality to assess the trade and, on that note, one cannot be wrong. Even when morally judged from European ecclesiastical and moral standards, chattel slavery, rape, torture, dehumanization, and kidnapping are all mortal sins in the eyes of God and man.

The Enslaved Instead of "Slaves"

Another area where scholars and students need to pay closer attention to is the designation and labeling of the victims of chattel slavery as "slaves." No doubt, all the textbooks since the 1990s rightly recognize, highlight, and depict the oppressive nature of slavery and its dehumanization of African descendants. Nevertheless, what nearly all fail to do is to situate the word "slave" in its proper historical and linguistic context. The American history textbooks examined for this article interchange between "African slaves," slaves, and enslaved Africans in describing the victims of the inhuman trade. But these words do not all mean the same thing. Saying "African slaves" implies that these Africans, who were held captives, turned into human cargoes, and molded into working and baby-making machines were "slaves" in Africa before being uprooted. However, the enslaved, terminologically, captures the historical reality by categorically stating that these individuals were Africans who were forced to become personal properties by someone.

Using the term "slaves" is pejorative as it is opprobrious; it takes away the victim's humanity by charting their identity based on the economic value to the enslavers. Further, it normalizes chattel slavery and unconsciously justifies the injustice of the past. By collectivizing them as slaves, historians repeat, affirm, and endorse one of the worst atrocities in human history. It will be akin to identifying a rape victim as a "raped girl" rather than by her name. The oppression thus becomes her identity due to ignorance and lack of empathy. The job of a historian is to act as an unbiased umpire with diligence and measured disinterestedness in dealing with the past.

Indigenous Americans Instead of "Native Americans"

The indigenous peoples of the Western Hemisphere have been consciously and unconsciously derided with different name labels because of both ignorance and arrogance. It is common knowledge that Columbus accidentally stumbled upon the Western Hemisphere en route to India. At first, he thought he had arrived at his destination and thus labeled the indigenous "Indians." Columbus, as well as historians, have since realized this error, but the name has seemingly stuck. From the perspective of Columbus's hosts, it is akin to an intruder coming to your house, robbing you of your valuables as well as family, and then renaming you derisively.

Historians have not only endorsed this apparent act of injustice, but they have also codified, advanced, and perpetuated it, thus ensuring that generation after generation the indigenous peoples of America are misrepresented by name. It is the job of us historians to hold Columbus accountable for his ignorance and arrogance rather than affirm it. Most history books since the 1990s, in a belated effort to correct this, have relabeled the indigenous peoples "Native Americans." This change of title or label does not solve the problem of name imposition. The word native literally means a person born in a particular geopolitical area. The reason this second label is problematic is that everyone qualifies as "Native American" by virtue of birth in the U.S. Therefore, every American-born individual is native to this land. This misrepresents facts and reality.

The proper name, in the absence of an indigenous one, for the peoples of the Western Hemisphere who were here first before everyone else should be "Indigenous Americans" rather than the former. Indigenous means to be natural to a place, to be original or first to a place. This seems like the best English word that describes their primacy to this land. Since Columbus did not ask his hosts if they had a general name for all the ethnicities, our duty in the present is to ensure historical accountability and to apply corrective measures where necessary.

"Discovery of America"

Since the late 1980s, most authors have begun to jettison the notion of Columbus discovering America. Nevertheless, some authors like Levine, writing in 1989 in *Who Built America?* continue to instill and pass that erroneous notion unto students in their texts (1989).[22] Arguing that Columbus "discovered" a continent is akin to suggesting that no one lived there, that the people who lived there did not know where they lived, or worse, that the land and its inhabitants equated inanimate objects that "smart" scientists discover. Eight years later in *Out of Many*, Faragher et al., was conscious of this point and rightly credited Columbus with not the discovery of land or its people, but "the clockwise circulation of the Atlantic winds."[23] By 2014, there has been some progress in that particular front as authors like Eric Foner in *Give Me Liberty!* rephrases it and perspicaciously calibrated it as "contact" which implies that two parties encountered each other without downplaying the repercussions.[24] The same author in a subsequent edition of his book doubled down on his critique of the misleading notion of "discovery," contending thus, "Historians no longer use the word 'discovery' to describe the European exploration, conquest, and colonization of a Hemisphere already home to millions of people."[25]

"New World"

Unfortunately, while scholars have discarded the erroneous term "discovery," they have paradoxically continued to call the undiscovered land new. This discrepancy is still prevalent at the time of this research. Even when some authors like Bender critiqued the phrase, they still fail to put it in parenthesis to contextualize it.[26] By so doing, these authors puncture their own arguments and demonstrate an inability to overcome a centuries-old historical opprobrium.

The problem with this term from a critical standpoint is that it feeds into the discovery mantra. If there was no discovery but only contact, then there should be no "New World" or old one. One of the biggest questions this phrase raises is from whose point of view are we writing history from? Clearly, to Indigenous Americans, this hemisphere is anything but new. Evidently, it was new to Columbus and his compatriots. We should strive to make it clear in our history books and to our students the various probable implications of what we say and write about. A common analogy would suffice—couple A buys a home and calls it a new house. However, the house was called "old house" by couple B, who had sold it to A. When interpreting such scenario and to capture the context, the historian's job is to be neutral because saying "new house" means interpreting the contested house narrative from the prism of couple A, while saying "old" means from that of B.

Above all, it is the job of a historian to hold past leaders accountable by raising necessary questions, even those questions past leaders failed to ask in the course of their exploits. In the case of the European encounter with the Indigenous Americans, some of the questions Columbus should have asked his hosts are: Where am I? Do you have a name for this entire hemisphere/world/continent? Do you have a group name for all the ethnic groups in this hemisphere? Rather than ask these salient questions and instead of historians chastising him and his cohorts for not doing so, the land was Europeanized and codified as America in history books, journals, and newspapers. The people were ignorantly and arrogantly lumped as "Indians." One may suggest that these indigenous people did not have a hemispheric concept nor a racial name for themselves. The truth is that we do not know, and Columbus should have asked, and historians should hold him accountable for not doing the right thing. This is exactly what normal rational people do when they travel. They introduce themselves, try to find out the name of the place they arrived, and ask their hosts their names rather than impose one on them.

Human Rights vs. Civil Rights

Interestingly, the struggle for human rights in the United States is popularly referred to as "Civil Rights" and the revolution, the "Civil Rights Movement." The revolution had its origin in Africa from the resistance from capture and kidnap by Europeans and their African agents. Naturally, humans resist oppression of any kind within the limits of their abilities. Even animals resist capture of any kind. Africans in the Americas continued to resist human trafficking, imprisonment, torture, rape, and forced labor with every means and tools available to them. After emancipation, they began to resist different kinds of oppression, most notably the successor to slavery, Jim Crow and later New Jim Crow. As discussed in the preceding chapters, Jim Crow laws and norms legalized and normalized the dehumanization of African people in the U.S. Therefore, the best words or phrase to capture the centuries-old struggle that reached a crescendo in the 1960s is the Human Rights Movement.

Jim Crow laws denied the humanity of African people by negating their freedom and ability to function not just as citizens of the United States, but as humans with flesh and blood. Explicit and implicit Jim Crow laws deprived and or limited African people's access to basic amenities of life in employment, education, housing, and transportation. It further placed African people in a position of inferiority or inanimate beings, whereby they were beaten, tortured, raped, publicly killed for fun both by the police and white mobs without recourse to rule of law that applied to European Americans. The second part of the Jim Crow laws and mores denied these individuals their civil rights as citizens of the United States. While the former are basic and natural rights humans have regardless of where they live, the latter are rights one has by virtue of citizenship and residency in a given country. These include the right to vote or be voted for, the right to access publicly owned facilities, and all kinds of discrimination and segregation. All these combined to impoverish and impugned Africans ability to climb to the social ladder.

Thus, the difference between the 1960s and other eras was that it was a period of boldness and fearlessness. A period when African Americans stood tall rather than stoop to assert their humanity. Even during the revolutionary movement, white police officers and mobs unhesitantly continued to assault and intimidate defenseless freedom marchers and protestors in the streets of America. They utilized water hoses, police dogs, batons, and even guns to terrorize people who were peacefully demanding freedom in an attempt to scare them into submission to the status quo. Hence, the movement was about freedom, it was about justice, it was about the right to be humans in America. A lynched, brutalized, or raped victim has not been denied their civil rights; it is their natural, human rights that have been violated. Civil Rights are rights and privileges accorded to one by the law. No one needs a law to exist, to eat, to bread or to walk. These rights are inherent regardless of where one lives. A lynched or brutalized individual has been dehumanized and denied his natural rights.

Interpreting this momentous revolution in American history as Civil Rights struggle or movement focuses on only one part of it —the secondary which is civil rights, right to citizenship. The major part of the struggle was the right to live, the right to be human, and the right to live a dignified right in pursuit of happiness. This narrative is misleading and undermines the essence of the struggle. The reason there are organizations and movements today such as the Black Lives Matter is because the war on the humanity of African people is not over yet. The federal government, by signing the Civil Rights and Voting Rights Acts as well as Affirmative Action dealt with the secondary concerns while the primary remains unattended. This misinterpretation and misconception give credence to the racist theories that abounded since the 1700s that African people were of subhuman species. It also lends credibility to the former constitutional provision that designated an African as a three-fifths of a person which is about 60 percent human. An individual who is 99 percent human is not a human being. Consequently, not recognizing the movement as a human rights struggle, the revolution as Human Rights Movement, definitely reinforces this racist and bigoted notion.

In the past few decades, authors of U.S. history survey textbooks are beginning to recognize the imperative of democratizing historical narratives to mirror America's collective and divergent experiences. Yet, more work needs to be done not just in ensuring diversity in content and perspective, but also in the language and choice of words used in conveying these stories to students.

The theory of multiperspectivity is instructive and as well as a deductive tool for historians in teaching and research as it provides a veritable platform to deepen historical research as well as offers new avenues for engaging students. For research historians, it has the potential of inspiring more curiosity and helping in reinvestigating facts of history. It is high time that historians began to question why Columbus and his contemporaries did not ask their Indigenous American hosts what they called their land as well as what they called themselves. If Columbus and his contemporaries failed to ask basic questions in the past, the contemporary historian must hold them accountable in the present. This can be accomplished by consciously reworking, rewording, and revamping U.S. history narratives. By so doing, the cardinal critical method is strengthened and instilled early in future historians. At the same time, the foundation for a better America based on true intellectual diversity and multiculturalism is laid. Thus, there would be no need for separatism because segregation and oppressive narratives would have been eliminated.

Survey textbooks, in general, need to challenge the students' preconceptions, because history survey courses, for some students, represent their only encounter with history in the academic setting. Therefore, historians should maximize the opportunity to teach and impart knowledge of the past, but at the same time encourage the students to be inquisitive rather than passive learners. By doing that, we bring the latter closer to history and history to them. Secondly, by challenging them through historical exposition and multi-perspectivity more "souls" are won for history and the question of is it "His story" or "Our-story?" is laid to rest.

NOTES

1. "Mainstream media favors business over workers," *Talking Biz News*, June 20, 2008, http://talkingbiznews.com/1/report-mainstream-media-favors-business-over-workers/ (accessed March 17, 2020).

2. Peter Huhn, Schmid, W., and Schonert, J. (2009). *Point of View, Perspective, and Focalization: Modeling Mediation in Narrative.* (1st ed.). (Berlin, Germany: De Gruyter, 2009); Marcus Hartner, "The Living Handbook of Narratology: Multiperspectivity," last modified April 22, 2014, http://www.lhn.uni-hamburg.de/article/multiperspectivity# (accessed March 17, 2020).

3. Shirley Hune, "Expanding the international dimension of Asian American Studies," *Amerasia Journal*, 15 no. 2 (1989): xix–xxiv; Taylor, U. (2010). Origins of African American Studies at UC-Berkeley. *The Western Journal of Black Studies* 34 (2).

4. Carl Anderson, "Misplaced Multiculturalism: Representations of American Indians in U.S. History Academic Content Standards," *Curriculum Inquiry*, 42 no. 4 (2012): 499–501.

5. Ibid.

6. Diane Vecchino, "Immigrant and Ethnic History in the United States Survey," *The History Teacher*, 37 no. 4 (2004): 494–500; Kriste Lindenmeyer, "Using Online Resources to Re-center the U.S. History Survey: Women's History as a Case Study," *The Journal of American History*, 89 no. 4 (2003): 1483–88.

7. Peter Vickery, "Progressive Pedagogy in the U.S. History Survey," *The Radical Teacher*, 83 (2008): 10–13.

8. Jim Hijiya, Changing United States History Survey Textbooks, *The History Teacher*, 28(2) (1995): 261–64; Lindenmeyer, "Using Online Resources,"; Carl Anderson, "Misplaced Multiculturalism."

9. Thomas Bender, *A Nation Among Nations: America's Place in World History* (New York, NY: Hill and Wang, 2006), 15.

10. Eric Foner, *Give me Liberty: An American History* (Seagul) (5th ed.) (New York, NY: W.W. Norton and Company, 2017), 1–2.

11. Neil Stout, *Getting the Most out of Your U.S. History Course: The Student's Vade Mecum* (Lexington, MA: D.C. Heath and Company, 1993), 4–20.

12. Bruce Levine, Joshua Brown and Roy Rosenzweig, *Who Built America?* (Vol. 1), (New York, NY: Pantheon Books, 1989), 8–9; J. Davidson, B. Delay, C. Heryman, M. Lytle, and D. Stoff, *Nation of Nations: A Narrative History of the American Republic* (2nd ed.) (New York, NY: McGraw-Hill, Inc., 1994), 10; J. Davidson, W. Gienapp, C. Heryman, and D. Lytle, *Nation of Nations: A Concise Narrative of the American Republic* (Vol. 1). (New York, NY: McGraw-Hill, Inc. 1996), 10; J. Faragher, D. Czitrom, M. Buhle, and S. Armitage, *Out of Many: A History of the American People* (2nd ed.), (Upper Saddle River, NJ: Prentice-Hall, 1997), 40-41; P. Hoffer, and W. Stueck, *Reading and Writing American History: An Introduction to the Historian's Craft*, (Vol. 1), (2nd ed.) (Boston, MA: Houghton Mifflin Company, 1998), 19.

13. John Henrik Clarke, *Christopher Columbus and the Afrikan Holocaust: Slavery and the Rise of European Capitalism* (Buffalo, NY: Eworld, Inc. 1998), 29, 66.

14. A. Bealer and K. Rodanas, *Only the Names Remain: The Cherokees and the Trail of Tears* (USA: Little, Brown Books, 1996).

15. H. James, D. Brody, S. Ware and M. Johnson, *America's History*, Fourth Edition (Boston, MA: Bedford/St. Martin's, 2000), 354; J. Davidson, and B. DeLay, *US: A Narrative History* (Vol. 1) (New York, NY: McGraw Hill, 2012), 210; J. Oakes, M. McGerr, E. Lewis, N. Cullather, J. Boydston, M. Summers and C. Townsend, *Of the People: A History of the United States* (2nd ed.) (New York, NY: Oxford University Press, 2013), 311.

16. James, *et al.*, 2000.

17. F. Sanborn, "John Brown in Massachusetts," *The Atlantic*, https://www.theatlantic.com/past/docs/issues/1872apr/sanborn.htm (accessed March 17, 2020); W. Connelly, *John Brown* (Topeka, KS: Crane and Company, 1900).

18. "John Brown, 1800-1859," *PBS*, https://www.pbs.org/wgbh/aia/part4/4p1550.html (accessed March 17, 2020).

19. Foner, (2017), 508.

20. Ibid.

21. Eric Williams, *Capitalism and Slavery*, (Chapel Hill, NC: University of North Carolina Press, 1944).

22. Levine, et al, 9.

23. Faragher, et al, 36.

24. Eric Foner, *Give me Liberty!* (Vol. 1.), (4th ed.) (New York, NY: W.W. Norton and Company, 2014), 16.

25. Foner, (2017), 1.

26. Bender, 17.

Chapter Seven

From Oppression to Freedom

Wherever there is any form of oppression, there is bound to be an instinctive resistance. African people have utilized multiple avenues to attempt to throw off shackles of oppression. Against the Arab slavery, European slavery and imperialism, and then Jim Crow, the victims of these oppressive schemes utilized means within the legal and outside it to defend their humanity. In recent times with New Jim Crow in the diaspora and Neocolonialism at home, Africans have similarly and sporadically fought against these injustices that masquerade as they oppress. The philosophy of African people's resistance can best be described as that of survivalism; to try to endure and manage the pains of racism rather than finding an eternal cure.

Every victim of oppression of any kind must strive to uphold their humanity, defend their honor and dignity. To attain that, Kwame Toure's thoughts become relevant. According to Toure, the only means of having a chance against the oppressive scourges of racist oppression is through organization rather than mobilization. It is easier to mobilize people around incidents of injustice and racial biases, but the masses of the oppressed have to start forming organizations that would be able to strategize and deal with multiple oppressive issues as well as systemic oppression rather than singularly and sporadically. Malcolm X and Marcus Garvey share this philosophical approach.[1] They were organizers as well as mobilizers. They formed organizations that attempted to solve socioeconomic and psychical problems within the African diaspora and on the continent. Garvey had the Universal Negro Improvement Association (UNIA), while Malcolm erected mosques, when he was with the Nation of Islam and then formed the Organization of African American Unity (OAAU), all geared toward uniting the oppressed to strategically tackle systems of oppression with unity and solidarity.

Unlike the duo, Martin Luther King, Jr. was a mobilizer, but not an organizer. He went from city to city mobilizing African Americans to fight racial segregation, after which everyone dispersed. Thus, his methodological approach was flawed as it did not provide an everlasting platform for strategic planning and discourses on multiple phases of oppression. The Human Rights Movement in the United States, though consisted of multiple organizations, was not organized nor structured just like the Million Man and More March on Washington in the 1990s. While both attained some degrees of success, they fizzled out because of this factor and became memorable circuses in the annals of history.

To counteract this and to attain victory over the subjugation of African people, the latter need to organize and move from survivalism as the goal to thriving as an end. The former is basic which is what every human has, but it is not and should not be the sole target. The objective should entail striving to thrive. Thriving means that Africans should, like everyone, pursue happiness, liberty, and excellence in all spheres of life. In the industries that African descendants dominate, it should not be enough to be salaried. The ultimate aim should be to be the employer, not just a happy employee, the boss not just the servant. This can be pursued within the legal parameters. Where the codes and norms are obstacles, there should be vociferous outcry, protests, and exposition of such bottlenecks as an example of the New Jim Crow or Neocolonialism.

Meanwhile, the nature of resistance to oppression in the post-Human Rights African world seems at odds to that of their forbearers who were conscious of their oppression and fervently wanted freedom. Recently, owing to the operational modus of new oppressions, African people often work within the confines of oppressions, in some cases submitting to them as natural, as inevitable, and as manageable. Unfortunately, they transfer such attitudes to upcoming generations. This scenario is apparent in nearly every spectrum of society. In the music industry, for instance, the African American music genre includes blues, jazz, R&B, rock and roll, soul, funk, and reggae among numerous others. Of all the top 10 music record labels in the world and the U.S. including the Atlantic Records, Def Jam Recordings, Red Hill Records, Virgin Records, ABC-Paramount Records, BMG Rights Management, Island Records, Warner Music Group, Universal Music Publishing Group, and Sony Music Entertainment, none is owned nor run by African descendants.[2]

The role of record labels in the lives and music of artists is akin to that between a book publisher and the author. While the latter does all the mental and physical work, the former uses its resources to publish, print, and distribute. The author, like the artist, who is the intellectual originator, the original owner of the piece, lost the right to his invention through the contract and is left with paltry royalty. The right to his work belongs to the record label company. Cognizant of this tragic reality late music maestro Prince, in 2015, warned current and future artists to desist from signing any form of contract with record label companies comparing the relationship between a musician and record label companies to that between the enslaved and the enslaver. Speaking in Minneapolis to the National Association of Black Journalists, Prince further likened the terms of the contract to that between the planter and indentured servants since, "the artists have little control or insight over how labels take their music and profit off it online."

According to a *Rolling Stone* article,

> This isn't the first time Prince has compared the music industry to slavery. In 1993, when Prince and Warner Bros. were warring over his record contract, the rocker frequently appeared in public and onstage [sic] with "slave" scrawled on his cheek. Prince would soon change his name to "the Artist Formerly Known As" and "the Love Symbol" in an effort to "emancipate" himself "from the chains that bind me to Warner Bros." Prince and the label later reconciled for 2014's Art Official Age. As fractious Prince's relationship with record labels have been, his dealings with the Internet have been even more contentious. In 2007, Prince called upon the Web Sheriff to strip all images, videos and torrents involving the rocker off the web. That same year, Prince feuded with his own fansites over the use of his image, which resulted in a diss track called "PFUnk."[3]

Rappers like Jay-Z have taken the bold step toward establishing their own record labels, thus becoming employers rather than a "big" employee. In appreciation of his efforts, Prince also decided to ditch the "plantation" to support a "brother" by working with Jay-Z in his "HitNRun" and subsequent releases. Jay-Z had set aside $100 million to build his own service company in an attempt to get off the musical plantation. And in appreciation, Prince told a reporter that "we have to show support for artists who are trying to own things for themselves."[4]

Jay-Z's effort and Prince's support illustrates the template for success. It underscores the philosophy of resistance within the legal parameters. Rather than tolerate, accommodate, or endure the torturous oppression of New Jim Crow, Prince fought it variously through vocalizations and by physically circumventing the record labels' entrapments. He achieved this relative victory by showing the rest of the African world how it could and should be done.

In the sporting arena, the master versus slave dynamic is even more glaring. In the U.S. leagues such as the NBA and the NFL, African Americans are overrepresented on one level and underrepresented in all others. In the playing category of the NBA during the 2010/2011 season, according to the data provided by the Institute for Diversity and Ethics in Sports of the University of Central Florida, 78 percent of the playing staff of

NBA teams are of African descent. On the other hand, only 18 percent is Caucasian during the same season. To contextualize this overrepresentation in one category and underrepresentation in others, one has to contrast these statistics with that of coaching and team management. During the course of the same season, the thirty-team NBA had only six African American CEOs or presidents, which translates to 20 percent. In the coaching category, only nine teams had African American coaches; one was Asian, while the rest was Caucasian. In the ownership cadre, only one out of the thirty teams had a black majority shareholder.[5]

In the NFL, the same trend applies. Out of the thirty-two teams in the league, eight of them had African descended coaches in the 2018 season. But by the start of the 2019 season, only two remained: Mike Tomlin of the Pittsburgh Steelers and Anthony Lynn of the San Diego Chargers. One other team, the Carolina Panthers had a Latino coach, Ron Rivera who was later sacked before the season ran its course and replaced by Perry Fewell on an interim basis. The rest are Caucasian. During the same period, 70 percent of the players in the league were African. "In 2009, a report by Janice Fanning Madden and Matthew Ruther at the University of Pennsylvania concluded that between 1990 and 2002, African American head coaches had to be significantly better than their European American counterparts in order to be hired as a coach in the NFL."[6] The same applies to quarterback position; African Americans always have to be twice as good to be considered for that skipper position. They not only have to be great at throwing, but many also have to be extremely athletic to have a shot. Lamar Jackson of the Baltimore Ravens, Russell Wilson of the Seattle Seahawks, Michael Vick formerly of the Atlanta Falcons and Philadelphia Eagles are few examples. White elite quarterbacks past and present do not have to be athletic to be considered great: Tom Brady, Aaron Rodgers, Peyton Manning, and Drew Brees. Certainly, based on the job description, the quarterback's position is more of a mental than physical position. It requires the player to be a leader, to be more mentally strong than physical. This prevailing trend of preferring whites in positions that demand mental toughness illustrates and compares favorably to the demography of slave plantation where the ownership, overseers, and security/vigilante were all Europeans, while the field laborers were Africans. The two systems also compare when one considers the nature of the two jobs, both are physically demanding jobs—more physical than mental. Therefore, players in both cases have to be extremely fit physically, but mentally weak and submissive to the authorities even at their own detriment.

To advance and therefore reverse this trend, African people have to change their approach toward Popular Oppression or New Jim Crow. There is an existing rule—the Rooney Rule—which is aimed at ensuring racial diversity in sports especially in the head coaching department. The rule requires NFL owners to interview at least one non-Caucasian coach when trying to fill a vacant head coach position. This rule can be utilized to a full extent and there should be a demand for a more stringent rule that should make the hiring process more transparent and based on competence rather than on skin color. From publicly advertising for positions, to listing the required and desired qualifications, to announcing the rationale for either hiring or rejecting and applicant—these should be basic.

Beyond coaching, African people will benefit a whole lot if they could operate in unity to effect desired rule changes in the league. Why are physical leagues like the NBA and NFL so oppressive to players that trivial issues like taunting and over celebration are punished while in NHL fisticuff is a norm? Why is it acceptable to tacitly discriminate and oppress within the system and illegal to protest verbally or otherwise during or before a game? How could these leagues support social causes including the fight against breast cancer and American veterans but also oppose to African people's causes? This situation is akin to beating someone and then forbidding them from crying—the least the victim could do. One cannot protest the persistent police brutality in any American leagues without repercussions; that is a clear signal that these leagues and team owners do not value the lives of African people. Like the slave traders, they value the labor, not humanity. How could taking a knee during the national anthem be more offensive than the barbaric killing and beating of African people on the streets of America every day?

The clear path to victory is to not give up protesting the injustices in society. It is unfortunate that unlike in the 1960s, when African people united and fought oppression with unison, they seem to be fighting it at individual levels in 2020. This makes the individual protestor an easy target for the oppressive forces. Like on the plantations of America, African Americans have the numerical advantage in these aforementioned league. They should make their numbers count and demand favorable rule changes. The rules must favor the players, not the media, not anyone else. The reason is simple. These sports are risky and extremely dangerous. The interest of the players must always come first, not just in concussion situations, but in terms of rules governing social conducts on or off the field.

Ownership, apart from the rules of the game, is another area unity and solidarity could address. Since the integration of the league from the decades of the 1950s and 1960s, there is no data on how much African American players have made from the league. Lack of unity meant that these players' financial successes are at the individual level and have not resulted in more African American team ownership. It also meant that the oppressive rules remain intact. Therefore, it is time these athletes started thinking about saving rather than spending. It is also about time they started organizing and putting some percentages of their earning toward team ownership. That should be the goal. It should not be enough to be drafted and earn some income; it should be time to start paving the way for future generations of

African American athletes. Other parts of sports like cheerleading, refereeing, sports administration, and journalism should reflect the demography of the playing staff. How could the powerful, numerically speaking, be so powerless that they could not even cry when beaten, could not at least take a knee to protest American racism? "There would be no NFL without black players. They can resist the anthem policy," therefore that numerical advantage can only count if the players are braver and wiser by uniting.[7]

Colin Kaepernick's story epitomizes persistence and perseverance amid adversity and odds. He began passively exposing American dehumanization and killings of blacks by kneeling while others stood during the playing of the national anthem starting in 2016. He sought to draw the attention of the world to that sort of gross injustice. According to him, "I am not going to stand up to show pride in a flag for a country that oppresses black people and people of color.... To me, this is bigger than football and it would be selfish on my part to look the other way. There are bodies in the street and people getting paid leave and getting away with murder."[8] The fact that the NFL as well as his team, the San Fransisco 49ers, dished out retributive actions against him for a peaceful protest rather than show support should concern every being with a conscience. According to a statement by the team,

> The national anthem is and always will be a special part of the pre-game ceremony. It is an opportunity to honor our country and reflect on the great liberties we are afforded as its citizens. In respecting such American principles as freedom of religion and freedom of expression, we recognize the right of an individual to choose and participate, or not, in our celebration of the national anthem.

Kaepernick joined the list of other African American athletes to bring oppression of African people to the forefront including former NBA player Dwyane Wade, and current players Chris Paul, LeBron James, and Carmelo Anthony and several WNBA players as of 2016. He follows the legacy of gold medalist Tommie Smith and bronze medalist John Carlos at the 1968 Olympics in protesting the injustices against African people in America. While many have stopped protesting, Kaepernick continues outside the league thus ensuring that his unofficial exile from the NFL is perpetual.[9] A significant amount of other players, including those in the 49ers, have defied oppressive injunctions and continued to protest during games. This is despite the NFL's move in 2018 to outlaw kneeling or sitting during NFL games. According to the NFL, any member of a team that kneels during the playing of the national anthem will be punished. Not only will he be punished, but his team will also be fined as well. The only option is to not be on camera or to be in the locker room during the singing of the anthem. Of course, the NFL hierarchy will not like oppression to be exposed on camera, hence their decree.

Commentators have criticized the policy as illegal and unilateral. Before adopting any policy, the league was duty-bound to negotiate with the players' union, but this did not happen. By so doing, the NFL is flagrantly violating the labor act, which requires every employer whose employees are represented by a union to negotiate terms and conditions of employment before modification and implementation. Also, employees are empowered to embark on workplace protests.[10]

To attain everlasting victory in this, African American players and indeed all players of good conscience should continue to voice out the evils of racism around the world. Players are the principal reason there are leagues and games. Therefore, their interest and opinions should be paramount rather than that of business owners whose sole concern is the profit margin.

Certainly, the education sector has been as oppressive as sports and the music industry for African people. On the surface, it seems that there is a lot of improvements in race relations, however, one has to consider the fact that the dwindling of African American own or run institutions is relatable to the crushing impact of New Jim Crow and Popular Oppression. This form of racial oppression, as discussed in chapters one and four, thrives by working through proxies and operates discreetly. It is popular because most European Americans, unlike African Americans, do not protest nor condemn it. The majority denounce open racism or racial epithet, but not this type that devastates African people socially and financially. The list of HBCUs that have closed down shop since the end of the Human Rights Movement is mind-blowing. Although the closures had started before the movement, the rate intensified thereafter. Many were shut down due to accreditation issues, others due to financial reasons occasioned by multiple factors including low enrollment and budget cuts. It makes one wonder if racial oppression is getting worse. These institutions were largely opened at the height of Jim Crow, but have been closing down during the era of New Jim Crow.

Eleven Historically Black Colleges and Universities That Have Closed

St. Paul College
Having unsuccessfully battled a crushing debt and a rejected accreditation, St. Paul College will soon join the ranks of HBCUs forced to close their doors for good. The major agents behind the 125-year-old school's closure have reignited discussions on the current state of HBCUs and possible ways to ensure their future.

Bishop College
Located originally in Marshall, Texas, Bishop College grew out of a desire to establish a Texas college for Black Baptists. The Baptist Home Mission Society founded the college in 1881. Accomplished clergymen like Martin

Luther King, Jr. and Jesse Jackson would often visit the religion-oriented institution. The school experienced a series of controversies and financial problems in the 1970s before closing in 1988.

Daniel Payne College

Daniel Payne College was a private four-year college located in Birmingham, Alabama. Founded in 1889, the college was named after the sixth bishop of the A.M.E. Church. Payne had been the first black president of a college in the United States. In 1977, a massive tornado left over $1 million worth of damages to the campus, forcing the college to close that same year.

Friendship College

Based in Rock Hill, South Carolina, Friendship College was founded in 1891 as "a place for young African-Americans to be educated so that they could move forward in society as ministers and educators." The institution held its final semester in 1981 after an investigation exposed a mismanagement of funds.

Guadalupe College

Members of the Guadalupe Baptist Association founded Guadalupe College in 1884 in Seguin, Texas. Primarily financed by black Baptists, the school was established to advocate educational pursuits among blacks in Texas. A disastrous fire forced Guadalupe to close in 1936.

Kittrell College

Kittrell College opened in 1886 in Kittrell, North Carolina. The North Carolina Conference of African Methodist Episcopal Church founded the historically black institution, which was originally a high school. Financial problems caused the school to shut down twice, before closing for good in 1975.

Leland University

Having wanted to establish an institution of higher learning for Louisiana's black population, Brooklyn resident Holbrook Chamberlain incorporated Leland University in 1870. A hurricane destroyed the original buildings in 1915, and consequently moved the school to Baker, Louisiana. Leland University served black students from first grade through university level, before closing in 1960.

Mary Holmes College

The Board of Freedmen of the Presbyterian Church founded Mary Holmes College as a high school in 1892 in Jacksonville, Mississippi. The school was made into a two-year private college in 1959. Toward the end of its legacy, a host of problems led the institution's Board of Trustees to declare bankruptcy and close in 2004.

Mississippi Industrial College

A private institution located in Holly Springs, Mississippi Industrial College was founded by the Mississippi Conference of the Colored Methodist

Episcopal Church in 1905. Young black students were trained in Christian ideals and provided with literary and industrial educations. The college closed in 1982.

Western University
The first black university in Kansas, Western University was established in 1865 as Freedman's University in the town of Quindaro. The school's nationally renowned music program produced many notable alumni, such as famed choral conductor Eva Jessye and the National Association of Negro Musicians co-founder Nora Douglas Holt. Following a fire in 1924 and a drop in admissions and private funding, Western University closed in 1943.

Prentiss Institute
Prentiss Institute opened in 1907 in Jefferson Davis County, Mississippi. Students initially paid for their education with eggs, chicken and produce, according to records. Heifer International partnered with the private two-year college in 1955, providing poor families with livestock to supplement their farm income. The school's decline and eventual closure in 1989 has been attributed to a gradual decline in admissions.[11]

Existing HBCUs around the United States are struggling and that is unimaginable. Parts of these problems as well as the perilous situations in African American communities are caused by not only the New Jim Crow Policies but also the fact that the "Talented Tenth" has abandoned the masses. They have fled the black communities in search of the so-called "nicer" neighborhoods. Educationally, they have taken their "smart kids" with them that the HBCUs have come to epitomize "dumping grounds." Sequel to this, the most talented African athletes join the "Talented Tenth" in search of "nicer schools." Conversely, African descendants dominate many sports at college and professional levels, but the fruits of these strides fall to other races because the best is outside the African American communities and institutions, not inside. Ironically, the solution to these quagmires lay in reversing the course. Just like the late nineteenth and early twentieth century's Great Migration was comprehensible, to achieve victory and to rejuvenate black communities and patrimonies, the elites need to retrace their steps en masse, not individually. Oppression applies to the mass of African people, and to counteract it there is a need for collective action. The success of the Human Rights Movement of the 1960s is traceable to this fact. Everybody, as they say, puts their best foot forward.

Having the best of African people in their communities and institutions would have a tremendous economic and psychical boost. History has shown that African Americans attain the highest group success not when they are fragmented and melted into other communities, but when leaders are in the communities leading. By so doing, their light shines from inside out. Giving back is not enough because whatever one gives will be barely enough to sustain the receiver. Giving back is key, as the poor have the opportunity to work for the rich, with the "not so smart" and the "smart" interacting in local black schools, the former learning from the latter. The best form of giving back is living back.

Added to the above is the fact that the "Talented Tenth" would be in a position to push for excellence in all African American institutions. How could African Americans' ancestors work so hard amid overt Jim Crow to establish so many institutions and the twentieth and twenty-first century generations let them shut down in the alter of integration? The "Talented Tenth" should be pushing for growth and advancement of HBCUs. It is quite unbelievable that none of the surviving HBCUs have a university press. Very few like Morehouse College and Howard University have law and medical schools. It is the job of the "Talented Tenth" to show their talent by working to reinvigorate African American institutions by stabilizing the existing programs and adding to them. Institutions like Fisk University, Morehouse College, Spelman College, Dillard University, Howard University, Clark Atlanta University, Morgan State University, Hampton University, and Tuskegee University should at least all have medical and law schools. These schools are also due for university presses. Unfortunately, the only notable HBCU university press operated by Howard University was shut down in 2011. That is unacceptable. One cannot measure black progress by recounting individual material success among the "Talented Tenth" who does not live in the African American community. Black progress means collective one determined by thriving institutions and communities, rather than personal accomplishments that do not benefit the mass.

As Booker T. Washington perceptively suggested, many of the HBCUs could benefit by going back to basics by adding vocational programs to their curricula. It will certainly benefit millions of African Americans and other Americans if the HBCUs revived trade schools and operate them alongside liberal arts programs. There is no doubt that trade schools offer practical skills in multiple fields. Thus, like Du Bois envisioned liberal education, and Washington vocational, both philosophies can combine and serve usefully in the twenty-first century. Certainly, not everyone whether African, Caucasian, or Asian will obtain or is inclined to obtain a liberal education. Therefore, reviving technical and vocational certificate programs will go a long way in solving some of the social vices in the African American communities. It is capable of breeding new generation entrepreneurs, employers and not just employees.

The "Talented Tenths" of today should think and function like that of the nineteenth century, the likes of David Walker, Harriet Tubman, Frederick Douglass, Marcus Garvey, and Booker T. Washington, who were selfless and worked to uplift the rest rather than gloating on their self-accomplishments. Tubman in particular epitomized community service. Unlike the modern era

African leaders at home and in the diaspora, she freed herself and went back risking it all to free more enslaved Africans. It was risky but the inspiration behind the risk was based on selfless articulation and appreciation that if others are in captivity her freedom was worthless. She perfectly understood the imperatives of group progress and the reality that racial progress trumps individual success. Since the 1960s, African American leaders, the middle and the upper class, have done the opposite by escaping and leaving others behind. They sneak out of the African American communities and institutions rather than stay back and use their influences to advance the race.

The "Talented Tenth" on both sides of the Atlantic needs to collaborate more in various areas like their Jewish counterparts. European descendants all over the world naturally understand the importance of racial solidarity. Apartheid could not have been so effective against the indigenous Africans in South Africa if the Boers did not have the material and moral support of their "cousins" in Europe and America. Likewise, Israel, as a nation would not be able to withstand the odds against its Arab adversaries if not for the tremendous sustenance and assistance from western nations. The level of cooperation between these Caucasian majority nations economically, culturally, and otherwise is a thing that African people should emulate.

There are incredible rooms for cooperation among African people. In the education sector, through the HBCUs, there should be more student exchange programs whereby students are sent to reciprocal institutions for learning and proper life experience. There are multiple foreign student program options for Jewish students around the world, which should serve as a template in this regard. Below are some of them, according to goabroad.com:

1. ISI Florence

Just last year ISI Florence, an independent, private educational organization that serves as an American center for higher education in Florence, collaborated in the opening of Shemah, a school of Jewish studies and culture in Florence. Students who choose to study abroad at ISI Florence can take part in a unique Jewish Studies track and enroll in courses at Shemah in Jewish history, thought and culture, ancient and modern, in and out of Italian context. Where: Italy; Cost: $17,000.

2. CET Jewish Studies Program in Prague

CET Prague is a one semester study abroad program for undergraduates, offered in the Fall and Spring semesters. Participants can choose a concentration in Jewish Studies. Instead of just reading about Jewish history in a textbook, this concentration allows you to use the city as your classroom. Students will visit WWII memorials for a Holocaust class, use the Jewish Museum in Prague to do research, and meet with Jews who live in Prague. Cost: $18,000

3. Paideia–The European Institute for Jewish Studies

Paideia offers a One-Year Program of Jewish Studies, which is the most intensive Jewish Studies program available in Europe today. A pluralistic, non-denominational institution, both Jewish and non-Jewish students study at Paideia each year, with students represented from Israel, the United States, and over 15 countries in Europe.... The One-Year Program focuses on text study from classical bible studies to modern Jewish philosophy. Modern Hebrew classes, a study trip to Israel, and a visiting lecture series are also included.... Where: Sweden. Cost: Price varies, there are available scholarships which include tuition-free studies, a study trip to Israel and a monthly stipend of ~800€ per month to cover rent and living costs.

4. Hebrew University of Jerusalem

While studying in a center of religious, historical, and political significance you will have the opportunity to take intensive Hebrew language studies, as well as classes on Israel, the Middle East, and Jewish Civilization, Religion and History. As a student at the Rothberg International School, you will be invited on trips, tours, and festivals all over Jerusalem and Israel that will enhance your in-class Jewish Studies. You will live with other international and Israeli students, providing you with the chance to not only learn globally, but to learn from those of different cultures. Students also have the option to participate in an internship at an organization in Jerusalem. Jewish Studies students can choose to intern at one of Israel's many Jewish Studies related organizations.... Where: Israel. Cost: $10,000.[12]

From the foregoing, it is not free nor cheap, but worthwhile. Trust funds could be established to raise the needed funds to finance such an essential program. Also, like the Jewish students are exposed and thus have a globalized experience, African people can do with such exposure. They will have the opportunity to learn about their true history, culture, and visit the land of their ancestors. Such collaboration makes connection to the continent easier and natural. It is not surprising that at least one NFL and NBA games are each played in London. It is also not surprising that during European soccer pre-season, major European soccer teams like Chelsea, Barcelona, Real Madrid, and Liverpool play some of their pre-season games in the United States. It follows this paradigmatic fraternal approach. It is natural and prevalent among every race except for the African. The only way to reverse it is to reverse the prevailing apathetic attitude.

On the continent, the "Talented Tenth" needs to correspondingly follow suit. It is disheartening to know that it is often easier and cheaper to go from Africa to Europe and America to Europe than to Africa. Statistics show that internal trade among African countries is poor. That is grossly unhealthy. The major part of the problems are anachronistic trade policies that deter trades such as high tariffs, uncomplimentary transportation and infrastructural networks all of which are part of the colonial legacies.[13] Added to the above are inexplicable border closure policies pursued by some African leaders and countries.

On so many occasions, Nigeria has closed its borders with the Benin Republic purportedly because of smuggling through those borders. One would think that the right policy approach would be to shore up security and activate an aggressive industrial policy that will foster domestic production. Local production, when enhanced, is capable of ending any form of smuggling as the latter becomes riskier and worthless. Defending the recent border closure, Nigeria's Minister of Information, Lai Mohamed, defended the policy stating that on " . . . Tuesday, there was a meeting between . . . the comptrollers of customs of all the three countries involved. We have not reached any agreement . . . but our insistence is that we must all respect the ECOWAS protocol on transit goods . . . ."[14] Individual Africans and countries should freely trade and travel within the continent to enhance economic and social development. Also, there should be a visa waiver for Africans in the diaspora. The elites of Africa owe that to their "cousins" abroad. It not only makes cultural sense; it makes economic sense as well.

African elites must do a better job to extinguish the burning flame of xenophobic policies and actions in all parts of Africa against the sons and daughters of the continent. It is as reprehensible as it is incomprehensible that rather than work together for common good, some individuals in different parts of Africa found an excuse and time to unleash terror against one another on the altar of nativity. Twenty-three years after most African countries were liberated from the clutches of colonialism, they began to turn on one another. One of the first incidences of xenophobic policies and action took place in Nigeria between 1983 and 1985 during which the Nigerian military government enacted an infamous policy generally known as "Ghana Must Go."[15] This policy required over 300,000 Ghanaians believed to have been working in Nigeria to obtain work permits or be expelled. Ghana's High Commissioner to Nigeria had asked Nigerian authorities to extend the deadline, but Nigeria's Interior Minister Maj. Gen. Mohammed Magoro refused to bulge. This caused untold hardships for these hundreds of thousands of Ghanaian masses.[16] Contrasted with the policies of the 1960s whereby Nigeria's foreign policy was premised on expelling all vestiges of colonialism, this stance becomes vexatiously inexplicable.

Thirty-six years later, in 2019, it is Ghana's turn to exert retributive actions not on Nigerian government that enforced the punitive measures, but on the masses of Nigerian residents in Ghana. Since 2010, there has been growing resentment in Ghana against Nigerians in general and traders in particular. In 2019, Ghana Electrical Dealers Association demanded a crackdown on their Nigerian counterparts operating in their nation claiming that many do not have necessary permits and licenses to do their businesses. They threaten to take laws into their own hands should their government failed to act. Responding to these threats, the National President of the Nigerian Union of Traders Association, Ghana (NUTAG) Chukwuemeka Nnaji, argued that the Economic Community of West African States (ECOWAS) protocol gives all citizens of member states equal rights and privileges to reside and conduct business within member states.[17]

Nevertheless, by November 2019, the Ghana trader's union had effected its threat by forcing the closure of foreign-owned businesses, especially those owned and operated by Nigerians. Joseph Obeng, president of the Ghana Union of Traders Association (GUTA) claimed that local traders were being undermined by foreigners arguing that they were being invaded by these foreigners with "cheaper products."[18] The inconsistency is apparent. While the association and NUTAG had complained of a lack of working papers and licensing, the former betrayed their real motive—fear of competition. These are in spite of existing regional and sub-regional agreements that allow member states and citizens to co-habit and trade freely.

A more severe form of xenophobia against Africans of varied nationalities and ethnicity is more rampant in South Africa than in other areas. These constant killings and destruction of properties belonging to foreign nationals are restricted to black Africa. There has been no report of a European or Asian resident attacked during the spike of these attacks. Unfortunately, years of Apartheid, a version of Jim Crow, meant that the natural resources and industries of South Africa were exclusively controlled by European descendants. Post-Apartheid policies of Nelson Mandela and Jacob Zuma did little if anything to address the wealth gap between Africans and Europeans in that country. Since African countries became free from imperialism in the 1960s, most devoted resources and personnel toward fighting the scourge of Apartheid. The unseen hand of Apartheid meant that the indigenous South Africans were miseducated and brainwashed as to whom their true enemies were. To this end, since the Mandela era and to this date, the indigenous population and their visiting African brothers and sisters have had a frosty relationship over scarce resources in terms of employment. The fight has never been about the natural resources controlled by other races, it has always been about the "left-over crumbs." These have seen hundreds killed, beaten, and their properties damaged in waves of xenophobic attacks that are reminiscent of the white mob attacks on African people in the United States in the nineteenth and early twentieth centuries.[19]

The latest waves of attack occurred in 2019. This has prompted the South African ambassador to Nigeria, Jeff Radebe, to issue an apology on behalf of his country to Nigeria's President Muhammadu Buhari. During a meeting in Abuja, the envoy expressed, "sincerest apologies" for the loss of lives and properties. But the attack and resultant apology are not new. Behind these atrocious assaults lay the same or similar excuses proffered by other culprits elsewhere; that foreigners are taking their jobs and that the former does not have proper documentation to reside or work in their country.[20]

While the latest incident left thousands of Nigerians stranded and in fear of their lives in the country, Nigerians and other Africans responded by attacking South African corporate entities domiciled in their countries. In Nigeria, firms like DSTV, MTN, Shoprite, and other known South African corporations were destroyed in some of the major cities like Lagos. A Nigerian citizen, Allen Onyema, amid the chaos, volunteered to use his private airline (Air Peace) to evacuate thousands of Nigerians at no cost. Nigeria's Diaspora Commission Chairwoman Abike Dabiri-Erewa complained to CNN about the slow pace of evacuation and the unfortunate bureaucratic bottlenecks put in place by South Africa making it impossible to evacuate Nigerians promptly: "The flight was supposed to come with 313 people, but only 187 people were cleared to fly, and the airline lost a lot of money in the process. We are asking the South African government to allow those who want to leave to leave."[21]

On a different level, there seems to exist a misguided frosty relationship between Africans born on the continent and their counterparts in America. Some people perceive real differences between what they term "African Americans" and "Africans" because of cultural and experience differences. In reality, there is no difference, just like there is none between an Asian in America and another in the Asian continent. Oppression recognizes this reality and does not distinguish between African people's nationality, cultural preferences, and accents when unleashing its venom. Why then would the victims of oppression not recognize that those differences exist because of oppression and that the latter is sustained through division? Are there differences between siblings raised in different homes, by different parents? The difference could be that they were exposed to different foods, music, and languages contingent upon that spoken by their foster parents or kidnapper and on the circumstances of separation. What ties the siblings together factually are stronger than what divides them. Biologically, their DNA is similar; history or genealogy is still the same. When one uses the superficial things to highlight the differences in any of these cases he or she is accentuating and therefore justifying the factors that separated them.

Regrettably, when a British Nigerian actress Cynthia Erivo was nominated to play the role of Harriet Tubman in the latter's biopic, there was a misguided outrage, especially online. A petition submitted by Tyler Holmes on Change.org garnered 1,123 signatures.[22] The signatories were numerically few compared to the masses of African Americans who have a heavy online presence. It is understandable where Holmes outrage is premised; that out of millions of African people in America, the producers could find a suitable actress to play the role perfectly. She completely went too far with the petition and her threat of boycott because of the casting. According to her, "We will boycott the film Harriet until you hire an actual black American actress to play the part." One wonders how many of such petitions have challenged the persistent casting of Caucasians as Egyptians by Hollywood. There is a reciprocal tendency by Hollywood to use whomever it deems fit for its movies. Many movies about the continent of Africa and its socio-economic conditions have seen the industry utilize diasporan Africans. Movies about Idi Amin and the Black Panther comes to mind. The latter has a diasporic title but was set in Africa. Why would an Africa-descended person in their logical mind be offended by that, including the use of actor Forest Whitaker as Idi Amin in the "Last King of Scotland?" The main concern should be on content, on narrative, and whether it misrepresented African people and reality in any way.

Ghana has been at the forefront of recognizing the imperatives for interconnectivity between Africans at home and in the diaspora. They have on several occasions granted African Americans Ghanaian citizenship, which others can do well to emulate. Again, in 2018, working with Pan-Africanists, the country launched "The Year of Return Ghana 2019." This initiative was spearheaded by the Ghana Tourism Authority (GTA) under the auspices of the Ministry of Tourism, Arts and Culture within the Office of Diaspora Affairs at the Office of the President. The forum was hosted in Washington, DC by the PANAFEST Foundation and the Adinkra Group. Accordingly, the goal of this mission is to get many African Americans to return to the motherland and gain first-hand knowledge and experience there.[23]

One year later in November 2019 in Accra, Ghana, over one hundred Africans from the diaspora were sworn in as citizens of Ghana by the president, Nana Akufo-Addo. This occasion is a big milestone and it is symbolic and historic in ensuring that African people separated by oppression unite in one accord in their homeland in the spirit of Pan-Africanism. A total of 126 Africans from the Caribbean, the United States, and elsewhere dressed colorfully in traditional African garbs and happily waved the Ghana flag at the swearing-in ceremony. In his welcome address, President Akufo-Addo said " . . . On behalf of the government and people of Ghana, I congratulate you once again on resuming your identity as Ghanaians." The president who also toured various Caribbean nations and the United States as part of the initiative added:

> We recognize our unique position as the location for 75 percent of the slave dungeons built on the west coast of Africa through which the slaves were transported. That is why we had a responsibility to extend the hand of welcome, back home to Africans in the diaspora . . .

In his response, Rabbi Kohain, who spoke on behalf of the returnee Africans stated that, "The most valuable possession that was taken away from us was our identity and our connection; it was like severing the umbilical cord . . . But tonight, our identity, the dignity, the pride that has been absent is restored here."[24]

Meanwhile, since the 1960s, thousands of Africans in the diaspora have been returning home in different ways. Some have been vacationing in Africa, others have moved back permanently. Few others like the Nuwaubian Nation have attempted to bring Africa to the diaspora. They did this by importing African material and immaterial cultures to give the diasporan Africans a sense of peoplehood.[25] Many like Jerome Thompson found out in one of such trips how cheaper and safer it is to own a home on the continent. His house in Ghana is just 500 meters from the Atlantic Ocean. Mr. Thompson, a Maryland-born retiree is proud of his home and one of the factors that makes it his dream home is the screen location and the fact that " . . . the ocean helps me fall asleep and wakes me up in the morning . . ." "Where else can I live this close to the ocean? It would cost me millions of dollars!" It is not surprising that according to a 2014 estimate, Ghana is home to over 3,000 African people from the diaspora.[26]

Other individuals have launched campaigns and companies to facilitate smooth relocation or vacationing in Africa for diasporic Africans. Eric Martin and Kent Johnson have a company known as "Black and Abroad" to encourage African people to travel to Africa. They aim to help correct the negative impression of Africa perpetuated in the western media. They post vacation pictures on their website and social media to advertise the continent and their company's services. They intend to reshape the narrative pejoratively employed by whites to intimidate African people, a phrase which was recently used by President Trump: "Go back to Africa." Their effort is geared toward reinventing and rebranding it making it possible for searches about going back to Africa to turn up positive things including their website and its positive contents. According to Johnson, " . . . we worked with a social listening company who checked various sites and found that the phrase had been used around 4,500 to 5,000 times a month, usually in a negative way."[27]

While African masses are doing their part, the "Talented Tenth" must do more to improve the lot of their people. It is unacceptable that the continent is treated with disdain on so many fronts. The English Premier League, which has become extremely popular on the continent since the turn of the twenty-first century grants viewership licenses to media companies, country by country. In the United States, the current license is held by NBC Sports. It was formally held by Fox Sports and later ESPN. Canada has its own. In Africa, one South African company, DSTV Multichoice has the right and license for all of the African countries except North Africa. They also monopolize popular content from U.S. cable TV. This situation deprives these Africans nations freedom of choice. It is also against every known convention for a company to obtain its right of operation and broadcast from one country and exercise that at another. Similar situations prevail in Africa, sadly, and the elites often collude with multinational corporations to exploit the unsuspecting public.

Africans at home and in the diaspora must work together to achieve sustainable victory against oppression because even oppression recognizes the reality of African oneness by oppressing the latter collectively without distinction. There is multiple evidence of collective success stories of African people. Some shackles and clutches of oppression are already falling apart in various parts of Africa. In ghana, the portrait of racist Mahatma Gandhi is down which represents a substantive and symbolic victory over miseducation, racism, and a victory for Pan-Africanism.

In Rwanda, Paul Kagame is showing leadership in his transformative strides and industrialization of the country. Under his leadership, "the East African nation recently launched Africa's first electronic cross-border trade platform with the help of Alibaba Group's Electronic World Trade Platform (eWTP) to engage small businesses across the continent." Also, Rwanda is erecting a multi-billion-dollar project for the production and development of soft and hardware technology. which is inspired by the U.S.'s Silicon Valley. The construction is ongoing in Rwanda's capital, Kigali.[28] In the United States, the ongoing suit, which has reached the Supreme Court, between Byron Allen and Comcast Cable Communications (Comcast), is illustrative of this fact. Allen is demanding justice and an end to Comcast's racist policies that exploit African American families on one hand but deny contract opportunities to African descendants who are seeking contracts from it on the other. He had already won victories at lower courts.[29] This case goes so far to expose the entrenched New Jim Crow policies of the twenty-first century that are masked, yet are as vicious and denigrating as its successor, old Jim Crow.

NOTES

1. "Kwame Ture - Organisation vs Mobilisation," *Youtube*, https://www.youtube.com/watch?v=fdHaFxsP5Bc (accessed March 17, 2020).
2. "Top 10 Major Record Labels," *Giglue*, last modified May 19, 2017, https://medium.com/giglue/top-10-major-record-labels-d776d158a463 (accessed March 17, 2020).
3. Daniel Kreps, "Prince Warns Young Artists: Record Contracts Are 'Slavery,'" *Rolling Stone*, August 9, 2015, https://www.rollingstone.com/music/music-news/prince-warns-young-artists-record-contracts-are-slavery-32645/ (accessed March 17, 2020).
4. Ibid.
5. Richard Lapchick, "The 2011 Racial and Gender Report Card: National Basketball Association," June 16, 2011, The Institute for Diversity and Ethics in Sports.
6. Lindsay Gibbs, "Only 2 Black Head Coaches Remain in NFL Despite the Rooney Rule Even Though 70 percent of NFL Players are Black," *ThinkProgress*, January 2, 2019, https://thinkprogress.org/rooney-rule-nfl-4d0f17baa469/ (accessed March 17, 2020).

7. Shaun R. Harper, "There Would be no NFL Without Black Players. They Can Resist the Anthem Policy," *The Washington Post*, May 24, 2018, https://www.washingtonpost.com/news/posteverything/wp/2018/05/24/there-would-be-no-nfl-without-black-players-they-can-resist-the-anthem-policy/ (accessed March 17, 2020).

8. Steve Wyche, "Colin Kaepernick Explains Why He Sat During National Anthem," *NFL*, August 27, 2016, http://www.nfl.com/news/story/0ap3000000691077/article/colin-kaepernick-explains-why-he-sat-during-national-anthem (accessed March 17, 2020).

9. Ibid.

10. Benjamin Sachs, "The NFL's 'take a knee' Ban is Flatly Illegal," *VOX*, May 25, 2018, https://www.vox.com/the-big-idea/2018/5/25/17394422/nfl-knee-kneeling-labor-law-kaepernick-free-speech-protest-owners (accessed March 17, 2020).

11. "11 Historically Black Colleges and Universities That Have Closed," *Urban Intellectuals*, https://urbanintellectuals.com/11-historically-black-colleges-universities-that-have-closed/ (accessed March 17, 2020).

12. Madison Jackson, "5 of the Best Programs for Jewish Studies Abroad," *GoAbroad.com*, last modified June 3, 2019, https://www.goabroad.com/articles/study-abroad/jewish-studies-abroad-best-programs (accessed March 17, 2020).

13. Joachim Jarreau, Cristina Mitaritonna, and Sami Bensassi, "Economists are Severely Underestimating the Amount of Trade Between African Countries," *Quartz Africa*, September 26, 2018, https://qz.com/africa/1402733/trade-between-african-countries-has-been-underestimated-by-economists/ (accessed March 17, 2020).

14. Felix Onuah, "Nigeria Meets with West African Neighbors on Border Closure," *Reuters*, November 27, 2019, https://www.reuters.com/article/us-nigeria-trade/nigeria-meets-with-west-african-neighbors-on-border-closure-idUSKBN1Y12HX (accessed March 17, 2020).

15. Nell Freudenberger, "Home and Exile," *The New York Times*, March 8, 2013, https://www.nytimes.com/2013/03/10/books/review/ghana-must-go-by-taiye-selasi.html (accessed March 17, 2020).

16. Sheila Rule, Ghanaian, Expelled by Nigeria, Return Home to Start Over," *The New York Times*, May 12, 1985, https://www.nytimes.com/1985/05/12/world/ghanaians-expelled-by-nigeria-return-home-to-start-over.html (accessed March 17, 2020).

17. "Ghana Traders Threaten Demo if Government no ban 'Foreign Retailers,'" *BBC PIDGIN*, July 25, 2019, https://www.bbc.com/pidgin/tori-49108389 (accessed March 17, 2020).

18. "Nigerian-owned Shops in Ghana Forced to Close by Traders: Union," *RFI*, November 1, 2019, http://www.rfi.fr/en/africa/20191101-nigerian-owned-shops-ghana-kumasi-forced-close-traders-union-borders-closed (accessed March 17, 2020).

19. Eusebius Mckaiser, South Africans Are Used to Being the Targets of Racist Hatred, Now They've Become the Haters," *ForeignPolicy.com*, September 19, 2019, https://foreignpolicy.com/2019/09/19/south-africans-are-used-to-being-the-targets-of-racist-hatred-now-theyve-become-the-haters-xenophobia-afrophobia/ (accessed March 17, 2020).

20. "South Africa Apologises to Nigeria Over Xenophobic Attacks," *BBC Africa*, September 17, 2019, https://www.bbc.com/news/world-africa-49726041 (accessed March 17, 2020).

21. Bukola Adebayo, "Nigerians Return Home, Fleeing Xenophobic Attacks in South Africa," *CNN*, September 13, 2019, https://www.cnn.com/2019/09/13/africa/nigerians-return-from-south-africa-xenopbobic-attacks-intl/index.html (accessed March 17, 2020).

22. Valerie Russ, "Who is Black in America? Ethnic Tensions Flare Between Black Americans and Black Immigrants," *The Philadelphia Inquirer*, October 19, 2018, https://www.inquirer.com/philly/news/cynthia-erivo-harriet-tubman-movie-luvvie-ajayi-american-descendants-of-slaves-20181018.html (accessed March 17, 2020).

23. Micha Green, "Ghana Welcomes African Americans Back Home," *Afro*, October 3, 2018, https://www.afro.com/ghana-welcomes-african-americans-back-home/ (accessed March 17, 2020).

24. Kwasi Gyamfi Asiedu, "Ghana Granted Citizenship to Over 100 African Americans and Afro-Caribbeans as Part of Year of Return," *Quartz Africa*, November 28, 2019, https://qz.com/africa/1757853/ghana-gives-citizenship-to-100-african-americans-year-of-return/ (accessed March 17, 2020).

25. See, Emeka Anaedozie, *Nuwaubian Pan-Africanism: Back to our Root* (Lanham, MD: Lexington Books, 2019).

26. Efam Dovi, "African-Americans resettle in Africa," *Renewal Africa*, April 2015, https://www.un.org/africarenewal/magazine/april-2015/african-americans-resettle-africa (accessed March 17, 2020).

27. Stephanie Busari, "African American Duo Launch 'Go back to Africa' Campaign to Take Hatred Out of Slur," *CNN*, July 17, 2019, https://www.cnn.com/travel/article/go-back-to-africa-campaign-intl/index.html (accessed March 17, 2020).

28. Munira Abdelmenan Awel, "Africa's First 'Silicon Valley' to be Built in Rwanda," *AA*, November 16, 2018, https://www.aa.com.tr/en/africa/africas-first-silicon-valley-to-be-built-in-rwanda/1313278 (accessed March 17, 2020).

29. Chauncey Alcorn, "Supreme Court Debates Merits of Black Media Mogul's Discrimination Suit Against Comcast," *CNN*, November 14, 2019, https://www.cnn.com/2019/11/13/business/comcast-byron-allen-scotus/index.html (accessed March 17, 2020).

Conclusion

African people are united by shared history, DNA, and reality, yet they act instinctively in disunity against conventional wisdom, against nature, and against their existential interests due to centuries of conditioning by oppression. Thus, their actions and attitudes become synonymous and in sync with the allegorical people with eyes but could not see. They are unable to see the blatant facts and inevitabilities in their faces. Yet, when they are able to see, the only things they see are the invisible, the impossible, the irrelevant—their imagined differences. To overcome the oppression of racism in the diaspora that manifests in multiple guises as well as Neocolonialism at home, African people must unite socioculturally, psychically, and ideologically to have a chance against a united adversary that created the disunity ab initio and thrives through it.

Contemporary African leaders on the continent and in the diaspora brazenly work against their people's collective interest. Thus, the "Talented Tenth" has morphed into another layer of oppression. Unlike their forebearers who knew the boundary between enmity and friendship, the post-1960s leadership around the world seemingly have no clue or are comfortable in oppression. They tend to look down derisively on the rest of the race rather than look up toward the bigger picture of collective freedom. By looking down, they seemingly derive succor in their material possessions and life of deprivation they have helped create for the most vulnerable within their race. To counteract this attitude, leadership must be redefined. Leadership has to mean selflessness rather than selfishness. It should be unacceptable for an African American member of the Democratic Party to put the party's interest first at the detriment of African American interest. Mantras such as "this election is about getting Trump out" is clearly a Democratic Party talking point and primary interest. African American interest has to be tailored to specific needs. It should be about policies and programs and plans. They must choose either to be in a beneficial relationship or remain single rather than a part of the prevailing status quo.

There is an abundance of so-called "black leaders" but very few are willing to serve. For example, African people defended President Obama and still do passionately at home and in the diaspora. Their defense of the former president is certainly based on emotion rather than on concrete policy executions. Sadly, this emotional defense lacks reciprocity as the former president, as well as other politicians, did not defend the people verbally and policy-wise enough while in office. It amounts to a travesty that the defenseless is bravely defending the strong, while the latter did not use his strengths (political clout, policies, programs, press briefings, executive order, etc) to return the favor. This unbalanced relationship also prevails on the continent whereby most African leaders brazenly work against the economic and social interests of their people. The African American leaders must stand up and be counted by going back to basics—selflessness and community service. Those were the virtues that drove African American leadership of the nineteenth century and before. The "Talented Tenth" must strive to make African Americans vote on interest rather than along party lines. Voting should be on substance, on reason, rather than on emotion.

Every well-meaning and conscientious being must jettison attitudinal imbalance and rise against racial oppression at all times not just race-neutral ones like bullying, rape, child trafficking, and so on. Caucasian liberals, especially the United States, ones owe African descendants their support and gratitude for their support and loyalty intergenerationally. Without the latter, the former could not have won the U.S. Civil War. Without the perpetual support for the liberal party (it was the Republican Party in the nineteenth century and Democratic Party became the liberal party since the 1930s), they would find it exceedingly hard to win general elections. Therefore, it is time for reciprocity. It is time for the redefinition of the relationship between African Americans and the Democratic Party. Is it a symbiotic relationship or not? Is it an inseparable marriage that was forged at someone's expense?

One of the troubling legacies of oppression upon the oppressed African people is the control of the latter's narrative leading to unfortunate self-indictments. Undoubtedly, for oppression to work and have an enduring impact, some elements within the oppressed are co-opted to work against the latter. This fact was apparent during the Arab and European traffic on African bodies for centuries. Unfortunately, the works of these few Judases—compared to the mass of African people—have been misread as a representation of Africa. It has led some to misguidedly argue that "Africans sold each other too." Some have cunningly brought up the roles of these Judases in the context of dissecting the causation, impact, and beneficiaries of the so-called Transatlantic Slave Trade.

The roles of these collaborators must be contextualized, otherwise we, for instance, blame a rape victim and her family for the injustices unleashed on her. That would amount todouble jeopardy. If one uses the roles of Judases and "house slaves" on the plantations of America as indicative of African participation in their enslavement in the diaspora it will certainly be preposterous. Oppression had always utilized the elements within the oppressed to accomplish its goals and overlooking this fact leads one to a shortsighted inference. One cannot ignore the reality that the engineer/technician designs a project on the basis of pre-established goals and executes same based on a plan and budget. In the process, he utilizes tools to craft his work to perfection. Will it be justifiable to give the tools credit for the work instead of the subject who conceived, designed, and used the tools to execute the plan? The answer is in the negative so is the question of African participation in the European trade on the former. Africans served as tools at the hands of engineers who conceived, designed, executed, and eventually stopped the trafficking across the Atlantic when they had no more needs for human labors.

African people must be reeducated to counteract the abusive impacts of miseducation. Eurocentric western education has operationally disabled African people intellectually and psychically abusing them to subconsciously hate their essences. As currently constituted in the most citadel of learnings across the globe, the Eurocentric curricula do not adequately address the social and psychological needs of African descendants. They implicitly validate the obnoxious stereotypes of African inferiority. This syndrome must be confronted head-on through Africa-centered education which is also termed Afrocentric education. Afrocentricity is, in a nutshell, amounts to placing African people at the center of their existential reality. In other words, it means evolving functional curricular that serves the peculiar needs of African people instead of a generic one. This also involves tailoring social education toward solving their social needs.

Proper education would go a long way in re-centering the minds of Africans, making them appreciate their essences, nature, community, and history. It will solve the problem of the best always seeking to leave the African community both at home and in the diaspora. No group can prosper without its best minds. The "Talented Tenth" must use its talent to serve the people. One cannot properly serve from outside; service is better done from the inside. Therefore, living outside of the African community and giving back is insufficient. Like Harriet Tubman, Frederick Douglass, Marcus Garvey, and many contemporary African leaders should appreciate their history, appreciate the selflessness of their ancestors, and apply that philosophy in their service to the people.

There is an urgent need for African people to wake up from slumber and reunite culturally and socially with their kith and kin across the Atlantic. That is what everyone is doing. The State of Israel could not have survived without the immense support it obtains from Europe and America. Also, Caucasian South Africans could not have succeeded for so long in applying the Apartheid (Jim Crow) system against the indigenous Africans if not for the support of their "cousins" across the Atlantic. Therefore, every evidence points toward unification and cooperation as a means of survival. For African people to survive oppressive regimes of Popular Oppression and Unpopular Oppression, it is imperative that they work together as Marcus Garvey, El-Hajji Malik El-Shabazz (Malcolm X), Kwame Nkrumah, Nnamdi Azikiwe, and Kwame Toure, among others, have demonstrated. The Black Power Movement was conscious of this reality as their symbol was a fist which stands for unity. Through unity, African people can exhume the destroyed legacies of their ancestors, chart a dignifying identity for themselves, rebuild the shattered cultural bridges, and move beyond survivalism.

Bibliography

PRIMARY SOURCES

Campbell, John. "African Migration Across the Sahara Is Down." *Council on Foreign Relations*, January 23, 2019. https://www.cfr.org/blog/african-migration-across-sahara-down (accessed March 17, 2020).

Jefferson, Thomas. "Declaration of Independence: Right to Institute New Government," *Library of Congress*. https://www.loc.gov/exhibits/jefferson/jeffdec.html (accessed March 17, 2020).

"Jefferson's Religious Beliefs." *Monticello.org*. https://www.monticello.org/site/research-and-collections/jeffersons-religious-beliefs (accessed March 17, 2020).

"Key Elements of Funding." *FundEd: State Education Funding Policies for all 50 States*, last modified November 21, 2019. http://funded.edbuild.org/ (accessed March 17, 2020).

Lapchick, Richard. "The 2011 Racial and Gender Report Card: National Basketball Association." The Institute for Diversity and Ethics in Sports.

Morton, Samuel. "Observations on the Size of the Brain in Various Races and Families of Man." From the Proceedings of the Academy of Natural Sciences, October, 1849.

Nwoko, Chinedum and Hyacinth Ichoku."Assessment of Public Finance Management in Anambra State, Using PEFA—Performance Management Framework," Consultant Report, 2007.

Richards, David A. R. and Janet T. Awokoya. "Understanding HBCU Retention and Completion." UNCF-Frederick D. Patterson Research Institute. (2012).

"UNICEF poll: More than a third of young people in 30 countries report being a victim of online bullying." *UNICEF*, last modified September 3, 2019. https://www.unicef.org/press-releases/unicef-poll-more-third-young-people-30–countries-report-being-victim-online-bullying (accessed March 17, 2020).

United Nations Human Rights. Office of the High Commissioner. "Democratic Republic of the Congo, 1993–2003 UN Mapping Report." https://www.ohchr.org/Documents/Countries/CD/FS-2_Crimes_Final.pdf (accessed March 17, 2020).

Wyche, Steve. "Colin Kaepernick Explains Why He Sat During National Anthem." *NFL*. August 27, 2016. http://www.nfl.com/news/story/0ap3000000691077/article/colin-kaepernick-explains-why-he-sat-during-national-anthem (accessed March 17, 2020).

Newspapers | Magazines

"80 percent Of Our Policemen Are Deployed To Protect Politicians And VIPS, Says Nigeria Police Chief," *Sahara Reporters*, February 8, 2018. http://saharareporters.com/2018/02/08/80-percent-our-policemen-are-deployed-protect-politicians-and-vips-says-nigeria-police (accessed January 17, 2020).

"African Chiefs Urged to Apologise for Slave Trade." *The Guardian*, November 18, 2009. https://www.theguardian.com/world/2009/nov/18/africans-apologise-slave-trade.

"Benin seeks forgiveness for role in slave trade," *Final Call*, last modified. October 8, 2002. http://www.finalcall.com/national/slave_trade10–08–2002.htm (accessed March 17, 2020)

Boffey, Daniel. "Who betrayed Anne Frank? Book Claims to Shed New Light on Mystery." *The Guardian*, May 25, 2018. https://www.theguardian.com/world/2018/may/25/who-betrayed-anne-frank-book-claims-to-shed-new-light-on-mystery (accessed March 17, 2020).

Chase, Jefferson. "RB Leipzig Seal Promotion to First Division." *DW*. May 8, 2016. https://www.dw.com/en/rb-leipzig-seal-promotion-to-first-division/a-19243190 (accessed March 17, 2020).

Chimurenga, Thandisizwe. "How Toxic is Black Hair Care?" *The Final Call*. February 8, 2012. http://www.finalcall.com/artman/publish/National_News_2/article_8598.shtml (accessed March 17, 2020).

Ekpu, Ray. "Geographical expression: So What?" *The Guardian*, August 15, 2017. https://guardian.ng/opinion/geographical-expression-so-what/ (accessed March 17, 2020).

Fraser, Dave. "Testament to The Game: Proportion of British Premier League Players from Black, Asian and Minority Ethnic Backgrounds Has Doubled Since the 1992–93 Season." *The Sun*, August 15, 2017. https://www.thesun.co.uk/sport/football/4246535/premier-league-black-asian-minority-ethnic-backgrounds-doubled-since-1992/ (accessed March 17, 2020).

Freudenberger, Nell. "Home and Exile." *The New York Times*, March 8, 2013. https://www.nytimes.com/2013/03/10/books/review/ghana-must-go-by-taiye-selasi.html (accessed March 17, 2020).

Green, Micha. "Ghana Welcomes African Americans Back Home," *The Afro*. October 3, 2018. https://www.afro.com/ghana-welcomes-african-americans-back-home/ (accessed March 17, 2020).

"George Zimmerman Raises $200,000 in Donations," *The Telegraph*. April 27, 2012. https://www.telegraph.co.uk/news/worldnews/northamerica/usa/9230457/George-Zimmerman-raises-200000–in-donations.html (accessed March 17, 2020).

Goodnough, Abby. "Harvard Professor Jailed; Officer Is Accused of Bias." *The New York Times*. July 20, 2009. https://www.nytimes.com/2009/07/21/us/21gates.html (accessed January 17, 2020).

Green, Ben. "Manchester United Fans Have a Hilarious New Romelu Lukaku Song." *101 Great Goals*.September 19, 2017. https://www.101greatgoals.com/news/social/new-romelu-lukaku-song/ (accessed March 17, 2020).

Grogg, Patricia. "Taking Efforts to Fight Prejudice in Cuba to the Barrios,"*The Final Call*, December 9, 2013. http://www.finalcall.com/artman/publish/World_News_3/article_101032.shtml. (accessed March 17, 2020).

Harper, Shaun R. "There Would be no NFL Without Black Players. They Can Resist the Anthem Policy." *The Washington Post*, May 24, 2018. https://www.washingtonpost.com/news/posteverything/wp/2018/05/24/there-would-be-no-nfl-without-black-players-they-can-resist-the-anthem-policy/ (accessed March 17, 2020).

Hughes, Rob. "Soccer: Racist Spanish Fans Push Eto'o to Edge." *New York Times*. February 26, 2006. https://www.nytimes.com/2006/02/26/sports/soccer-racist-spanish-fans-push-etoo-to-edge.html (accessed March 17, 2020).

Kazeem, Yomi. "The Harrowing, Step-by-step Story of a Migrant's Journey to Europe," *Quartz Africa*. October 25, 2018. https://qz.com/africa/1341221/the-harrowing-step-by-step-story-of-a-migrants-journey-to-europe/ (accessed March 17, 2020).

Kimeria, Ciku. "The Most Unusual Ways Many African Countries Got their Names." *Quartz Africa*, October 6, 2019. https://qz.com/africa/1722919/how-many-african-countries-got-their-names/ (accessed March 17, 2020).

Kreps, Daniel. "Prince Warns Young Artists: Record Contracts Are 'Slavery.'" *RollingStone*, August 9, 2015. https://www.rollingstone.com/music/music-news/prince-warns-young-artists-record-contracts-are-slavery-32645/ (accessed March 17, 2020).

Liew, Jonathan."Football Must Face up to an Indisputable Truth: Black Managers do not get the Same Chances as White Managers." *Independent*, June 1, 2018. https://www.independent.co.uk/sport/football/news-and-comment/rooney-rule-black-managers-indisputable-data-football-jonathan-liew-a8379111.html (accessed March 17, 2020).

Meckler, Laura. "Report Finds $23 Billion racial Funding Gap for Schools," *Washington Post*. February 26, 2019. https://www.washingtonpost.com/local/education/report-finds-23-billion-racial-funding-gap-for-schools/2019/02/25/d562b704-3915-11e9-a06c-3ec8ed509d15_story.html (accessed March 17, 2020).

Meyer, Pamela. "Foxes Foretell the Future in Mali's Dogon Country" *National Geographic* (1969).

Mock, Brentin. "What New Research Says About Race and Police Shootings." *CityLab*, August 6, 2019. https://www.citylab.com/equity/2019/08/police-officer-shootings-gun-violence-racial-bias-crime-data/595528/ (accessed March 17, 2020).

Muhammad, Charlene. "Legislation Protecting Natural Hair Styles Makes Progress." *The Final Call*, May 1, 2019. https://www.finalcall.com/artman/publish/National_News_2/Legislation-protecting-natural-hair-styles-makes-progress.shtml (accessed March 17, 2020).

Muhammad, Charlene. "The Constant Fight Against Disrespect Of The Black Female." *The Final Call*. April 6, 2017. http://www.finalcall.com/artman/publish/National_News_2/article_103592.shtml (accessed March 17, 2020).

Ogbeche, Emmanuel. "Removal of History from School Curriculum." *The Abuja Inquirer*. https://www.theabujainquirer.com/?page=920&get=920 (accessed March 17, 2020).

Rule, Sheila."Ghanaian, Expelled by Nigeria, Return Home to Start Over." *The New York Times*. May 12, 1985. https://www.nytimes.com/1985/05/12/world/ghanaians-expelled-by-nigeria-return-home-to-start-over.html (accessed March 17, 2020).

Russ, Valerie. "Who is Black in America? Ethnic Tensions Flare Between Black Americans and Black Immigrants." *The Philadelphia Inquirer*. October 19, 2018. https://www.inquirer.com/philly/news/cynthia-erivo-harriet-tubman-movie-luvvie-ajayi-american-descendants-of-slaves-20181018.html (accessed March 17, 2020).

Silverstein, Jason. "George Zimmerman Goes on Depraved Twitter Rant after Retweeting Picture of Trayvon Martin's Corpse." *New York Daily News*. September 28, 2015. https://www.nydailynews.com/news/national/george-zimmerman-retweets-picture-trayvon-martin-corpse-article-1.2376777 (accessed March 17, 2020).

Specia, Megan. "The African Currency at the Center of a European Dispute." *The New York Times*, January 22, 2019. https://www.nytimes.com/2019/01/22/world/africa/africa-cfa-franc-currency.html (accessed March 17, 2020).

"Stakeholders Condemn Removal of History from School Curriculum."*Dailypost*. October 26, 2015. https://dailypost.ng/2015/10/26/stakeholders-condemn-removal-of-history-from-school-curriculum/ (accessed March 17, 2020).

"The Foreign Coach Nigeria Needs!," *Complete Sports*, last modified July 19, 2015. https://www.completesports.com/the-foreign-coach-nigeria-needs/ (accessed March 17, 2020).

Vandercook, John. "The Mandate of Cameroun: A Vast African Territory Ruled by Petty Sultans Under French Sway." *National Geographic* (1931).

Wickenden, Dorothy. "NYPD Sergeant Blows the Whistle on Quotas." *The New Yorker*, August 27, 2018. https://www.newyorker.com/podcast/political-scene/an-nypd-sergeant-blows-the-whistle-on-quotas (accessed March 17, 2020).

Wilkes, Neil. "Manchester United Fans to Keep Singing About Romelu Lukaku's Penis." *SportsMole*. https://www.sportsmole.co.uk/off-the-pitch/man-utd/racism-in-football/news/fans-to-keep-singing-about-lukaku-penis_307734.html (accessed March 17, 2020).

"Willie Lynch letter: The Making of a Slave." *Final Call*, May 22, 2009. http://www.finalcall.com/artman/publish/Perspectives_1/Willie_Lynch_letter_The_Making_of_a_Slave.shtml (accessed March 17, 2020).

Online Sources

"11 Historically Black Colleges & Universities That Have Closed." *Urban Intellectuals*. https://urbanintellectuals.com/11-historically-black-colleges-universities-that-have-closed/ (accessed March 17, 2020).

"2015 Volkswagen Tiguan Prom Night TV Commercial." *Youtube*. https://www.youtube.com/watch?v=0Lu765vTn8U (accessed January 17, 2020).

"ACE Brief Illustrates HBCU Funding Inequities," *ACE*, last modified January 22, 2019. https://www.acenet.edu/News-Room/Pages/ACE-Brief-Illustrates-HBCU-Funding-Inequities.aspx (accessed March 17, 2020).

Adebayo, Bukola. "AU Faces Backlash after Terminating Ambassador's Appointment." *CNN*. October 16, 2019. https://www.cnn.com/2019/10/16/africa/petition-over-sacking-of-au-ambassador/index.html (accessed March 17, 2020).

Adebayo, Bukola. "Nigerians Return Home, Fleeing Xenophobic Attacks in South Africa." *CNN*. September 13, 2019. https://www.cnn.com/2019/09/13/africa/nigerians-return-from-south-africa-xenopbobic-attacks-intl/index.html (accessed March 17, 2020).

"Ahmadu Bello on Igbos."*YouTube*. https://www.youtube.com/watch?v=5_odAy4rVz8.

Alcorn, Chauncey. "Supreme Court Debates Merits of Black Media Mogul's Discrimination Suit Against Comcast." *CNN*, November 14, 2019 (accessed March 17, 2020). https://www.cnn.com/2019/11/13/business/comcast-byron-allen-scotus/index.html.

"A list of George Zimmerman's past run-ins with the law." *Fox News Channel*. January 13, 2015. https://www.foxnews.com/us/a-list-of-george-zimmermans-past-run-ins-with-the-law (accessed March 17, 2020).

"Asian Store Owner that Punched Black Woman in Face Give 50% Off Sale." *YouTube*. https://www.youtube.com/watch?v=xI-7mHrcWjA (accessed March 17, 2020).

Asiedu, Kwasi Gyamfi. "Ghana Granted Citizenship to Over 100 African Americans and Afro-Caribbeans as Part of Year of Return." *Quartz Africa*. November 28, 2019. https://qz.com/africa/1757853/ghana-gives-citizenship-to-100-african-americans-year-of-return/ (accessed March 17, 2020).

"AU Ambassador To The U.S. Offers Masterful History Lesson Dissecting The Legacy Of Colonization."*YouTube*.https://www.youtube.com/watch?v=jOTEs2UHego (accessed March 17, 2020).

Awel, MuniraAbdelmenan. "Africa's First 'Silicon Valley' to be Built in Rwanda." *AA*. November 16, 2018. https://www.aa.com.tr/en/africa/africas-first-silicon-valley-to-be-built-in-rwanda/1313278 (accessed March 17, 2020).

"Bob Marley 'Redemption Song'—Lyrics."*YouTube*. https://www.youtube.com/watch?v=h_a3hh5nRrY (accessed March 17, 2020).

Boyle, Alan. "Genetic Quest Leads to African Apology for Role in Slave Trade." *NBC NEWS*. October 13, 2013. https://www.nbcnews.com/sciencemain/genetic-quest-leads-african-apology-role-slave-trade-8C11467842 (accessed March 17, 2020).

Brown, Carolyn. "Over $500,000 in Crowdfunding Raised For Ferguson Officer Darren Wilson." *Black Enterprise*. September 5, 2014. https://www.blackenterprise.com/over-500000-raised-for-ferguson-officer-darren-wilson-before-sites-shut-down/ (accessed March 17, 2020).

Busari, Stephanie. "African American Duo Launch 'Go back to Africa' Campaign to Take Hatred Out of Slur." *CNN*. July 17, 2019. https://www.cnn.com/travel/article/go-back-to-africa-campaign-intl/index.html (accessed March 17, 2020).

Charles, Nick. "Racist Abuse of Inter Milan Star Romelu Lukaku Shows 'Widespread Ignorance' Persists in Soccer." *NBC NEWS*, last modified September 25, 2019. https://www.nbcnews.com/news/nbcblk/racism-soccer-widespread-ignorance-n1056921 (accessed March 17, 2020).

Bibliography

"Christie Claims Sister was Racially Abused by Own Fans," *RTE*. August 3, 2019. https://www.rte.ie/sport/soccer/2019/0803/1066855-christie-claims-sister-was-racially-abused-by-own-fans/ (accessed March 17, 2020).

"College of Humanities and Social Science." *Virginia State University*. http://www.sola.vsu.edu/departments/history-and-philosophy/index.php (accessed March 17, 2020).

"Colonial Mentality - FelaKuti (1977)." *YouTube*. https://www.youtube.com/watch?v=9Q2F2TaRghE (accessed March 17, 2020).

"'Colonial tax' or important currency stability? Debate rages over CFA Franc." *Africa Check*, September 6, 2019. https://africacheck.org/fbcheck/colonial-tax-or-important-currency-stability-debate-rages-over-cfa-franc/ (accessed March 17, 2020).

Cole, Ngozi. "The Real Meaning Behind Sierra Leone's Beautiful Name." *Culture Tip*, last modified, September 3, 2018. https://theculturetrip.com/africa/sierra-leone/articles/the-real-meaning-behind-sierra-leones-beautiful-name/ (accessed March 17, 2020).

"Demo Farxiga." *YouTube*. https://www.youtube.com/watch?v=i5uDfLs4Yy4 (accessed January 17, 2020).

"Department of History." *Grambling State University*. https://www.gram.edu/academics/majors/arts-and-sciences/history/curriculum/ (accessed March 17, 2020).

Dovi, Efam. "African-Americans resettle in Africa." *Renewal Africa*. April 2015. https://www.un.org/africarenewal/magazine/april-2015/african-americans-resettle-africa (accessed March 17, 2020).

"Dying to be White." *University of Cape Town News*. September 10, 2014. https://www.news.uct.ac.za/article/-2014-09-10-dying-to-be-white (accessed March 17, 2020).

"Execution of Mathias Kanu, A Biafran by Nigeria Army." *YouTube*. https://www.youtube.com/watch?v=Yb7Z_7AiGr8 (accessed March 17, 2020).

"FelaKuti—Colonial Mentality," *Song Meanings*. https://songmeanings.com/songs/view/3530822107858727873/ (accessed March 17, 2020).

FIFA. https://www.fifa.com/ (accessed March 17, 2020).

Fihlani, Pumza. "Africa: Where Black is not Really Beautiful." *BBC*. January 1, 2013. https://www.bbc.com/news/world-africa-20444798 (accessed March 17, 2020).

Gänsler, Katrin. "English Threatens Nigeria's Native Languages," *DW*. May 14, 2019. https://www.dw.com/en/english-threatens-nigerias-native-languages/a-48730346 (accessed March 17, 2020).

Gates, Henry L. "Who Really Invented the 'Talented Tenth'?" *PBS*. https://www.pbs.org/wnet/african-americans-many-rivers-to-cross/history/who-really-invented-the-talented-tenth/ (accessed January 17, 2020).

"Ghana Traders Threaten Demo if Government no ban 'Foreign Retailers.'" *BBC PIDGIN*, July 25, 2019. https://www.bbc.com/pidgin/tori-49108389 (accessed March 17, 2020).

Gibbs, Lindsay. "Only 2 Black Head Coaches Remain in NFL Despite the Rooney Rule Even Though 70% of NFL Players are Black." *ThinkProgress*. January 2, 2019. https://thinkprogress.org/rooney-rule-nfl-4d0f17baa469/ (accessed March 17, 2020).

"Girls Shopping State Farm TV Commercial." *YouTube*. https://www.youtube.com/watch?v=BFhP6f02Euw (accessed January 17, 2020).

"Global Poll on Bullying." UReport. https://ureport.in/v2/opinion/575/ (accessed March 17, 2020).

"Graduate Programs in History –Seventh Edition 2019," *Morgan State University*. https://www.morgan.edu/college_of_liberal_arts/departments/history_geography_and_museum_studies/graduate_program_handbook.html (accessed March 17, 2020).

"IgboAlphabet," Ezinaulo. https://ezinaulo.com/igbo-lessons/pronunciation/igbo-alphabet/ (accessed March 17, 2020).

"It's Time for Africa to Take a Stand on Skin Lightening Creams." *University of Cape Town News*. January 14, 2016. https://www.news.uct.ac.za/article/-2016-01-14-its-time-for-africa-to-take-a-stand-on-skin-lightening-creams (accessed March 17, 2020).

Jackson, Madison. "5 of the Best Programs for Jewish Studies Abroad." *GoAbroad.com*, last modified June 3, 2019. https://www.goabroad.com/articles/study-abroad/jewish-studies-abroad-best-programs (accessed March 17, 2020).

Bibliography

Jarreau, Joachim, Cristina Mitaritonna, and Sami Bensassi. "Economists are Severely Underestimating the Amount of Trade Between African Countries." *Quartz Africa*. September 26, 2018. https://qz.com/africa/1402733/trade-between-african-countries-has-been-underestimated-by-economists/ (accessed March 17, 2020).

"John Brown, 1800–1859." *PBS*. https://www.pbs.org/wgbh/aia/part4/4p1550.html (accessed March 17, 2020).

"Kimberly Daniels Thanks God For Slavery." *YouTube*. https://www.youtube.com/watch?v=CKCSUbJceeU&feature=emb_logo (accessed March 17, 2020).

"Kimberly Daniels Candidate for City Council at Large Group 1." *News4Jax*, last modified March 12, 2015. https://www.news4jax.com/news/2015/03/12/kimberly-daniels/ (accessed March 17, 2020).

Konkobo,Lamine. "African Protests Over the CFA 'Colonial Currency.'" *BBC*, August 30, 2017. https://www.bbc.com/news/world-africa-41094094 (accessed March 17, 2020).

"Kwame Ture - Organisation vs Mobilisation." *YouTube*. https://www.youtube.com/watch?v=fdHaFxsP5Bc (accessed March 17, 2020).

Lombardo,Clare. "Why White School Districts Have So Much More Money," *NPR*. February 26, 2019. https://www.npr.org/2019/02/26/696794821/why-white-school-districts-have-so-much-more-money (accessed March 17, 2020).

"Love Hurts." *YouTube*. https://www.youtube.com/watch?v=Y09z8lwOEYA (accessed January 17, 2020).

"Lucky Dube—Back To My Roots."*YouTube*. https://www.youtube.com/watch?v=AktF2MT9wF4 (accessed March 17, 2020).

"Lucky Dube—Reggae Strong (lyrics)."*YouTube*. https://www.youtube.com/watch?v=R0B6BhwpR3w (accessed March 17, 2020).

Macguill,Dan. "Did Florida State Rep. Kimberly Daniels Once Say, 'I Thank God for Slavery'?" *Snopes*, last modified January 2, 2019. https://www.snopes.com/fact-check/kimberly-daniels-thank-god-slavery/ (accessed March 17, 2020).

"Mainstream media favors business over workers." *Talkingbiz*. http://talkingbiznews.com/1/report-mainstream-media-favors-business-over-workers/ (accessed March 17, 2020).

"Malcolm X - The House Negro and the Field Negro." *YouTube*. https://www.youtube.com/watch?v=7kf7fujM4ag (accessed March 17, 2020).

Mckaiser, Eusebius."South Africans Are Used to Being the Targets of Racist Hatred, Now They've Become the Haters." *ForeignPolicy.com*, September 19, 2019. https://foreignpolicy.com/2019/09/19/south-africans-are-used-to-being-the-targets-of-racist-hatred-now-theyve-become-the-haters-xenophobia-afrophobia/ (accessed March 17, 2020).

McLaughlin, Eliott C. "George Zimmerman's Auction for Gun that Killed Trayvon Martin Ends." *CNN*, last modified May 18, 2016. https://www.cnn.com/2016/05/18/us/george-zimmerman-gun-auction/index.html (accessed March 17, 2020).

"Negritude: A Dialogue Between Wole Soyinka and Senghor - Trailer - Available from TWN." *YouTube*. https://www.youtube.com/watch?v=VPjmRGvkFZE (accessed January 17, 2020).

"Nigeria: Corruption Fueling Police Abuses," *Human Right Watch*, August 17, 2010. https://www.hrw.org/news/2010/08/17/nigeria-corruption-fueling-police-abuses (accessed January 17, 2020).

"Nigerian-owned Shops in Ghana Forced to Close by Traders: Union." November 1, 2019. http://www.rfi.fr/en/africa/20191101-nigerian-owned-shops-ghana-kumasi-forced-close-traders-union-borders-closed (accessed March 17, 2020).

Obioma,Chigozie. "There Are No Successful Black Nations." *Foreignpolicy.com*, August 9, 2016.https://foreignpolicy.com/2016/08/09/there-are-no-successful-black-nations-africa-diginty-racism-pan-africanism/ (accessed March 17, 2020).

Omoruyi, Omo. "The Origin of Nigeria: God Of Justice Not Associated with an Unjust Political Order. Appeal to President Obasanjo not to Rewrite Nigerian History (PART 1)."Rework Nigeria. January 19, 2010. http://reworknigeria.blogspot.com/2010_01_19_archive.html (accessed March 17, 2020).

1 Corinthians 14:33–36. BibleGateway. https://www.biblegateway.com/passage/?search=1+Corinthians+14%3A33–36&version=NIV (accessed March 17, 2020).

Bibliography

1 Timothy 2:12–15. BibleGateway. https://www.biblegateway.com/passage/?search=1+Timothy+2%3A12–15&version=NIV (accessed March 17, 2020).

Onuah, Felix. "Nigeria Meets with West African Neighbors on Border Closure." *Reuter*. November 27, 2019. https://www.reuters.com/article/us-nigeria-trade/nigeria-meets-with-west-african-neighbors-on-border-closure-idUSKBN1Y12HX (accessed March 17, 2020).

Peak Milk. https://www.peakmilk.com.ng/ (accessed January 17, 2020).

"Redemption Song Bob Marley & The Wailers." *Genius*. https://genius.com/Bob-marley-and-the-wailers-redemption-song-lyrics (accessed March 17, 2020).

Sachs, Benjamin. "The NFL's 'take a knee' Ban is Flatly Illegal." *VOX*,May 25, 2018. https://www.vox.com/the-big-idea/2018/5/25/17394422/nfl-knee-kneeling-labor-law-kaepernick-free-speech-protest-owners (accessed March 17, 2020).

Schlein, Lisa. "Thousands of African Migrants Die Crossing Sahara Desert."*VOA NEWS*. December 23, 2018.https://www.voanews.com/africa/thousands-african-migrants-die-crossing-sahara-desert (accessed March 17, 2020).

"South Africa Apologises to Nigeria Over Xenophobic Attacks." *BBC Africa*. September 17, 2019. https://www.bbc.com/news/world-africa-49726041 (accessed March 17, 2020).

"State Farm Commercial Robbed Hoopers." *YouTube*. https://www.youtube.com/watch?v=DDGjASZToyM (accessed January 17, 2020).

"Statistics." *Rape Crisis Center*. https://rapecrisis.com/statistics/ (accessed March 17, 2020).

"Stop and Frisk." *Cornel Law School: Legal Information Institute*. https://www.law.cornell.edu/wex/stop_and_frisk (accessed March 17, 2020).

"Stop Speaking Vernacular in Class." *Orijin Culture*. http://www.orijinculture.com/community/stop-speaking-vernacular-class/ (accessed March 17, 2020).

StopBullying.gov. https://www.stopbullying.gov/ (accessed March 17, 2020).

Taiwo, Kwabena. "Indigenous African Languages are Dying Out and it's a Good Thing." *International Policy Digest*. June 6, 2018.https://intpolicydigest.org/2018/06/06/indigenous-african-languages-are-dying-out-and-it-s-a-good-thing/ (accessed March 17, 2020).

"The 2015 Cadillac Escalade Commercial."*YouTube*. https://www.youtube.com/watch?v=3im23e4Z-gY (accessed January 17, 2020).

"The American Civil War Society." *ACWS*. https://acws.co.uk/historyalive/ACWS_InfoPack.pdf (accessed March 17, 2020).

"The Fading Use of Indigenous Languages in African Households," *This is Africa*, May 17, 2018. https://thisisafrica.me/arts-and-culture/the-fading-use-of-indigenous-languages-in-african-households/ (accessed January 17, 2020).

"This Video Will Shock South African People - American Politics."*YouTube*. https://www.youtube.com/watch?v=17m8OnHC7dQ (accessed March 17, 2020).

"To Be Sold & Let: On Monday 18th of May. 1829," *South African History Online*, last modified August 27, 2019. https://www.sahistory.org.za/sites/default/files/article_pics/2_1_slave_poster_big%5B1%5D.gif (accessed March 17, 2020).

"Top 10 Major Record Labels." *Giglue*, last modified May 19, 2017. https://medium.com/giglue/top-10–major-record-labels-d776d158a463 (accessed March 17, 2020).

"Two Minute History | Aunt Jemima." *YouTube*. https://www.youtube.com/watch?v=grkgS4y5_1c (accessed January 17, 2020).

"United States Incarceration Rates by Race and Ethnicity, 2010," *Prison Policy Initiative*. https://www.prisonpolicy.org/graphs/raceinc.html (accessed March 17, 2020).

"Woman-Like MrIbu 2 - John Okafor Nigerian Movies 2017 | African Movies | Nigerian Movies."*YouTube*.https://www.youtube.com/watch?v=NSHbLLZLlp0 (accessed January 17, 2020).

"World Cup South Africa 2010 Commercial."*YouTube*. https://www.youtube.com/watch?v=G9hHyZiHZNs (accessed January 17, 2020).

"Young Couple State Farm Insurance Commercial (2011)."*YouTube*. https://www.youtube.com/watch?v=VA14cagdtwo (accessed January 17, 2020).

SECONDARY SOURCES

Adelabu, M. A. "Teacher Motivation and Incentives in Nigeria," (2005):1–20.
Adi, Hakim. *Pan-Africanism: A History*. London: Bloomsbury Academic, 2018.
Adi, Hakim. "Pan-Africanism: An Ideology and a Movement," in *Global Africa: Into the Twenty-First Century*, edited by Hodgson Dorothy L. and Byfield Judith A. Oakland, California: University of California Press, 2017.
Aiello, Thomas. *Jim Crow's Last Stand: Nonunanimous Criminal Verdicts in Louisiana*. Baton Rouge: Louisiana State University Press, 2015.
Alexander, Michelle. *The New Jim Crow: Mass Incarceration in the Age of Colorblindness*. New York: The New Press, 2010.
Amoah, Michael. *The New Pan-Africanism: Globalism and the Nation State in Africa*. New York: I.B. Tauris, 2019.
Amole, Bayo. "The Boys Quarters: An Enduring Colonial Legacy in Nigeria." In Socio-Environmental Metamorphoses: Proceedings 12th International Conference of the IAPS. IAPS. Halkidiki, Greece: Aristotle University Press, 1992.https://iaps.architexturez.net/doc/oai-iaps-id-iaps-12-1992-1-008. (accessed March 17, 2020).
Anaedozie, Emeka. "American Media, Public Opinion, and the Nigerian Civil War, 1967–1970." *OFO: Journal of Transatlantic Studies* 4 no2 (2014): 1–20.
Anaedozie, Emeka.*Nuwaubian Pan-Africanism: Back to Our Root*. Lanham: Lexington Books, 2019.
Anderson, Carl. "Misplaced Multiculturalism: Representations of American Indians in US History Academic Content Standards." *Curriculum Inquiry*, 42 no. 4 (2012): 497–509.
Anyanwu, Esther Chikaodi, Queen Ugochi Njemanze, and Mark Chitulu Ononiwu. "English Usage Pattern In Nigerian Religious Settings perspectives From Selected Worship Centers In Imo State." *Journal Of Humanities And Social Science*, 21, no 6 (June 2016): 1–6.
Apfelbaum, Marian. *Two Flags: Return to the Warsaw Ghetto*. Jerusalem, Israel: Gefen Publishing House, 2007.
Asante, Molefi K. *Afrocentricity*. Trenton, NJ: Africa World Press, Inc., 1988.
Awoniyi,Timothy A. "The Yoruba Language and the Formal School System: A Study of Colonial Language Policy in Nigeria, 1882–1952." *The International Journal of African Historical Studies* 8, no. 1 (1975): 63–80.
Bealer, Alex and Kristina Rodanas.*Only the Names Remain: The Cherokees and the Trail of Tears*. USA: Little, Brown Books, 1996.
Banks, Jalen. "Community or Funding: How American Universities Are Failing Black Students." *Berkeley Political Review*, March 18, 2018. https://bpr.berkeley.edu/2018/03/18/community-or-funding-how-american-universities-are-failing-black-students/ (accessed March 17, 2020).
Baron, Lawrence. *Projecting the Holocaust into the Present: The Changing Focus of Contemporary Holocaust Cinema*. Lanham, MD: Rowman & Littlefield, 2005.
Battle, J. and Earl Wright. "W.E.B. Du Bois's Talented Tenth: A Quantitative Assessment." *Journal of Black Studies* 32, no. 6 (2002): 654.
Bender, Thomas. *A Nation Among Nations: America's Place in World History*. New York, NY: Hill and Wang, 2006.
Bird, Elizabeth and Fraser Ottanelli. *The Asaba Massacre: Trauma, Memory, and the Nigerian Civil War*. Cambridge, UK: Cambridge University Press, 2017.
Bird,Elizabeth and Fraser Ottanelli. "The Asaba Massacre and the Nigerian Civil War: Reclaiming Hidden History." *Journal of Genocide Research* 16 Issue 2–3 (2014): 379–399.
Blanchard, Pascal, et al, eds. *Human Zoos: Science and Spectacle in the Age of Colonial Empire*. Liverpool: Liverpool University Press, 2008.
Bradford, Phillips V. *Ota Benga: The Pygmy in the Zoo*. New York: St Martin's Press, 1992.
Brantlinger, Patrick. *Rule of Darkness: British Literature and Imperialism, 1830—1988*. Ithaca: Cornell University Press, 1988.
Brauss,Minerva, Xi Lin, and Barbara Baker. *A Gender Comparison of HBCUs and PWIs in the Southeast*. Women's Leadership Institute, 2016.

Bibliography

Clarke, John Henrik. *Christopher Columbus and the Afrikan Holocaust: Slavery and the Rise of European Capitalism.* Buffalo, NY: Eworld, Inc.1998.

Connelly, W. *John Brown.* Topeka, KS: Crane and Company, 1900.

Corbey, Raymond. "Ethnographic Showcases, 1870–1930," *Cultural Anthropology* 8, no. 3 (1993): 338–69.

Curthoys, Ann and John Docker. *Is History Fiction?* Sydney: University of New South Wales, 2006.

Davidson, James and Brian DeLay. *US: A Narrative History* (Vol. 1). New York, NY: McGraw Hill, 2012.

Davidson, James, Brian Delay, Christine Heryman, Mark Lytle, Michael Stoff. *Nation of Nations: A Narrative History of the American Republic* (2nd ed.). New York, NY: McGraw-Hill, Inc., 1994.

Davidson, James, William Gienapp, Christine Heyrman, and Mark Lytle. *Nation of Nations: A Concise Narrative of the American Republic* (Vol. 1). New York, NY: McGraw-Hill, Inc.1996.

Dubois, W. E. B. *The Talented Tenth.* Scotts Valley, CA: CreateSpace Independent Publishing Platform, 2017.

Durbach, Nadja. *Spectacle of Deformity: Freak Shows and Modern British Culture.* Berkeley, CA: University of California Press, 2009.

Elkins, Caroline. *Imperial Reckoning: The Untold Story of Britain's Gulag in Kenya.* New York: Henry Holt and Company, 2005.

Faragher, John, Daniel Czitrom, Mari Buhle, and Susan Armitage. *Out of Many: A History of the American People* (2nd ed.). Upper Saddle River, NJ: Prentice-Hall, 1997.

Festinger, Leon. *A Theory of Cognitive Dissonance.* Palo Alto, CA: Stanford University Press, 1957.

Foner, Eric. *Give me Liberty: An American History* (Seagul) (fifth edition.). New York, NY: W.W. Norton & Company, 2017.

Foner, Eric.*Give me Liberty!* (Vol. 1.), (fourth edition). New York, NY: W.W. Norton & Company, 2014.

Foster, Hal. "The 'Primitive' Unconscious of Modern Art." *October* (1985): 45–70.

Frazier, Franklin. *Black Bourgeoisie: The Book That Brought the Shock of Self-Revelation to Middle-Class Blacks in America.* New York: Free Press, 1997.

Freire, Paulo. *Pedagogy of the Oppressed.* https://selforganizedseminar.files.wordpress.com/2011/08/freire_pedagogy_oppresed1.pdf (accessed March 17, 2020).

Gale, Thomas S. "Segregation in British West Africa (La Ségrégation En Afrique Occidentale Britannique)." *Cahiers D'Études Africaines* 20, no. 80 (1980): 495–507.

Garvey, Marcus. *Emancipated From Mental Slavery: Selected Sayings of Marcus Garvey.* Cleveland, OH: Universal Negro Improvement Association, 2016.

Gilman, Sander L. "Black Bodies: Toward an Iconography of Female Sexuality in Late Nineteenth-Century Art, Medicine, and Literature" in Henry Louis Gates, Jr. ed. *"Race," Writing, and Difference.* Chicago: University of Chicago Press, 1986.

Graham, Lawrence O. *Our Kind of People: Inside America's Black Upper Class.* New York: Harper Perennial, 1999.

Haggard, Rider. *King Solomon's Mines.* New York: Penguin Books, 2007.

Hartner, Marcus. "The Living Handbook of Narratology: Multiperspectivity." Last modified April 22, 2014. http://www.lhn.uni-hamburg.de/article/multiperspectivity# (accessed March 17, 2020).

Henretta, James, David Brody, Susan Ware, and Marilyn Johnson. *America's History* (fourth edition).Boston, MA: Bedford/St. Martin's, 2000.

Hijiya, Jim. "Changing United States History Survey Textbooks." *The History Teacher*, 28 (2) (1995): 261–64.

Hoffer, Peterand William Stueck. *Reading and Writing American History: An Introduction to the Historian's Craft* (Vol. 1) (second edition). Boston, MA: Houghton Mifflin Company,1998.

Home, Robert. "'Culturally Unsuited to Property Rights?': Colonial Land Laws and African Societies." *Journal of Law and Society*, 40, no. 3 (September, 2013): 403–19.

Huhn, Peter, Wolf Schmid, and Schonert, Jorg, eds. *Point of View, Perspective, and Focalization: Modeling Mediation in Narrative* (1st ed.). Berlin, Germany: De Gruyter, 2009.

Hune, Shirley. "Expanding the International Dimension of Asian American Studies." *Amerasia Journal*, 15 no. 2 (1989): xix–xxiv.

Iyer, Lakshmi. "Direct versus Indirect Colonial Rule in India: Long-Term Consequences." *The Review of Economics and Statistics*, 92, No. 4 (November 2010): 693–713.

Jacques-Garvey, Amy. ed. *Philosophy and Opinions of Marcus Garvey*. The Journal of Pan African Studies, 2009 eBook.

Jaji, Tsitsi Ella. *Africa in Stereo: Modernism, Music, And Pan-African Solidarity*. New York and Oxford: Oxford University Press, 2014.

James, C. L. R. *A History of Pan-African Revolt*, Oakland, CA: P.M. Press, 2012.

James, Leslie. *George Padmore and Decolonization from Below: Pan-Africanism, the Cold War, and the End of Empire*. London: Palgrave Macmillan, 2015.

Jeyifo, Biodun. "Wole Soyinka and Tropes of Disalienation," in Biodun Jeyifo (ed.), *Perspectives on Wole Soyinka: Freedom and Complexity*. Jackson: University Press of Mississippi, 2001.

Kerchy, Anna and Andrea Zittlau. *Exploring the Cultural History of Continental European Freak Shows and 'enfreakment'*. Newcastle, UK: Cambridge Scholars Publishing, 2012.

Landau, Paul and Deborah Kaspin, eds. *Images and Empires: Visuality in Colonial and Postcolonial Africa*. Los Angeles: University of California Press, 2002.

Lindenmeyer, Kriste. "Using Online Resources to Re-center the US History Survey: Women's History as a Case Study." *The Journal of American History*, 89 no. 4 (2003): 1483–1488.

Levine, Bruce, Brown, J. and Roy Rosenzweig. *Who built America?* (Vol. 1). New York, NY: Pantheon Books, 1989.

Lutz, Catherine and Jane Collins. *Reading National Geographic*. Chicago: University of Chicago Press, 1993.

Marenin, Otwin. "Policing Nigeria: Control and Autonomy in the Exercise of Coercion." *African Studies Review* 28, no. 1 (1985): 73–93.

McClintock, Anne. *Imperial Leather: Race, Gender and Sexuality in the Colonial Contest*. New York: Routledge, 1995.

Miller, Joshua and Anne Marie Garran. *Racism in the United States: Implications for the Helping Professions* (second edition). New York: Springer Publishing Company, 2017.

Morton, Janks and Ivory A. Toldson. *Black People Don't Read: The Definitive Guide to Dismantling Stereotypes and Negative Statistical Claims About Black Americans*. Scotts Valley, CA: CreateSpace Independent Publishing Platform, 2012.

Muhammad, Maryam Salihu, Rozilah Kasim, and David Martin. "A Review of Residential Segregation and Its Consequences in Nigeria." *Mediterranean Journal of Social Sciences* 6, no 2 (March, 2015): 376–84.

Nantambu, Kwame. "Pan-Africanism Versus Pan-African Nationalism: An Afrocentric Analysis." *Journal of Black Studies*, 28, No. 5 (May, 1998): 561–74.

Nkrumah, Kwame. *Neocolonialism: the Last Stage of Imperialism*. London: Thomas Nelson and Sons, Limited, 1965.

Nwabughuogu, Anthony I. "The Role of Propaganda in the Development of Indirect Rule in Nigeria, 1890–1929." *The International Journal of African Historical Studies*, 14, No. 1 (1981): 65–92.

Oakes, James, Michael McGerr, Ellen Lewis, Nick Cullather, Jeanne Boydston, Mark Summers, and Camilla Townsend. *Of the People: A History of the United States* (2nd ed.). New York, NY: Oxford University Press, 2013.

Okebukola, Peter. *Towards Innovative Models for Funding Higher Education in Africa*. Accra, Ghana: Association of African Universities, 2015.

Omego, Christie. "The Igbo Language Development: The Challenges of the Igbo Lexicographer." In Convergence: English and Nigerian Languages: A Festschrift for Munzali A. Jibril, edited by NdimeleOzo-mekuri, 689–706. Port Harcourt: M & J Grand Orbit Communications, 2016. www.jstor.org/stable/j.ctvh8r1h7.59 (accessed March 17, 2020).

Osborn, Emily Lynn. "'Circle of Iron': African Colonial Employees and the Interpretation of Colonial Rule in French West Africa." *Journal of African History*, 44, No. 1 (2003): 29–50.

Philips, U. B. *American Negro Slavery*. Gutenberg's Edition, 2004.

Philips, U. B. "The Economic Cost of Slaveholding in the Cotton Belt." *Political Science Quarterly*, 20 (2) (1905): 257–75.

Philips, U. B. "The Origin and Growth of the Southern Black Belts," *American Historical Review*, 11 (4) (1906): 798–816.

Philips, U. B. "The Slave Labor Problem in the Charleston District." *Political Science Quarterly*, 22 (3): 416–39.

Pieterse, Jan N. *White on Black: Images of Africa and Blacks in Western Popular Culture* New Haven: Yale University Press, 1992.

Rodney, Walter. *How Europe Underdeveloped Africa*. Washington, DC: Howard University Press, 1982.

Said, Edward. *Orientalism*. New York: Vintage Books, 1978.

Sanborn, F. "John Brown in Massachusetts." https://www.theatlantic.com/past/docs/issues/1872apr/sanborn.htm (accessed March 17, 2020).

Stout, Neil. *Getting the Most out of Your US History Course: The Student's Vade Mecum*. Lexington, MA: D.C. Heath and Company, 1993.

Strother, Z. S. "Display of the Body Hottentot" in Bernth Lindfers, ed. *Africans on Stage: Studies in Ethnological Show Business*. Bloomington: Indiana University Press, 1999.

Taylor, Elizabeth D. *The Original Black Elite: Daniel Murray and the Story of a Forgotten Era*. New York: Amistad, 2017.

Taylor, Ula. "Origins of African American Studies at UC-Berkeley."*The Western Journal of Black Studies* 34 (2), (2010): 256–65.

Torgovnick, Marianna. *Gone Primitive: Savages Intellects, Modern Lives*. Chicago: The University of Chicago Press, 1990.

Ture, Kwame and Mumia Abu-Jamal. *Stokely Speaks: From Black Power to Pan-Africanism*. Chicago: Lawrence Hill Books, 2007.

Vecchino, Diane. "Immigrant and Ethnic History in the United States Survey." *The History Teacher*, 37 no. 4 (2004): 494–500.

Vickery, Peter. "Progressive Pedagogy in the US History Survey." *The Radical Teacher*, 83 (2008): 10–13.

Walker, David. *David Walker's Appeal to the Coloured Citizens of the World*. Eastford, CT: Martino Fine Books, 2015.

Walters, Ronald. *Pan Africanism in the African Diaspora: An Analysis of Modern Afrocentric Political Movements*. Detroit, MI: Wayne State University Press, 1997.

Wengraf, Lee. "Legacies of Colonialism in Africa: Imperialism, Dependence, and Development." *International Socialist Review*, 103. https://isreview.org/issue/103/legacies-colonialism-africa (accessed March 17, 2020).

Williams, Eric. *Capitalism and Slavery*. Chapel Hill, NC: The University of North Carolina Press, 1944.

Williams, Justin. *Pan-Africanism in Ghana: African Socialism, Neoliberalism, and Globalization*. Durham, NC: Carolina Academic Press, 2016.

Index

Abike Dabiri-Erewa, 135
Abraham Lincoln, 58, 111
Active Oppression, 16
African Diaspora Congress, 72
African historiography, xv
African Union (AU), vii, xv, 71, 72
Afrocentric, viii, xvi
Action Group (AG), 67
Aimé Césaire, xiv
Air Peace, 135
Akufo-Addo, 136
American Civil War Society, 3
American Colonization Society (ACS), 58
Andrew Jackson, 107–109
Anglican church, 22, 99
Anglo-Saxon, 21, 22, 24, 89
Apollos Nwauwa, 72
Arikana Chihombori-Quao, 71
Asaba Massacre, 2

Balkanized, 68
Baltimore Museum of Arts (BMA), 45–48
bandana, 48, 88
Bantu, 22
Barcelona, 13, 15, 132
BBC, 68, 70, 94
Berlin Conference, 69, 71
Biafran, 2–3
Bible, 5, 6, 26
binary paradigm, 36, 39
"Black is Beautiful", 92

Black Lives Matter, 73, 118
Black Nationalist, xvi, 79
Bob Marley, 80
Booker T. Washington, xii, 79, 130
Boys Quarters, 69
British, xi, 10, 22–23, 29, 30, 43, 67, 68, 69, 71, 84, 86, 89, 99, 135
Brown v. Board of Education, 60
bullying, 7, 10–11, 13, 142
Bundesliga, 15

Cadillac Escalade, 49
California, 61, 97
Cameroonians, 44
Cape Town, 23, 29, 79, 92
Caribbean, 107, 111, 136
Cataluña of Spain, 68
CFA, 70, 72
chattel slavery, 4, 5, 114
Cherokee, 108
China, 71
Christians, 5, 26
Columbus, Christopher, 105–107
classism, viii, x, xiv
CNN, 9, 72, 135
cognitive dissonance, viii, ix
colo-mentality, 81–82
Columbian Exchange, 106
Confederacy, 111–112
continuum, vii, 57
Coons, 5

157

Cote d'Ivoire, 83
creamy crack, 96
criminal record, 60
Creating a Respectful and Open Workplace for Natural hair (CROWN), 97

D. W. Griffith, 52
"dark continent", 22, 48

Wilson, Darren, 9
Walker, David, ix, xiii, 79, 109, 130

Declaration of Independence, 6
Demo Farxiga, 52
Democrats, 75
deportation to Africa, 57
Deuteronomy, 5–6
Djibouti, 71
Dr. S. E. Onwu Committee, 85
DSTV, 135, 137

East Indian Company, 29
Ebba Kalondo, 72
Egyptians, 22, 23, 136
El-Hajj Malik El-Shabazz: Malcolm X, 32, 81, 82, 83, 90, 121, 144
Emancipation Proclamation, vii, 58
England, 14, 17, 69
Eric Williams, 28, 113
Eurocentric, xiv, xvi, 4, 22, 25, 32, 46, 48, 69, 88, 97, 143
Europa League, 15
European Imperialism, vii, 22, 28, 38, 48
European Industrial Revolution, 28
European Slave Trade, 27, 82, 114
Exodus, 5, 6

Faki Mahamat, 71
Fela Anikulapo Kuti, 80
FIFA, 18
Fourth Amendment, 8
France: French, xiv, 38, 70, 71, 72
Frederick Douglass, xiii, 109, 143

Genesis, 6
Geneva Conventions, 2
George Padmore, xvi
George Zimmermann, 8, 9

Ghana, xv, 15, 61, 72, 83, 85, 99, 100, 133, 134, 136, 137
Ghana Electrical Dealers Association, 133
Government Reserved Area (GRA), 69
Grandfather Clause, 59
Great Depression, 43
Greek, 4, 87
Guadalupe, 86, 128
Guardiola, 86
Guinea: Guinean, 47

Hague Conventions, 2
Hakim Adi, xvii
Hausa, 69
HBCUs, 60, 63, 64, 65, 66, 97, 98, 100, 104, 127, 129, 130, 131
Henry Louis Gates, xi
House Negro, 5, 82
human rights, viii, 7, 41, 117, 127, 129
Human Rights Movement, viii, 7, 41, 127
human trafficking, 5, 23, 25, 80, 114
human zoos, 41, 48

Igbo, viii, 3, 46, 68, 83, 85, 86
inferiority complex, xiv
International Criminal Court, 2
Israelite, 5
Italian Deputy Prime Minister, 70
Italy, 13, 14, 106, 131

James David Manning, 27
Jay-Z, 123
Jerry Rawlings, 72
Jesus, 6, 26, 110
Jews, 22, 23, 26, 85, 131
Jim Crow, 6, 7, 13, 50, 57, 59, 60, 66, 73, 79, 117, 121, 127, 130, 134, 138, 144
Johannesburg, 27
John Brown, 109, 110, 111
John Quincy Adam, 107
Judas, 5, 142, 143
jungles, 36

Kenya, 30, 62
Khoi Khoi, 40
Kimberly Daniels, 26
King Solomon's Mines, 21
Klimmende, 38
Ku Klux Klan (KKK), 58, 73

Index

Kwame Nkrumah, xv, 32, 66, 67, 71, 73, 83, 85, 144
Kwame Ture: Stokely Carmichael, xv, 83, 138

La Liga, 15
Leon Festinger, ix
Leopold Senghor, xiv
Libya, 74
"Love Hurts", 51
Lucky Dube, 81
Luigi Di Maio, 70
lynching, 6, 57

Major League Baseball (MLB), 46
Mali, 42, 43
Manchester United, 13, 14
Manifest Destiny, 24
Marcus Garvey, ix, xiv, 32, 79, 96, 121, 130, 144
Martin Delaney, ix
Martin Luther King, 32, 122
Matthias Kanu, 3
Mike Brown, 9
Mike Tomlin, 124
Minstrel Shows, 41, 48, 50
Mitchell Alexander, 58
Modern-day Slave, 59
Molefi Kete Asante, viii, 83
Mr. Macron, 70
MTN, 135
multiculturalism, 105, 119
multiperspectivity, 103, 104, 105, 107, 109, 111, 113, 115, 117
Muslim, 48, 69

National Geographic, 41, 42, 43, 44
Native Americans, 115
Nazis, 28
NBA, 17, 46, 50, 87, 103, 105, 123, 124, 125, 126, 132
NBC, 14, 137
NCNC, 67
Negritude, xiv
Nelson Mandela, 27, 32, 134
Neocolonialism, xvii, 57, 59, 61, 63, 65, 66, 67, 69, 70, 71, 73, 74, 75, 82, 121, 122, 141
Netherlands, 2, 48

New Jersey, 60, 61
New Jim Crow, x, xiv, xvii, 57, 58, 59, 60, 61, 63, 65, 66, 67, 69, 71, 73, 75, 79, 117, 121, 122, 124, 127, 129, 138
New Testaments, 5
New World, 116
New York, 7, 8, 32, 50, 61
NFL, 15, 17, 46, 51, 87, 123, 124, 125, 126, 127, 132, 138
Niger, 2, 29, 83, 84, 135
Nigeria, xi, 2, 61, 67, 68, 69, 70, 74, 84, 85, 89, 92, 94, 96, 98, 99, 100, 133, 134, 135
Nigeria Civil War, 2
Nnamdi Azikiwe, 32, 83, 144
Nomasonto "Mshoza" Mnisi, 94
NPC, 67
NYPD, 8

Obafemi Awolowo, 67

Chukwuemeka Odumegwu, 32

Old Testament, 110
Orange, 83
Ota Benga, 50

PANAFEST, 136
Passive Oppressor, 17, 18, 46
Paul Kagame, 138
Peak Milk, 48
Pepsi Max, 51, 53
Picasso, 46, 47
plantation South, 57
police brutality, xi, 7
popular oppression, x, 13, 14, 17, 18, 35, 37, 39, 41, 43, 45, 46, 47, 49, 51, 53, 124, 127, 144
Premier League, 14, 15, 18, 137
Prince, 123, 138
Process Racism, x, 61
PWIs, 63, 64, 66, 98, 100

Rabbi Kohain, 136
Rape Crisis Center, 11
RB Leipzig, 15
Real Madrid, 15
"Redemption Song", 80
Republicans, 75

Rome Statute, 2
Romelu Lukaku, 13, 14
Royal Niger Company, 29
Rwanda, 138

Saartjie Baartman, 40
Sabon Gari, 69
Sahara Desert, 73
Samuel Eto'o, 13
Samuel George Morton, 4
Second World War, 2, 28
Shoprite, 135
slave culture: relaxer, 40, 88; skin bleaching, 90; wig, 88
slave trade, 27, 113
slavocracy, 5, 31, 57, 60, 110
State Farm Commercial Robbed Hoopers, 50
State Farm Insurance, 49, 51
Stockholm Syndrome, viii
sub-Saharan, 30
Super Bowl, 15

Tafawa Balewa, 68
Talented Tenth, ix, x, xii, xiii, xiv, 27, 75, 87, 90, 97, 100, 129, 130, 131, 132, 137, 141, 142, 143
terrorism, 57, 58
13th Amendment, 58, 59

Thomas Jefferson, 6
Thucydides, 4
Togo, 71
Tom Brady, 124
Trans-Atlantic Slave Trade, 18, 113, 142
Trayvon Martin, 8, 9

Donald J. Trump, 137, 141
2015 Volkswagen Tiguan Prom Night TV Commercial, 52

U. B. Phillips, 24
UEFA Champions League, 15
UNIA, 96, 121
UNICEF, 11
United Nations, 2, 3
United Negro College Fund (UNCF), 65
unpopular oppression, x, 17, 18, 144

Virginia Company, 29
Virginia State University, 64, 98

W. E. B. DuBois, xii, xvi
Washington Post, 61, 138
whiteness, viii, 39, 50, 94
Willie Lynch Letter, 5, 6
WNBA, 103, 126
Wole Soyinka, xiv
World Cup South Africa, 2, 50

About the Author

Emeka C. Anaedozie is a lecturer and researcher. His teaching and research interests are in the subfields of Pan-Africanism, the Black Resistance Movement, and Cultural and Intellectual History. He is the author of *Nuwaubian Pan-Africanism: Back to Our Root*.